The Memoirs of Lt. Henry Timberlake

The Memoirs of

LT. HENRY TIMBERLAKE

The Story *of a* Soldier, Adventurer, *and*
Emissary *to the* Cherokees, 1756–1765

EDITED BY Duane H. King

MUSEUM OF THE CHEROKEE INDIAN PRESS

Cherokee, North Carolina

Publication of this work and the exhibit "Emissaries of Peace:
the 1762 Cherokee & British Delegations," a We the People Exhibit,
have been made possible by support from:
   The National Endowment for the Humanities
   The Cherokee Preservation Foundation
   First Citizens Bank
   Harrah's Foundation
   The Cannon Foundation

Published by the Museum of the Cherokee Indian Press, Cherokee, NC.
All photographs by John Warner unless otherwise noted.
Endpapers from the cover of the original, 1765 edition of Timberlake's *Memoirs*,
courtesy of William Reese.
Design and composition by BW&A Books, Inc., Durham, NC.
Printed in Canada by Friesens Corp.

Distributed by The University of North Carolina Press
116 South Boundary Street
Chapel Hill, NC 27514
Additional copies of this publication may be ordered by calling
1-800-848-6224 or from UNC Press's web site, www.uncpress.unc.edu.

Library of Congress Cataloging-in-Publication Data
Timberlake, Henry, d. 1765.
  [Memoirs of Lieut. Henry Timberlake]
  The memoirs of Lieutenant Henry Timberlake : the story of a soldier, adventurer, and
emissary to the Cherokees, 1756–1765 / edited by Duane H. King.
    p. cm.
  Originally published: The memoirs of Lieut. Henry Timberlake. London :
Printed for the author, 1765. With new annotations.
  Includes bibliographical references and index.
  ISBN 978-0-8078-3126-7 (cloth : alk. paper) — ISBN 978-0-8078-5827-1 (pbk. : alk. paper)
  1. Cherokee Indians. 2. United States—History—French and Indian War, 1755-1763.
I. King, Duane H. II. Museum of the Cherokee Indian. III. Title.
E99.C5T62 2007
973.2'6092—dc22   2007013174

cloth ISBN 10: 0-8078-3126-3   ISBN 13: 978-0-8078-3126-7
paper ISBN 10: 0-8078-5827-7   ISBN 13: 978-0-8078-5827-1

Third printing, 2016

Contents

Color plates fall after book page xxxii

Illustrations

Color Plates (following book page xxxii)

14. *Warriors by Robert Griffing (2003). (Courtesy Robert Griffing and Paramount Press)*

15. *Cunne Shote by Francis Parsons at his studio in Queens Square, London beginning on June 29, 1762. Oils, 35" × 28". (Courtesy of the Gilcrease Museum, Tulsa, Oklahoma)*

16. *Reverse of proclamation medallion of King George III by royal engraver J. Kirk (1760) as seen in the portrait of Cunne Shote by Francis Parsons. (Collection of Duane King)*

17. *Silver wedding medallion by J. Kirk (1761) as seen in Cunne Shote portrait by Francis Parsons. (Collection of Duane King)*

18. *British military gorget. 18th century. (National Museum of the American Indian collection)*

19. *Silver armband. French and Indian War period. (National Museum of the American Indian collection)*

20. *British military gorget in gilt with royal coat of arms. French and Indian War period. (Museum of the Cherokee Indian collection)*

21. *Silver peace medal of King George III. After 1760. (National Museum of the American Indian collection)*

22. *Syacust Ukah, Cherokee Chief by Sir Joshua Reynolds (1762). Inscribed at right "Scyacust Ukah 1762." Oils, 47½ × 35". (Courtesy of the Gilcrease Museum, Tulsa, Oklahoma)*

23 & 24. Two Images of The Harlequin Cherokee: or, The Indian Chiefs in London, 1772. *Published by Robert Sayer, London. 7¾" × 4¼" (19.7 cm × 10.7 cm). (Courtesy of the Department of Special Collections, Charles E. Young Research Library, University of California at Los Angeles, Catalogue number: CBC P26.H2272 1772)*

Figure 1. The Memoirs of Lt. Henry Timberlake, *1765 edition.*
(Collection of William Reese)

Introduction

DUANE H. KING

ALTHOUGH Lt. Henry Timberlake spent only three months in the Over-hill country in early 1762, his observations provide an unparalleled eyewitness account of Cherokee life at the time. No other single source provides so much information on Cherokee culture and traditions while at the same time providing insights into a larger story of Cherokee politics and international relations. Apart from Timberlake, documentation of Cherokee customs, traditions and lifestyle in the eighteenth century was sparsely recorded, composed mostly of scattered references in letters, journals, and newspaper accounts. James Adair, William Bartram, and William De Brahm provide eyewitness accounts that describe southeastern tribes, including the Cherokees, and confirm many of Timberlake's observations. Timberlake's writings convey unique personal perceptions of a first-time observer. Supported by recent archaeological excavations, his *Memoirs*, combined with other historical records, provide an accurate, verifiable, and detailed look at Cherokee material culture and life. We can also recognize the deficiencies in his observations due to his limited time among the Cherokees.

To a large extent, our good fortune in having his account was the result of Timberlake's misfortunes. Intertwined with the rich narrative of Cherokee ethnography are the adventures of a young army officer. His account is replete with accidents, mishaps, errors of judgment, and illusions of grandeur ending in personal financial ruin and public disgrace. Timberlake's memoirs were published, in part, as an anticipated reprieve of his staggering debts and, perhaps more importantly, to publicly respond to the charges brought against him of profiteering and fraud. He had hoped to extricate himself from the precarious financial and social position in which he found himself in mid-1765. Imprisoned for debt and stranded in London far from his Virginia home, he penned his memoirs because that was the only outlet for his voice to be heard. His words occasionally vacillate between self-pity and righteous indignation in a final futile attempt for vindication. The anguish and stress of defending himself against his creditors and detractors and his decline into abject poverty no doubt contributed to his early demise. He died during the prime of his life, on September 30, 1765, shortly after his memoirs were completed but before there was any chance for a reversal of his fortunes.

BACKGROUND

By 1762 the British population of the American colonies had reached 1.5 million. The Cherokee population at the time was no more than 20,000.[1] In spite of the overwhelming numbers, Cherokee settlements were not yet threatened by white encroachment. At the beginning of the French and Indian War, the British viewed the Cherokees as an important buffer between the Virginia and Carolina colonies and French outposts on the Ohio and Mississippi rivers.[2] A strong alliance with the Cherokees was critical to British interests. During this period British settlement was more or less confined to the eastern seaboard. Prior to the war, Cherokee contact with whites was primarily through fur traders and diplomatic envoys, as it had been for the past two centuries.

Although the Cherokees first saw Europeans in 1540 when the expedition led by Hernando DeSoto crossed their territory, they attracted little attention from European observers until the eighteenth century. Unlike the Muskogean chiefdoms encountered by the Juan Pardo expedition of 1566–68, which controlled large expanses of agricultural land with population centers, the Cherokee people in the sixteenth century lived in farming hamlets in the valleys of the Appalachian summit area.[3] The remote location provided a buffer against European diseases that ravaged the coastal tribes during the early contact period. Trade with the Europeans during the first century and a half after initial contact was limited and insignificant. It is unlikely that the Cherokees had any contact with English speakers until the late seventeenth century. In 1693, a delegation of seven Cherokees traveled to Charleston to sign a treaty of friendship with the South Carolina colonists and asked for firearms to protect themselves against other Indians who were already well-armed. The necessity of European technology for self-defense brought about a new economic reality that would forever change Cherokee culture and political alliances. The Cherokees were able to supply only one commodity, deerskins, for which the Europeans would trade manufactured goods.

By the first decade of the eighteenth century, the deerskin economy was fully established with more than 50,000 deerskins exported from Charleston annually. In exchange, the Cherokees received an array of items that included firearms, ammunition, iron axes, knives, and hoes, and an assortment of glass beads, mirrors, and clothing. Metal tools and firearms enabled the Cherokees to become more efficient hunters and horticulturalists. As a result, the population expanded and the lands over which they could exert control increased. Firearms proved essential in acquiring more deerskins to procure more European manufactured goods, but they were also necessary for self-

Figure 2. Reproduction of an 18th century trade gun. (Made by the Colonial Williamsburg Foundation)

defense and territorial expansion. Consequently, the Cherokees successfully competed for previously shared or contested hunting grounds, driving other tribes out and securing a larger portion of the deerskin market. In the second decade of the eighteenth century, the Cherokees fought wars with most of their neighbors, including the Shawnees, the Tuscaroras, the Catawbas, and the Creeks. During this period, the Cherokees moved into present-day east Tennessee, formerly occupied by Muskogean speakers.[4] The towns along the lower Little Tennessee Valley in present-day Monroe County, Tennessee, which were occupied by Alabama or Koasati speakers when visited by Juan Pardo in 1568, were overtaken by Cherokees. In 1721, one these towns, Tanasi, became the capital of the Cherokee Nation by virtue of the town chief being appointed "Emperor" by Governor Nicholson of South Carolina. When Lt. Henry Timberlake visited the area in 1762, most of the towns still had Muskogean names, i.e. Tallassee, Chilhowie, Settiquo (recorded as Satapo by Pardo 200 years earlier), Tanasi, Toquo, Tommotley, and Tuskeegee, even though they were occupied by Cherokee speakers. Only Chota (Itsodiyi, "fire place"), founded about 1735, and Mialaquo (amayeli equa, "big island"), founded about 1755, bore Cherokee names.[5]

During the first half of the eighteenth century, the Cherokees and the British became interdependent, economically and politically. The Cherokee economy was dependent on a steady supply of European manufactured goods, and the security of British colonies in the Southeast was dependent upon a strong Indian ally in the interior to serve as a bulwark and buffer against French incursions from the Ohio and Mississippi valleys. As a result, the most important conduit of information and supplies between the two groups was the white fur traders, who lived in Cherokee towns most of the year and made seasonal trips to Charleston for more supplies. For their personal security and credibility, many fur traders aligned themselves with specific Cherokee leaders. A number of traders married or cohabited with women from prominent families. This contact hastened the acculturation process by virtue of the fact that the most influential families had the greatest access to European material

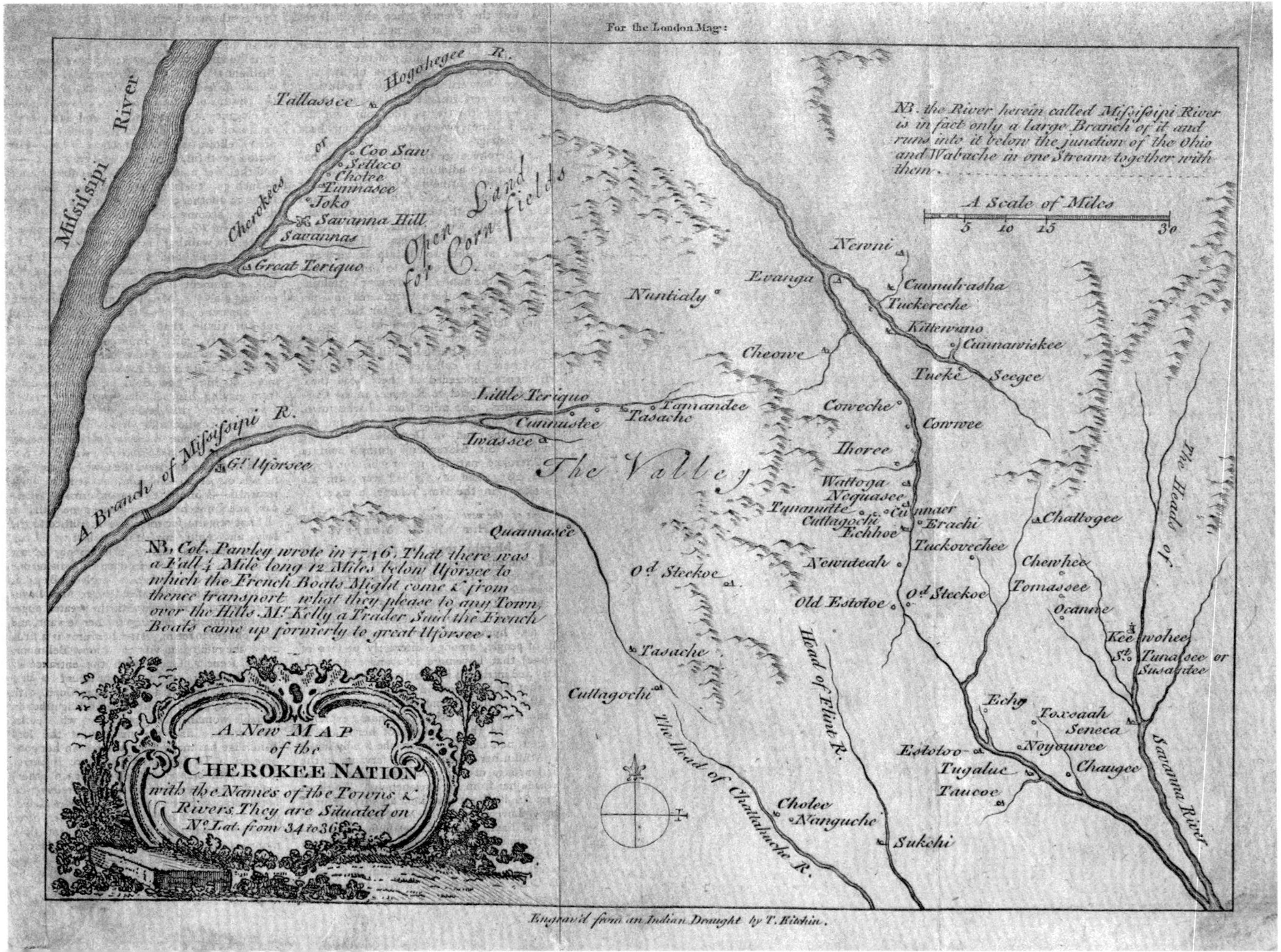

Figure 3: Kitchin's Map of the Cherokee Nation was published in the February 1760 edition of the London Magazine to acquaint readers with the area about to be invaded by the British Army. (Museum of the Cherokee Indian collection)

culture, and the offspring of some of these families grew up in homes that were bilingual and bicultural.

In 1730, after the Moytoy of Great Tellico was elected Emperor, seven Cherokee leaders (including 19-year-old Attakullakulla), escorted by Sir Alexander Cuming, traveled to London for an audience with King George II. While there they signed a treaty by which the Cherokee "(1) would submit to the sovereignty of the King and his successors; (2) they would not trade with any other nation but the English; (3) they would not permit any other nations but the English to build forts or cabins or plant corn among them; (4) they would apprehend and deliver runaway Negroes; and (5) they would surrender any Indian killing an Englishman."[6] This treaty would prove to be problematic in many ways, not the least of which was to place the Cherokees at odds with their own law of "corporate responsibility" as opposed to individual responsibility in cases of international homicide.[7] As subjects of the King, the Cherokees were obligated to fight all enemies of the Crown, both foreign and domestic.

At the time the French and Indian War broke out in 1753, only one member of the 1730 delegation, Attakullakulla, was still alive.[8] Invoking the Treaty of 1730, the British demanded that the Cherokees fight against the enemies of King George. The Cherokees, while amenable to the British request, were reluctant to send warriors to the Virginia frontier unless the British provided protection for the vulnerable Overhill settlements. So, after both Virginia and South Carolina built forts in the Overhill country,[9] the Cherokees sent several hundred warriors to fight on the frontier and distinguished themselves in service.

The beginning of difficulties between the British and the Cherokees began when some returning Cherokee warriors were killed by Virginia frontiersmen, and outraged Cherokee clansmen of the dead were obligated by traditional law ("corporate responsibility") to avenge their deaths. The Cherokees took their revenge on nearby Carolina settlements, rather than the offending and more distant settlements in Virginia. The South Carolina government, in turn, demanded satisfaction according to British law.

In an effort to avoid further confrontation, the great warrior Oconostota led a peace delegation to Charlestown in 1759 to offer reassurances of Cherokee loyalty. But the delegation was marched back to Cherokee country in chains, accompanied by 1,300 militia. At Fort Prince George, South Carolina governor William Lyttelton offered to exchange members of the peace delegation on an individual basis for the twenty-four warriors guilty of murders in Carolina.

This was an impossible situation for the Cherokees. According to their traditional law, they could not surrender men for execution when they had only acted in good conscience as agents of society. But they could not abandon innocent leaders who had only sought to reaffirm their loyalty to South

Figure 4. A silver gorget based on a traditional Cherokee design was inscribed "South Carolina" to reinforce the alliance about the time of the construction of Fort Loudoun in 1756. (Frank McClung Museum collection)

(far right) Figure 5. A silver bracelet inscribed "SC" for South Carolina dates to about 1756. (Collection of Tommy Beutell)

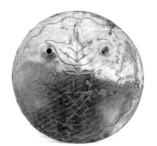

Figure 6. Fort Prince George, built near Keowee in South Carolina, was the scene of a massacre of Cherokee prisoners in February 1760. (Artist's reconstruction of Fort Prince George by Denison B. Hall, Museum of the Cherokee Indian collection)

Carolina. Finally, three of the alleged murderers were surrendered and the British released several Cherokee captives, including Oconostota.

But their troubles did not end there. In the ensuing difficulties, twenty-two members of the Cherokee peace delegation were murdered by soldiers from Fort Prince George. On March 20, 1760, Standing Turkey began a four-day unsuccessful assault on Fort Loudoun. In the meantime, an army of 1,650 soldiers, led by Colonel Archibald Montgomery, moved toward the Cherokee country.[10] He destroyed five Lower Towns but was defeated when he attempted to continue into the Middle Settlements. The Cherokees, regarding their encounter with Montgomery's army as a victory, pressed their siege of Fort Loudoun. On August 7, 1760, the garrison, weakened by desertions and

Figure 7. *Fort Loudoun 1756–1760 near the town of Tuskeegee was built to protect the Overhill towns from the French and their Indian allies. It was surrendered to the Cherokees on August 9, 1760. (Courtesy of the Tennessee Department of Conservation, Doug Henry, artist)*

Figure 8. *Detail of reproduction Indian trade gun. Firearms and metal tools were important trade items for the Cherokees during the 18th century. (Made by the Colonial Williamsburg Foundation)*

near-famine conditions, surrendered. The surrender terms allowed them to march to Fort Prince George. On August 10, they were attacked by seven hundred Cherokees at Cane Creek, where Captain Demere and more than two dozen soldiers were killed. Of the officers, only Captain John Stuart survived. He was captured before the battle began and was spared. He later made his escape, with the help of Attakullakulla, to Virginia.[11]

The following spring brought another British invasion, this time led by Lt. Colonel James Grant. The Cherokees attempted to stop Grant close to the place where they had engaged Montgomery the year before. The battle, which took place on June 10, 1761, resulted in substantial losses on both sides. Grant and his army of 2,600 men subsequently burned fifteen Middle Towns, destroyed 1,500 acres of crops, and created great human suffering, driving "five thousand Cherokees into the mountains to starve."[12] The war was also

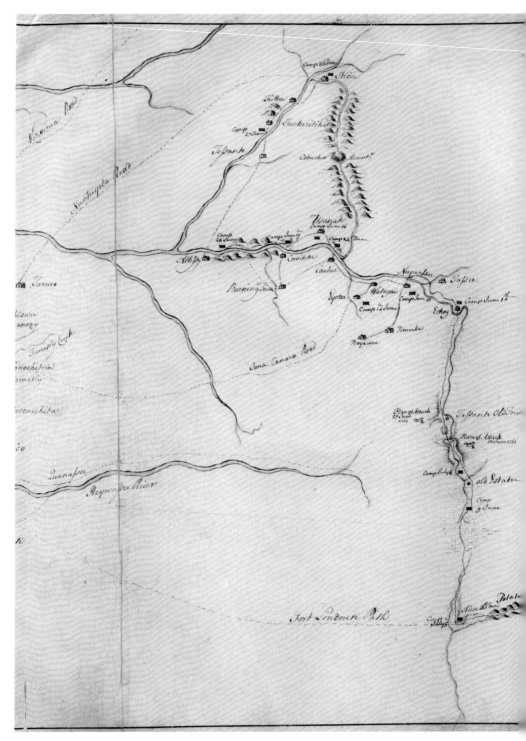

Figure 9. Military cartographers accompanying the Grant expedition charted the movement of the troops and the locations of encounters with the Cherokees. (British Public Records Office W. O. 34/37. SR01751, courtesy of William Anderson)

16

xxi

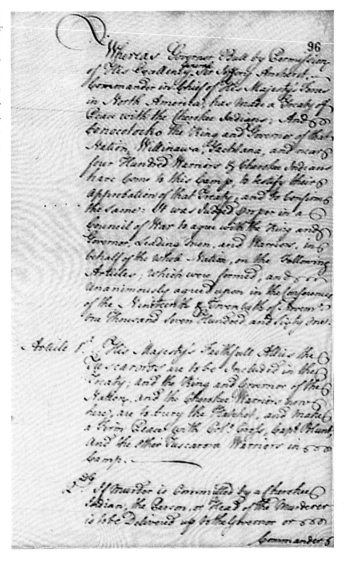

costly for the British. In addition to the loss of life, there was a heavy financial burden. The war cost £100,000 sterling to prosecute.[13]

The Overhill Towns feared the same fate if the Virginia Army reached their settlements. The Cherokees again attempted to sue for peace. A party of about 400 Cherokees set out to intercept an army of Virginians marching toward the Overhill towns, which were overflowing with refugees from the Lower and Middle Towns destroyed by the Montgomery and Grant expeditions. The Cherokees met the Virginians at Long Island (present-day Kingsport, Tennessee) about 140 miles from the Cherokee towns. A peace treaty was negotiated at the partially constructed Fort Robinson, and the Cherokee

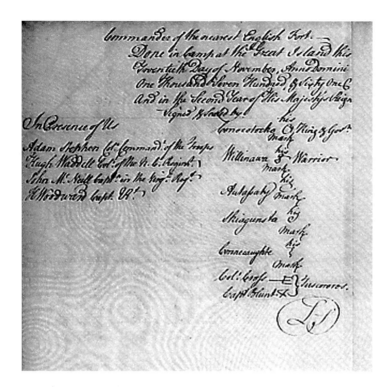

delegation requested that an ambassador be sent back with them to serve as a symbol of British good faith, which for the Cherokee would also reflect British culpability in the late war. A junior officer, Ensign Henry Timberlake, volunteered for the perilous mission.

Samuel Cole Williams concluded:

> *"Little is known or ascertainable of Timberlake beyond what is disclosed in his Memoirs. He was, almost certainly, of the Timberlake family of very early colonial days, the representatives of which in later generations lived in the counties of Hanover, Fluvanne, Louisa, and Albemarle, Virginia. Henry Timberlake died while in London in 1765, and probably before his book was off the press; certainly before he could have profited from sales of it."*[14]

According to the *Dictionary of American Biography*, Henry Timberlake was born in 1730 in Hanover County, Virginia, and was a third-generation American.[15] When Timberlake applied for a marriage license in January 1763, he listed his age as 27, which would suggest a birth date of 1735.[16] His grandfather Joseph Timberlake emigrated from England, and his parents, Francis and Sarah Austin Timberlake, lived in Hanover County. His father died when Timberlake was young and left him with a small inheritance.

Timberlake entered the military in 1756 with a local militia unit called the "Patriot Blues." He applied for but did not receive a commission in the Vir-

Figure 11. George Washington in 1762 at age 30. (Collection of Duane King)

ginia Regiment commanded by Col. George Washington. He thought about giving up the military, but was dissuaded when George Washington, a man whom Timberlake believed had no future, was replaced by Colonel William Byrd III of James River as commander of the old regiment, and Timberlake was induced to accept another commission.[17]

Timberlake applied for and received a commission as ensign and was assigned to a troop of light horse. He served on the Pennsylvania frontier in 1758. He lost three horses in the campaign and was close enough to hear the fleeing French blow up powder magazines at Fort Duquesne.[18] He entered the ruined post with the British troops on November 25, 1758.

He returned to Pittsburg, formerly Fort Duquesne, in 1759 for another campaign under General Stanwix. He spent nine months in command of a small post sixty miles east of Pittsburg. In the spring of 1760, he was relieved by a company of the Pennsylvania Regiment and returned to Pittsburg to find Colonel Byrd and half the regiment prepared to move against the Cherokees. The troops, under Col. Stephen, were destined to serve on the Ohio. Timberlake remained at Pittsburg until autumn and then received permission to spend the winter at home in Virginia.

In the spring of 1761, Timberlake was ordered to return to his division under Colonel Stephen and join with Colonel Byrd, then en route to the Cherokee country. At the camp at Stalnakres, Virginia, Byrd left the troops and passed the command of the Regiment to Col. Adam Stephen.

Colonel Stephen led the expeditionary force sent to chastise the Cherokees for a series of transgressions against the British, including the massacre of the capitulated garrison of Fort Loudoun the previous year. The troops halted at the Long Island of the Holston (present-day Kingsport, Tennessee), and began the construction of Fort Robinson. The fort was nearly completed by the middle of November 1761, when a large delegation of Cherokees arrived.

After the signing of the peace treaty at Long Island of the Holston on November 19, 1761, the Cherokee emperor, Kvna Katoga (Standing Turkey), told the British commander that he "had one more favour to beg of them, which was, to send an officer back with them to their country, as that would effectually convince the nation of the good intentions and sincerity of the English towards them." More importantly, it would signal to the Cherokee populace that the English were the egregious party in the late war and the officer, under the traditional law of "corporate responsibility," would be the first victim of Cherokee vengeance if the English broke the treaty.[19] Unwittingly, Ensign Henry Timberlake volunteered for the assignment and spared Colonel Stephen the dilemma of ordering an officer to accept a perilous fate. Timberlake described the Cherokee leaders who made the request as "now tolerably sincere, and had, seeing me employed in drawing up the articles of peace, in a manner cast their eyes upon me as the properest person to give them an account of it to their countrymen."[20] In this statement, Timberlake suggests that he was either author or scribe for the 1761 Treaty of Long Island. The copy of the Treaty in the British Archives is not attributed, but in comparing the handwriting with Timberlake's signature on his marriage allegation at Lambeth Palace Archives, it does appear that they were penned by the same person.

Although Timberlake readily accepted the role of diplomat, he also saw an opportunity to be a spy. He declined an offer to be escorted in safety to the Overhill Towns by hundreds of Cherokees by the overland route, and opted instead to travel by canoe because he "thought a thorough knowledge of the navigation would be of infinite service, should these people ever give us the trouble of making another campaign against them. . . ."[21] Thus on November 28, 1761, Timberlake, Sergeant Thomas Sumter, John McCormack the interpreter, and a servant departed Long Island by canoe. They arrived at the mouth of the Tellico River, 140 miles downstream, twenty-two days later. The journey was marked by a series of comical mishaps, and the length of time it took resulted in the group being given up for dead by the Cherokees.

THE OVERHILL TOWNS

Timberlake stayed in the Overhill country from about December 20, 1761, through March 10, 1762, as a guest in the home of Ostenaco at Tommotley. He was amazed by what he saw and experienced. He found the Cherokee peo-

Figure 12. The Townhouse at Chota, visited by Timberlake in 1762, was excavated by the University of Tennessee in 1969. (Photo courtesy of the Frank McClung Museum)

ple fascinating and their culture curious. He was a conscientious observer and recorded many details of Cherokee life that would have only appeared curious or interesting to the uninitiated. His ethnographic descriptions encompass many aspects of Cherokee society. He described Cherokee architecture, including council houses, long houses, and paired summer and winter houses. He described items of aboriginal manufacture and their use, and the adaptation and modification of European trade items.

The accuracy of his observations was verified in the 1960s and 1970s when the towns he had visited two hundred earlier were excavated by the University of Tennessee in advance of the inundation of the Little Tennessee Valley by the Tellico Reservoir. The map he drew provided an identification and guide for archaeologists searching for town sites long since abandoned.[22] The specific buildings he entered, such as the Townhouses at Chota and Tommotley, were excavated. Examples of every item of material culture and architectural feature described by Timberlake were discovered in the investigations.

TRIPS TO ENGLAND

For historians, Timberlake is primarily remembered for conducting a delegation of three Cherokees, led by Ostenaco of Tommotley, to London in 1762. The purpose of the embassy, ostensibly, was to reaffirm with the British Crown a recently concluded peace ending a three-year war in which there were substantial losses on both sides. In reality, both Timberlake and Ostenaco hoped to use the diplomatic mission to bolster their own political standings. Both realized that failure of their peace mission could have had disastrous consequences, particularly for the Cherokees who for decades had been dependent upon, but in recent years at war with, the British.

In England, the Cherokees were cordially received by King George III and government officials, although effective communication was impossible because of the untimely death at sea of the interpreter, William Shorey. London, with a population of 700,000, was, at the time, the largest city in the world. The visit of the Cherokee delegation was a sensation. Virtually every public and social engagement was followed by the press. In the end, their visit was marred by a series of public embarrassments and a heated debate over responsibility for their travel expenses. By early August, orders were given that they should not be taken to any more places of public entertainment because of the scenes of "rioting and mischief" that seemed to follow them. The group returned to North America with royal gifts and a promise that the King would read Ostenaco's message after it was translated and mailed from Charleston.

A subordinate of Timberlake in the Virginia militia, Sergeant Thomas Sumter, also accompanied the Cherokees. Timberlake spent his entire inheritance and his life savings, and pawned personal effects and mortgaged his

Figure 13. The caption for this engraving reads: "The Three Cherokees, came over from the head of the River Savanna to London, 1762. / Their interpreter that was Poisoned." The depiction was mostly fictitious. Although the interpreter, William Shorey, died before reaching England, he was not poisoned. The depictions of the three Cherokees and the wolf/ dog are primarily copied from portraits of Mohawk kings painted by Jan Vereslidt in 1710, as a commission from Queen Anne. One of the faces appears to be from an 1762 engraving of Ostenaco by Joshua Reynolds. The original image size is 8½" × 11¼". (Museum of the Cherokee Indian collection)

future earnings, to cover the costs of the trip. Sumter, who accompanied the Cherokees back to their home, petitioned the colony of South Carolina, where he was stranded, for reimbursement of his travel expenses. Sumter's petition was denied. He was imprisoned for debt and abandoned by the government he thought he was serving.

After his escape from the Staunton jail in 1766, he led a remarkable life in the back country of South Carolina, for which he gained fame and notoriety in his lifetime and is still highly regarded today. Timberlake, on the other hand, was rewarded for his services by the King with a Lieutenancy in the

Figure 14. Thomas Sumter in his Revolutionary War uniform alongside an unidentified man from a copper plate engraving, printed on wove about the time Sumter visited London. Artist, subject, and original publication are unknown. ([a] Museum of the Cherokee Indian collection and [b] Collection of Duane King)

42nd Regiment of Royal Highlanders, the Black Watch.[23] Timberlake and his new bride, Eleanor Binel, returned to Virginia in March 1763. He hoped that his meager salary as a soldier would permit him to pay off debts incurred attending to the Cherokees. With the French and Indian War winding down, the British government sought to reduce expenses by cutting the pay of many soldiers by fifty per cent. After an arduous and life-threatening journey to New York to report for duty, Timberlake learned that his name was on a list of officers to be reduced to half pay. Disillusioned, he returned to his home in Virginia.

In 1764, he was sought out by a group of five Cherokees led by Chucatah of Settico, proposing another trip to England. They wanted to appeal to King George to enforce the Proclamation Line of 1763, which forbade white settlement beyond the Appalachian Mountains, citing daily encroachments on Cherokee lands. Timberlake repeatedly declined the invitation, citing his financial embarrassment and public humiliation two years earlier. He reluctantly acquiesced, possibly to accommodate his wife's desire to return to England to visit her family, when a Virginian planter named Aaron Truehart and his son agreed to sponsor the trip. If the 1762 trip was a disaster, the one in 1764–65 was a genuine catastrophe. Two of the Cherokees and both of the Truehearts died at various points in the journey.

Just before they left Virginia, one of the Cherokees died. During the voy-

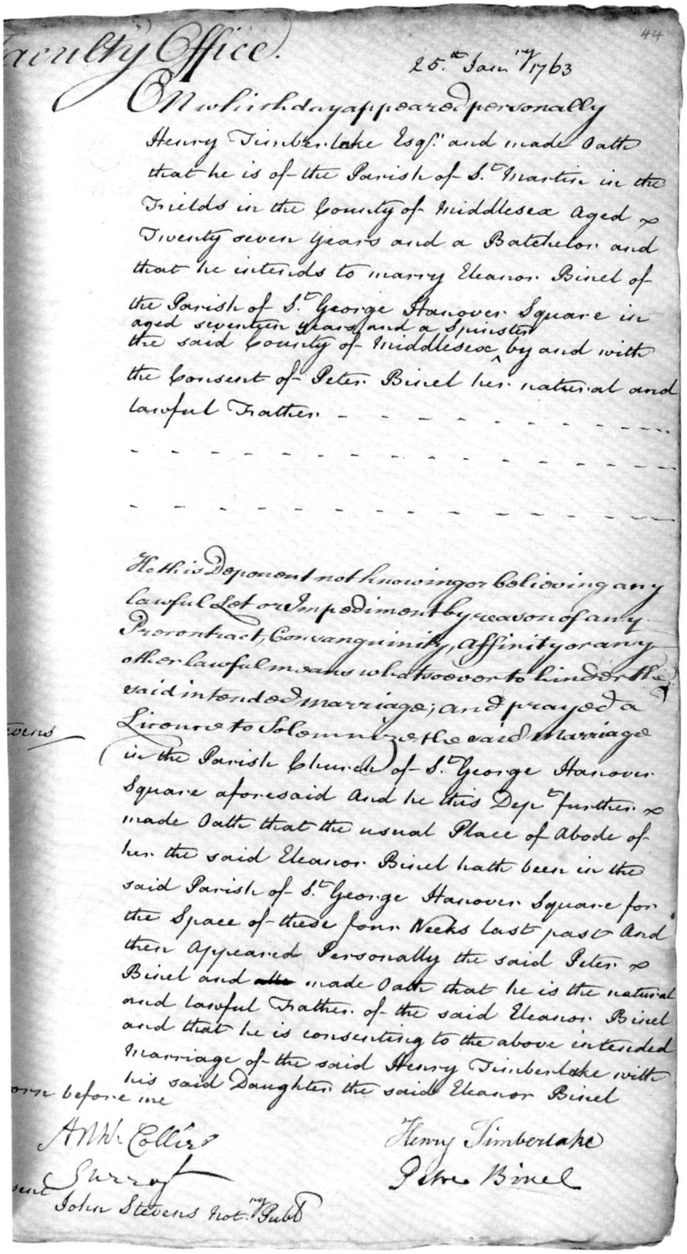

[F]aculty Office.

25th Jan 1763

On which day appeared personally
Henry Timberlake Esqr. and made Oath
that he is of the Parish of St. Martin in the
Fields in the County of Middlesex aged
Twenty seven Years and a Batchelor and
that he intends to marry Eleanor Binel of
the Parish of St. George Hanover Square in
aged seventeen years and a Spinster
the said County of Middlesex by and with
the Consent of Peter Binel her natural and
lawful Father - - - - - - - -

He this Deponent not knowing or believing any
lawful Let or Impediment by reason of any
Precontract, Consanguinity, Affinity or any
other lawful means whatsoever to hinder the
said intended marriage; and prayed a
Licence to solemnize the said Marriage
in the Parish Church of St. George Hanover
Square aforesaid and he this Depont further
made Oath that the usual Place of Abode of
her the said Eleanor Binel hath been in the
said Parish of St. George Hanover Square for
the Space of these four Weeks last past And
then appeared Personally the said Peter
Binel and ~~also~~ made Oath that he is the natural
and lawful Father of the said Eleanor Binel
and that he is consenting to the above intended
marriage of the said Henry Timberlake with
his said Daughter the said Eleanor Binel

[Sw]orn before me

A.W. Collier — Henry Timberlake

Peter Binel

John Stevens Not. Publ.

Figure 15. In his marriage allegation of January 1763, Henry Timberlake asserts that he is 27 years old, ten years older than his bride-to-be, Eleanor Binel. (Lambeth Palace Archives)

age, Mr. Trueheart's son died. The day they landed at Bristol, another Cherokee, Chucatah's brother, suddenly died. After arriving in London, Timberlake attempted to obtain an audience for the delegation with Lord Halifax, who would not receive them. Mr. Trueheart and the Indians were greatly displeased and probably greatly disappointed in Timberlake, who obviously by this time was not highly regarded by government officials. To lessen expenses, Mr. Trueheart took "cheap lodging in Long's Court, Leicester-Fields, for himself and the Indians, where, after a short illness, he died on the 6th of November, 1764." Timberlake again was left alone in London to attend a Cherokee delegation, who were without money and spoke a language that no one else in the country understood. This time there was no royal audience, and, as with the first trip, charges were leveled at Timberlake and others about profiteering by charging admission to see the delegation.

With no financial resources, Timberlake also found that he had no friends. Former acquaintances in the government refused to receive him or even acknowledge his requests for appointments. To make matters worse, according to Timberlake, someone impersonated Chucatah, using his name and dressing like an Indian. Stories of the imposter became so widespread that when Chucatah did appear in public, people believed that he was the imposter. A group of three Mohawks, who were in London at the same time after completing a tour of England and Ireland, made a show at the Strand. The public confused the two groups, and Timberlake was accused of taking his delegation, which had not left London since their arrival, all over England for paid sideshows.

To prevent further embarrassment, the Cherokees were quickly put back on a boat for America, with the government paying for their passage. At the same time, Timberlake's request for reimbursement for expenses was denied on the basis that the trip was made without authority. Timberlake was subsequently arrested for failing to make good on a note for 29 pounds 13 shillings and 6 pence, the last bill for lodging for himself and the Cherokees. Timberlake may have passed the time while incarcerated penning his memoirs in the hope of personal vindication.

It is unknown how many copies of Timberlake's *Memoirs* were published or how well they sold. The book was popular enough to be later translated into German and included in J.T. Kohler's Collection of Travels titled *Sammling neuer Reise-Beschreibungen*, Volume I, part 2, in 1767. A French translation by J. B. L. J. Billecocq was published in Paris in 1796. Robert Southey, an English poet, relied heavily on Timberlake's account in his epic poem, *Madoc* (1805), which recounts the adventures of a mythical twelfth-century Welsh prince who supposedly journeyed to North America.[24]

The first edition was quite rare and virtually unknown to American scholars by the 1920s. In 1927, an American edition of *Timberlake's Memoirs* was published by the Watauga Press with annotations by Samuel Cole Williams, a respected Tennessee historian. Williams's version was reprinted in 1948 by the Continental Book Company in Marietta, Georgia. All of these editions, long out of print, are now prized by libraries and collectors.

Although Williams's footnotes and annotations provide valuable insights into the life and times of Henry Timberlake, considerable additional infor-

mation has come to light since the time of Williams's research in the mid-1920s. Archaeological fieldwork during the 1960s and 1970s at the Cherokee town sites visited by Timberlake has resulted in a wealth of knowledge about the Cherokees during the eighteenth century and confirmed many of the observations reported in the *Memoirs* and previously considered speculative. Timberlake's map of the area led archaeologists to important sites and the correct identification of long-abandoned towns. His descriptions of buildings, implements, ornamentation, and customs ensured proper interpretation of the archaeological record.[25] His accounts of the people he encountered brought to life for his readers the bustling villages that had been silenced by the ravages of time.

As his memoirs attest, Timberlake endured many hardships and difficulties during his brief period of public service. He died embittered and impoverished on September 30, 1765. His wife had been a teenager when they married, only two years before. In 1786–87 his widow, now using the name Helena Theresa Timberlake Ostenaco, petitioned the government for assistance in securing passage to North America, citing her late husband's service to the crown. Her petition was supported by Lord Amherst and others.[26]

Timberlake's work constitutes an enigma for today's readers. The text was written for an eighteenth-century British audience familiar with the leading personalities of the British court and the customs of contemporary European society. He appealed to his readers' interest in the wilderness of America and the strange inhabitants of that distant part of the British Empire beyond the Appalachian Mountains. He perpetuated a widely held European notion that

American Indian life was the antithesis of European life and emphasized, to the point of exaggeration, the differences between Cherokee culture and that of his audience. Timberlake's writing is elusive. His circumspect descriptions and accounts leave the reader with a desire for more detail and greater depth of explanation. It can still be debated, however, whether Timberlake was motivated, as one contemporary suggests, by personal "pleasure and profit," or by a nobler cause of securing lasting peace between warring nations.

ooooo

The *Memoirs* are provided here in their entirety. Annotations and descriptions are offered to provide additional information in cases where the original *Memoirs* are lacking in sufficient detail, along with commentary to better allow the reader to understand the context of Timberlake's writings. The editorial notes follow the sequence of events described in the memoirs, with additional editorial notes added for ease of reading. The original page numbers are shown at the end of the page on which they appeared. This follows the convention that Williams used in the 1927 and 1948 reprints of the *Memoirs*. The notes that Timberlake appended to his text are indicated in this reprint, as in the original, by the reference marks star (*), dagger (†), etc., and also by the suffix (T). Timberlake's spellings and punctuation are left intact. Explanations and notes of the present editor are indicated with (K).

Plate 1. Ostenaco Triumphant *by Keith Bearly (2006). This portrait depicts Ostenaco defeating Montgomery's forces at the battle of Cohowee Pass, June 27, 1760. (Museum of the Cherokee Indian collection)*

Plate 2. Captain Hugh Montgomery 77th Highlanders *by John Singleton Copley (1780) depicts Montgomery recounting his exploits during the Cherokee campaign of 1760 but wearing the uniform of his Revolutionary War unit, the Argylle Fencibles. (Los Angeles County Museum of Art)*

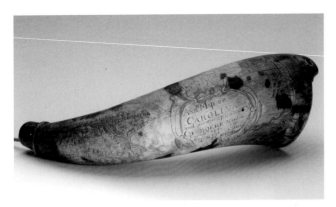

Plate 3. Grant expedition commemorative powder horn (1761). The map of the Cherokee towns destroyed suggests that the powder horn was carved by a soldier in either the 17th or 22nd British Regiments. Although the horn was discovered as a family heirloom in Ireland in 1976, the carver has not been identified. (Museum of the Cherokee Indian collection)

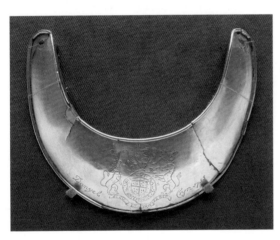

Plate 5. Danyel Cryn gorget. This gorget was made by the noted silversmith Van Eyck in Albany, NY in 1755 and found near the Nikwasi Mound in Franklin, NC in 1887. Cryn may have participated in the 1760 Montgomery expedition against the Cherokees. (National Museum of the American Indian collection)

(above) Plate 6. This rare Cherokee beaded garter, about sixteen inches long, was given by Attakullakulla to Rev. John Martin, one of the first missionaries among the Cherokees, in 1758. (Collection of Patrick R. Meguiar)

(right) Plate 7. Cherokee overhills cooking pot from Great Hiwassee. Circa 1750. Shell-tempered, plain surface, hand-built, open-fired Cherokee cooking pot with applied and notched rim strip. (Museum of the Cherokee Indian collection)

Plate 8. *Warriors of AniKituhwa, dance group sponsored by the Museum of the Cherokee Indian (2006). This group performs the Cherokee War Dance as described by Timberlake. Left to right: Ty Oocumma, Robert "Hoss" Tramper, John Grant Jr., Will Tuska, Daniel Tramper, John "Bullet" Standingdeer Jr., Jeremy Sequoyah, James "Bo" Taylor. Photo by Barbara R. Duncan.*

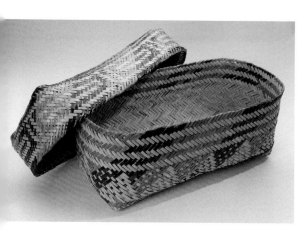

Plate 10. *Bead necklaces. 18th century. Blue, white, and red trade glass beads. (Frank McClung Museum collection, University of Tennessee)*

Plate 9. *Cherokee double weave river cane basket with lid. Mid-20th century. Made about 1950 in Cherokee N.C., it is patterned after a Cherokee basket circa 1730 in the British Museum. (Museum of the Cherokee Indian collection)*

Plate 11. *Military commission given to Oconastota by the French Governor of Louisiana, Louis de Kerlerec, in 1761. Oconastota sought help from the French during the Cherokee war with the British. (U.S. National Archives)*

Plate 12. *Timberlake and Ostenaco (2006). Life-sized figures by Gerry Embledon. Timberlake is wearing the uniform of his Virginia regiment, and Ostenaco is wearing the clothing as described from his audience with King George III. (Museum of the Cherokee Indian collection)*

Plate 13. *Official coronation portrait of George III by Allan Ramsay (1760). Copies of this portrait were painted by artists in Ramsay's studio and distributed throughout the British Empire. One from William and Mary College was subsequently transferred to the National Portrait Gallery in Washington, D.C. It is believed that this is the portrait that Ostenaco saw in Williamsburg before departing for England in May 1762. (Museum of the Cherokee Indian collection)*

Plate 14. Warriors *by Robert Griffing (2003). A Cherokee warrior and a Highlander scout in advance of Grant's disastrous expedition against Fort Duquesne, which was captured by the British on November 25, 1758. (Courtesy Robert Griffing and Paramount Press)*

(left) *Plate 15. Cunne Shote by Francis Parsons at his studio in Queens Square, London beginning on June 29, 1762. Oils, 35" × 28". (Courtesy of the Gilcrease Museum, Tulsa, Oklahoma)*

Plate 18. British military gorget. 18th century. (National Museum of the American Indian collection)

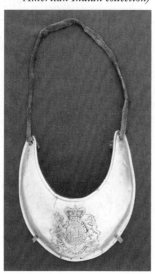

(above, top) *Plate 16. Reverse of proclamation medallion of King George III by royal engraver J. Kirk (1760) as seen in the portrait of Cunne Shote by Francis Parsons. The obverse is the draped bust of George III with long hair tied in queue with the inscription GEORGIVS.III. REX. The reverse (seen in portrait) has a heart in the center of a wreath of laurel and oak on a plinth inscribed BORN MAY 24 / 1738 / PROCLAIMED / OCT^r 26. 1760. The patriotic legend around the medallion reads: ENTIRELY BRITISH. (Collection of Duane King)*

(above) *Plate 17. Silver wedding medallion by J. Kirk (1761) as seen in Cunne Shote portrait by Francis Parsons. The obverse shows the conjoined busts of George III and Queen Charlotte facing right. On the reverse is Eros, Roman god of love, standing and fanning flames of two hearts burning on an altar. THE FELICITY OF BRITAIN. In exergue: MARRIED SEPT. THE / VIII MDCCLXI. (Collection of Duane King)*

Plate 19. *Silver armband. French and Indian War period. (National Museum of the American Indian collection)*

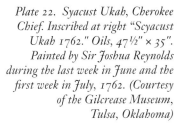

Plate 20. *British military gorget in gilt with royal coat of arms. French and Indian War period. (Museum of the Cherokee Indian collection)*

Plate 21. *Silver peace medal of King George III. After 1760. (National Museum of the American Indian collection)*

Plate 22. *Syacust Ukah, Cherokee Chief. Inscribed at right "Scyacust Ukah 1762." Oils, 47½" × 35". Painted by Sir Joshua Reynolds during the last week in June and the first week in July, 1762. (Courtesy of the Gilcrease Museum, Tulsa, Oklahoma)*

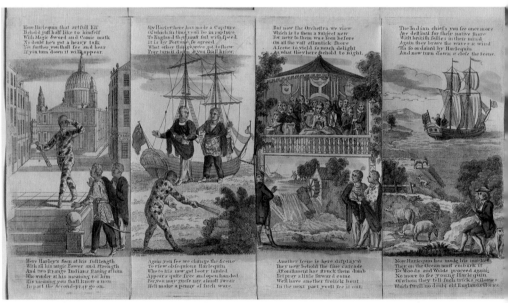

Plates 23 & 24. Two Images of The Harlequin Cherokee: or, The Indian Chiefs in London, 1772. *Published by Robert Sayer, London. 7¾″ × 4¼″ (19.7 cm × 10.7 cm). (Courtesy of the Charles E. Young Research Library, University of California at Los Angeles, Catalogue number: CBC P26.H2272 1772)*

THE

M E M O I R S

O F

Lieut. HENRY TIMBERLAKE,

*(Who accompanied the Three Cherokee Indians to England
in the Year* 1762)

C O N T A I N I N G

Whatever he obferved remarkable, or worthy of public
Notice, during his Travels to and from that Nation;
wherein the Country, Government, Genius, and Cuf-
toms of the Inhabitants, are authentically defcribed.

A L S O

The PRINCIPAL OCCURRENCES during their Refidence
in LONDON.

Illuftrated with

An ACCURATE MAP of their Over-hill Settlement, and a curious
Secret JOURNAL, taken by the Indians out of the Pocket
of a Frenchman they had killed

L O N D O N:

Printed for the AUTHOR; and fold by J RIDLEY, in St.
James's-Street; W. NICOLL, in St. Paul's Church-Yard;
and C. HENDERSON, at the Royal-Exchange.
MDCCLXV.

THE PREFACE

*A*FTER extracting this detail from my Journal, and supplying many circumstances from my memory, I was very much at a loss what title to give it. MEMOIRS seemed to answer my design with the greatest propriety; but that being so commonly misapplied, I was afraid the public would expect a romance, where I only intended laying down a few facts, for the vindication of my own conduct. I do not, however, by this mean to suggest to my reader, that he will find here only a bare uninteresting narrative; no, I have added all in my power to make it useful and agreeable to others, as it was *[v]* necessary to myself; and indeed it was highly so, since a person who bears ill treatment without complaining, is generally held by his friends pusillanimous, or believed to be withheld by secret motives from his own justification. I know not what mine think, but it will not be amiss to inforce their good opinion of me, by laying all my actions open to their view. And as once publishing will be more general, and save many repetitions of a disagreeable narration, this motive first induced me to write, to exchange my sword for a pen, that I wield as a soldier, who never dreamt of the beauties of stile [sic], or propriety of expression. Excuse then, gentle reader, all the faults that may occur, in consideration that these are not my weapons, and that tho' I received almost as good an education as Virginia could bestow on me, it only sufficed to fit me for a soldier, and not for a scholar; but tho' this was the chief end I proposed from it, I have, occasionally deviating from my main design, added whatever I thought curious and [enter]taining, that occurred to my observation, in the Cherokee country, and my travels to and from it, not omitting the principal dan- *[vi]* gers I have passed through, and the expences I have been at, that the reader, weighing them and the rewards I have received, may judge where the balance is due. I do not doubt but I shall be censured for exposing so freely the actions of Mr. Kaxoanthropos;[27] but to this I was constrained by the clamours made against the unnecessary and extravagant expences into which the reception of the Indians had drawn the government. To unveil where the unnecessary and extravagance of it lay, became my duty; and I cannot say but I took some pleasure in detecting the person in the crime he so artfully had laid to my charge: It is, I presume, very pardonable in a person who has so much reason to complain of his unfair practices towards him. As to the manners of the Indians, I grant they have been often represented, and yet I have never seen any account to my perfect satisfaction, being more frequently taken from the reports of traders, as ignorant and incapable of making just observations as the natives themselves, than from the writer's own experience. These I took upon the [vii] spot, and if I have failed in relating them, it is thro' want of art in expression, and not of due knowledge in point of facts. As, however, I did not take upon me to write as an author who seeks applause, but compelled by the necessity of vindicating myself, I once more beg the public to pass over, with a candid indulgence, the many faults that may deserve their censure. [viii]

THE MEMOIRS, &c.

○○

NOTWITHSTANDING my aversion to formal beginnings, and any thing that may relish of romance, as the reader may desire some knowledge of the person who has submitted his actions to his judgment, I shall, in hastening to my principal design, just acquaint him, that my father was an inhabitant of Virginia,[28] who dying while I was yet a minor, left me a small fortune, no ways sufficient for my support, without some employment. For some time, by the advice of my friends, I proposed *[1]* following the more lucrative one of commerce, but after my minorship was elapsed, my genius burst out. Arms had been my delight from my infancy, and I now resolved to gratify that inclination, by entering into the service. Pursuing this resolution, I made my first campaign in the year 1756, with a company of gentlemen called the Patriot Blues,[29] who served the country at their own expence; but whether terrified by our formidable appearance, or superior numbers, the enemy still avoided us; so that, notwithstanding many recent tracks and fires, we never could come to an engagement.[30] On our return, I made application for a commission in the Virginia regiment, then commanded by Col. Washington;[31] but there being at that time no vacancy, I returned home.[32]

In the year 1758, a new regiment was raised for that year's service, to be commanded by the Hon. William Byrd, Esq;[33] from whom I not only received an ensigncy, but as subalterns were to be appointed to a troop of lighthorse, *[2]* he honoured me with the cornetcy of that also.[34] I was soon after ordered on an escort, in which service I continued till July, when I joined the army at Ray's-Town,[35] where I found General Forbes[36] already arrived. The army then marched to Fort Ligonier,[37] on the way to Fort Du Quesne.[38] I was seized here by a violent fit of sickness, caught in searching for some of the troop-horses that were lost, by over-heating myself with running, and drinking a large quantity of cold water, which rendered me incapable of duty. I got something better about the time the troops marched for Fort Du Quesne, and could sit my horse when helped on, but was ordered back by the General, who, however, on my telling the doctor I hoped to do duty in a day or two, permitted me to continue the march.[39] We heard the French blow up their magazine, while yet some miles off; and, on our arrival, we found the barracks, and every thing of value, in flames.[40] My malady rather increased, so that I was at last compelled to petition for my return. I lost my horse at Fort Ligonier, the third I had lost during the [3] campaign; and being obliged to mount a very weak one, I met with great difficulty in crossing the Allegany mountains; and before I reached Ray's Town my horse was entirely knocked up. I bought another, and proceeded to Winchester, where, in a little time, I got perfectly recovered.

Those light-horsemen that survived the campaign, were here in want of all necessaries; and no money being sent up from Williamsburg to pay them, I advanced upwards of an hundred pounds, intending to reimburse myself from the first that should arrive; mean while the troops I belonged to were disbanded, and I, in consequence, out of pay. I had no further business at Winchester than to wait for this money, which I did, till my patience being quite exhausted, I resolved to go down the country in search of it. On my arrival at Williamsburg,[41] I was informed the money had been sent up to me by the paymaster. I returned immediately to Winchester, near 200 miles, where I found the paymaster had paid [4] it to the Lieutenant of the troop, who had appropriated it to his own use. He returned me fifty pounds, but it has never been in his power to pay me the remainder, and to all appearance it never will.

After such unfortunate essays I began to give over all thoughts of the army, when Col. Byrd was appointed to the command of the old regiment, in the room of Col. Washington, who resigned;[42] on which I was unfortunately induced to accept another commission. I served another campaign in the year 1759, under General Stanwix,[43] in the same quarter; but on our arrival at Pittsburg, formerly Fort Du Quesne, I had little employment except looking over the men at work, till the fall of the leaf, when the General gave me the command of Fort Burd,[44] about sixty miles to the eastward of Pittsburg, where I continued about nine months at a very great expence, partly through hospitality to those who passed to and from Pittsburg, and the dearness of necessaries, and partly by building myself a [5] house, and making several improvements, and finishing the half-constructed fort, for which I never received any gratuity. I was relieved by a company of the Pensylvania regiment in the spring, and returned to Pittsburg, but found Col. Byrd with one half of the regiment ordered against the Cherokees, now become our most inveterate enemies; while the remainder under Col. Stephen[45] were destined to serve on the Ohio. I will not fatigue the reader with an account of campaigns wherewith all our news-papers were filled, but confine myself to what more immediately concerned me.[46]

FRENCH CHAPTER II

I REMAINED at Pittsburg till autumn, when I obtained permission to pass the winter at home. I accordingly set out in company with an Ensign named Seayres,[47] who had obtained the same permission: we found great difficulties from the badness of the road of which I may quote the following instance. After marching three whole days from Pittsburg to the place where General Braddock *[6]* first crossed the Yawyawgany river (little better than sixty miles), and leaving one of my horses fast in the mire, we found, to our great surprize, the river about twelve feet high. We waited a whole day in hopes of its falling, but had the mortification to find it had rather rose a foot; our provisions beginning to run short, we hunted to recruit them, but without any success, which obliged us to come to an immediate determination. We at last resolved to look for some other crossing-place; we found about two miles lower, a part of the river, which by its breadth we judged to be fordable; but as the water was muddy, and the bottom could not be seen, there was a considerable risk in attempting it, especially as it lay under a fall, from whence the current darted with great impetuosity. After some deliberation, we resolved to venture it; pushed on by the fears of starving, if we remained any longer where we were, Mr. Seayres proposed himself to try it first; mounting therefore the best of our horses, he plunged into the stream: for the first hundred yards the wa-*[7]*ter reached little higher than the horse's belly, but before he got to a small island in the middle, which we had resolved to rest at, he was quite up to the saddle-skirts; after halting a little time, he set out again for the opposite side, but found it impossible to proceed, a deep channel lying between him and the shore, into which he often plunged, but was as often obliged to turn back, at a great hazard of being carried away by the current. Despairing at last of being able to cross it, yet unwilling to return, he forced up the shallow part about an hundred yards, towards the falls, making several attempts to cross, which he at last effected; but the banks being excessively steep, he found as much difficulty and danger in climbing them, as he had before done in crossing. We then followed and tho' we now knew exactly what course to keep, as our horses were weaker, and more heavily loaded, our task was not less dangerous or difficult. We found the bottom so rocky and irregular, that the horses staggered with their loads. The rapidity of the stream, and the false steps they made, *[8]* threatened every moment to leave their burthens and lives in the middle of the stream. One of them, on which my servant was mounted, actually fell, letting my portmantua[48] into the water, which luckily lodged among the limbs of an old tree that had been washed down by the current; the horse recovered himself, and all the damage occasioned by this accident was the spoiling of my cloaths, and to the amount of forty pounds in paper money, which got so wet, and stuck so fast together, that the greatest part of it was rendered entirely useless. Happy, however, that this was our only loss, and that we escaped with our lives.

In the spring 1761, I received orders to return to my division, which was to proceed to the southward, and join the other half against the Cherokees.[49] Soon after this junction we began our march towards the Cherokee country.[50] Col. Byrd parted from us at a place called Stalnakres,[51] and returned down the country, by which the command devolved on Col. [9] Stephen. We marched,[52] without molestation, to the great island[53] on Holston's River, about 140 miles from the enemy's settlements, where we immediately applied ourselves to the construction of a fort,[54] which was nearly completed about the middle of November, when Kanagatucko,[55] the nominal king of the Cherokees, accompanied by about 400 of his people, came to our camp, sent by his countrymen to sue for peace, which was soon after granted by Col. Stephen, and finally concluded on the 19th instant.[56] All things being settled to the satisfaction of the Indians, their king told Col. Stephen he had one more favour to beg of them, which was, to send an officer back with them to their country, as that would effectually convince the nation of the good intentions and sincerity of the English towards them.[57] The Colonel was embarrassed at the demand; he saw the necessity of some officer's going there, yet could not command any on so dangerous a duty. I soon relieved him from this dilemma, by offering my service; my active disposition, or, if I may venture to say, a love [10] of my country, would not permit it's losing so great an advantage, for want of resolution to become hostage to a people, who, tho' savage, and unacquainted with the laws of war or nations, seemed now tolerably sincere, and had, seeing me employed in drawing up the articles of peace, in a manner cast their eyes upon me as the properest person to give an account of it to their countrymen. The Colonel seemed more apprehensive of the danger than I was myself, scarce giving any encouragement to a man whom he imagined going to make himself a sacrifice, lest he should incur the censure of any accident that might befall me.

The 28th was fixed for our departure; but on making some inquiries about our intended journey, the Indians informed me that the rivers were, for small craft, navigable quite to their country; they strove, however, to deter me from thinking of that way, by laying before me the dangers and difficulties I must encounter; almost alone, in a journey so much further about, and continually infested with [11] parties of northern Indians,[58] who, though at peace with the English, would not fail to treat, in the most barbarous manner, a person whose errand they knew to be so much against their interest. They professed themselves concerned for my safety, and intreated me to go along with them: but as I thought a thorough knowledge of the navigation would be of infinite service, should these people even* [Williams gives this as 'ever'] give us the trouble of making another campaign against them, I formed a resolution of going by water; what much conduced to this, was the slowness they march with when in a large body, and the little pleasure I could expect in such company.

FRENCH CHAPTER III

ON THE DAY appointed the Indians set out on their journey, and a little after I embarked on board a canoe to pursue mine: my whole company consisted of a serjeant,[59] an interpreter,[60] and servant, with about ten days provisions, and to the value of twenty odd pounds in goods to buy horses for our return: this was all our cargo, and yet we had not gone far before I perceived we were much too heavy loaded; the canoe being small, *[12]* and very ill made, I immediately ordered my servant out, to join the Indians, giving him my gun and ammunition, as we had two others in the canoe; little could I foresee the want we were soon to experience of them. We then proceeded near two hundred weight lighter, yet before we had gone a quarter of a mile ran fast a-ground, though perhaps in the deepest part of the stream, the shoal extending quite across. Sumpter the serjeant leaped out, and dragged us near a hundred yards over the shoals, till we found deep water again. About five miles further we heard a terrible noise of a water-fall, and it being then near night, I began to be very apprehensive of some accident in passing it: we went ashore to seek the best way down; after which taking out all the salt and ammunition, lest it should get wet, I carried it along the shore, while they brought down the canoe; which they happily effected. It being now near dark, we went ashore to encamp[61] about a mile below *[13]* the fall. Here we found a party of seven or eight Cherokee hunters, of whom we made a very particular inquiry concerning our future route: they informed us, that, had the water been high, we might from the place we then were reach their country in six days without any impediment; but as the water was remarkably low, by the dryness of the preceding summer, we should meet with many difficulties and dangers; not only from the lowness of the water, but from the northward Indians, who always hunted in those parts at that season of the year. I had already been told, and fortified myself against the latter, but the former part of this talk (as they term it) no way pleased me; it was however too late, I thought, to look back, and so was determined to proceed in what I had undertaken. We supped with the Indians on dried venison dipped in bears oil, which served for sauce. I lay (though I was too anxious to *[14]* sleep) with an Indian on a large bear-skin, and my companions, I believe, lodged much in the same manner.

Early next morning we took leave of our hosts, and in less than half an hour began to experience the troubles they had foretold us, by running a-ground; we were obliged to get out, and drag the canoe a quarter of a mile before we got off the shallow; and this was our employment two or three hours a-day, for nineteen days together, during most part of which the weather was so extremely cold, that the ice hung to our cloaths, from the time we were obliged to get in the water in the morning, till we encamped at night. This was especially disagreeable to me, as I had the courses of the river to take for upwards of two hundred and fifty miles.

We kept on in this manner, without any remarkable occurrence, till the 6th of December, when our provisions falling short, I went on shore, with the interpreter's gun, to [15] shoot a turkey; singling one out, I pulled the trigger, which missing fire, broke off the upper chap and screw-pin; and, as I could find neither, after several hours search, rendered the gun unfit for service. M'Cormack was not a little chagrined at the loss of his gun; it indeed greatly concerned us all; we had now but one left, and that very indifferent; but even this we were shortly to be deprived of, for we were scarce a mile from this unlucky place, when seeing a large bear coming down to the water-side, Sumpter, to whom the remaining gun belonged, took it to shoot; but not being conveniently seated, he laid it on the edge of the canoe, while he rose to fix himself to more advantagè; but the canoe giving a heel, let the gun tumble over-board. It was irreparably gone, for the water here was so deep, that we could not touch the bottom with our longest pole. We were now in despair: I even deliberated whether it was not better to throw ourselves overboard, as drowning at once seemed preferable to a lingering death. Our provisions were consumed to an ounce of meat, [16] and but very little flour, our guns lost and spoiled, ourselves in the heart of woods, at a season when neither fruit nor roots were to be found, many days journey from any habitation and frequented only by the northern Indians from whom we had more reason to expect scalping than succour.

We went ashore as it was in vain to proceed, and, desponding, began to make a fire; while thus employed, several large bears came down a steep hill towards us. This, at another time, would have been a joyful sight; it now only increased our affliction. They came within the reach of a tommahawk; had we had one, and the skill to throw it, we could scarce have failed of killing. In short, they were as daring as if they had been acquainted with our misfortunes. Irritated by their boldness, I formed several schemes for killing, among which, as mending the broken gun seemed most probable, I instantly set about trying the experiment. Notching a flint on each side, I bound it to the lower chap with a [17] leather thong. This succeeded so far, that in ten or twelve times snapping, it might probably fire, which was matter of great joy to us. Before I had finished it, the bears were frightened away; but as we had now mended our gun, we conceived great hopes. It was very probable they might return; and we were not long in expectation, for in less than a quarter of an hour, another very large one stalked down towards us, tho' not so near as the former ones had done. M'Cormack snatched up his gun, and followed him near a quarter of a mile. I had sat down in expectation of the event, and pulled my shoes and stockings off to dry; when I heard the report of the gun, my heart leaped for joy, since I imagined M'Cormack would have certainly taken all imaginable precautions; but judge of my despair, when, after running myself out of breath, and bare-footed among the rocks and briars, I found he had missed, and that having left the ammunition at the place where we had encamped,* [Williams gives this as 'camped'] he could not charge again, till I returned for it. I ran back, unable as I was, and brought it; then [18] sat down, and he continued the chace. By this time Sumpter, who had been gathering wood, joined me, and, we soon heard M'Cormack fire again; upon which, running with all our speed, to the place from whence the report came, we had the inexpressible joy of seeing a large bear, that might weigh near 400 weight, weltering in his blood. It being late, we propped him for that night, on an old tree, to prevent his being devoured by other beasts. Next morning my companions skinned him, and taking as much of his meat as we could conveniently carry, we left the camp in much better spirits than when we came to it.

Nothing more remarkable occurred, unless I mark for such the amazing quantity of buffaloes, bears, deer, beavers, geese, swans, ducks, turkeys and other game, till we came to a large cave;[62] we stopped to examine it, but after climbing, with great difficulty, near 50 feet almost perpendicular, to get to it, we saw nothing curious, except some pillars of the petrified drop-[19] pings, that fell from the roof, of a prodigious size. I could not, indeed, penetrate very far, for want of light. Coming back to the edge of the rock, we perceived our canoe adrift, going down with the stream. Sumpter scrambled down the rock, and, plunging into the river, without giving himself scarce time to pull off his coat, swam a quarter of a mile before he could overtake her. When he returned, every thing on him was stiff frozen. We instantly made a fire to recover him; but this accident, joined to the severity of the weather, obliged us to stay the day and night following. We laid ourselves down to sleep in the mouth of the cave, where we had made our fire, which we no sooner did, than, oppressed with the fatigues of the preceding day, we fell into a sound sleep, from which we were awaked before midnight, by the howling of wild beasts in the cave, who kept us awake with this concert till a little before day. About four o'clock in the morning, we had a more terrifying alarm, we were stunned with a noise, like the splitting of a rock. As there had never been, to all ap-[20] pearance, a fire near that place, I could no otherwise account for it, than by laying it to the, fire, which refining the air, might have occasioned some pressure in the cavities, or fired some collected vapour, the explosion of which had been the noise that waked us; yet, as I could not clearly comprehend it, I was under the greatest apprehensions, especially as I could perceive it hollow just under us. The severity, however, of the weather obliged us to stay the next night likewise, but the howling of the beasts, and thinking of the preceding night's noise, prevented me from getting any sleep. On the morning of the 9th instant we were, to my great satisfaction, obliged to decamp for want of wood. We passed the place where the canoe was taken up, and came to a fall about a quarter of a mile further, which, had she reached, we should never have seen the least atom of her cargoe more.

FRENCH CHAPTER IV

WE CONTINUED our journey much in the same manner till the 11th:[63] as during the whole time we had seen or heard nothing of [21] the northward Indians, the Cherokees had so menaced us with, we began to imagine ourselves secure, and that they had, for some reasons, imposed on us, when the report of a gun on one side of the river undeceived us; for as the Cherokees had told us how much the northward Indians frequented this place, it was reasonable to conclude, that they themselves came only here to fight, at which time they seldom fire, as that gives notice to the enemy where to come and reconnoitre them, but seek to hear their adversaries fire, that their scouts may measure their forces, and they take all advantages of the enemy before they come to action. We therefore concluded that this must certainly be a party of northern hunters. We were talking of this, when another gun from the opposite shore declared us in the midst of our enemies, whom there was no resisting; we heard several more some time after, which made us go as far as we possibly could before we encamped, which we did very cautiously, retiring into a thicket of canes, and chusing to lay on our wet and cold blankets, rather than make a [22] fire to dry them, by which we might be discovered. Next day[64] we heard several more guns on both sides of the river, which made us conjecture that the Indians had watched us, but not finding our encampment the night before, were still following us. I was resolved, however, to encamp in such an inconvenient manner no more, and to make a fire at night, whatever might be the consequence. We took all other imaginable precautions, encamping in a thicket of canes, impenetrable to the eye, as we had done the preceding night. About midnight some drops falling on my face from the trees under which we lay, awaked me, on which I imagined I heard something walk round our camp. I lay still some time to consider what could be patroling at that time of night in the rain, a thing unusual for wild beasts to do, when M'Cormack, who had been awake for some time, asked me if I heard the noise. I told him yes, very plain, for by the cracking of the sticks that lay on the ground I could perceive it approached us. M'Cormack starting up, [23] swore directly it was a party of northern Indians, and ran down, in a pannic, to the canoe, and, had not I followed to prevent him would certainly have made off with it, and left us exposed to the mercy of the enemy, if there were any pursuing us, without any means of escape; but for my part, I imagined it some half-starved animal looking for food; and Sumpter had been so certain of this, that he never moved from where he lay; for when, in an hour after, I had persuaded M'Cormack to return to the camp, we found Sumpter fast asleep, and the noise entirely gone. We set out early the next day,[65] on account of this alarm, and about 12 o'clock heard a noise like distant thunder. In half an hour we reached the place called the Great Falls, from which it proceeded. The river was here about half a mile broad, and the water falling from one rock to another, for the space of half a mile, had the appearance of steps, in each of which, and all about the rocks, the fish were sporting in prodigious quantities, which we might have taken with ease, had we not been too busy in working the [24] canoe down, to look after them. I observed here the same method I had with the other falls, by going ashore and looking out the safest way for the canoe to pass; and lest some accident should happen to it, I took what salt and ammunition we had left, and carried it along the shore: if this was not so dangerous, it was quite as difficult a task; and were I to chuse again, I should prefer the danger in the canoe to the difficulty of passing such rocks, both hands occupied, with the care of the gun and ammunition. Theirs was no ways easy. Before they had passed half the fall, the canoe ran fast on a rock, and it was with the greatest difficulty they got her clear; notwithstanding which I was at last so entangled among the rocks, that I was obliged to order the canoe ashore, at a place where the current was more practicable than others, and proceed in it. We scarce advanced a hundred yards, when we ran with such violence against another rock, that Sumpter, breaking his pole in attempting to ward the shock, fell over-board; and we narrowly escaped being [25] partakers of the same accident. Had not the canoe been of more than ordinary strength, she must certainly have dashed to pieces; she turned broadside too, shipping in a great deal of water, by which all the things were wet that I had so much laboured to preserve. We got out to right her; and as I observed some bad places below, I resolved to wade to the shore, being as much an incumbrance as a help. The water was not then above knee-deep; but, before I reached the shore, I got into a sluice as high as my arm-pits, and was near forced away by the rapidity of the stream, entangled in my surtout,[66] and a blanket I had wrapped about me: when I got on shore, examining the damage I had sustained, I found my watch[67] and papers spoiled by the wet, and myself almost frozen; so that, after shivering on three miles further, we were constrained to encamp, and make a fire to dry ourselves; but as it continued snowing, hailing, and raining alternately, we were again obliged to lie in wet blankets; which, though more intolerable, after the hardships we had sustained this [26] day, we had done half the time since our departure from the Great Island.

Next morning,[68] when we decamped, it was so excessive cold, that coming to a still place of the river, we found it frozen from bank to bank, to such a degree, that almost the whole day was spent in breaking the ice to make a

Figure 17. Mid–18th-century pocket watch. Timberlake ruined his pocket watch when he fell into the Holston river on his way to the Cherokee country. (Museum of the Cherokee Indian collection)

passage. This, indeed, had already happened some days before, but never so severe as now.

Next morning[69] we had the pleasure of finding the ice entirely gone, thawed, probably, by a hard rain that fell over-night, so that about two o'clock we found ourselves in Broad River,[70] which being very high, we went the two following days at the rate of ten miles an hour, till we came within a mile of Tennessee river,[71] when, running under the shore, we on a sudden discovered a party of ten or twelve Indians, standing with their pieces presented on the bank. Finding it impossible to resist or escape, we ran the canoe ashore to-wards them, *[27]* thinking it more eligible to surrender immediately, which might entitle us to better treatment, than resist or fly, in either of which death seemed inevitable, from their presented guns, or, their pursuit. We now imag-ined our death, or, what was worse, a miserable captivity, almost certain, when the headman of the party agreeably surprized us, by asking, in the Cherokee language, to what town we belonged? To which our interpreter replied, To the English camp; that the English and Cherokees having made a peace, I was then carrying the articles to their countrymen. On this the old warrior, com-monly called the Slave Catcher of Tennessee,[72] invited us to his camp, treated us with dried venison, homminy, and boiled corn. He told us that he had been hunting some time thereabouts and had only intended returning in seven or eight days, but would now immediately accompany us.

We set out with them next morning to pursue our voyage; but I was now obliged to give over taking the courses of the river, lest the In- *[28]* dians, who, tho' very hospitable, are very suspicious of things they cannot compre-hend, should take umbrage at it.

Entering the Tennessee River,[73] we began to experience the difference be-tween going with the stream, and struggling against it; and between easy paddles, and the long poles with which we were constrained to slave to keep pace with the Indians, who would otherwise have laughed at us. When we en-camped about ten miles up the river, my hands were so galled, that the blood trickled from them, and when we set out next morning I was scarce able to handle a pole.

Within four or five miles of the nation, the Slave Catcher sent his wife forward by land, partly to prepare a dinner, and partly to let me have her place in his canoe, seeing me in pain, and unaccustomed to such hard labour, which seat I kept till about two o'clock, when we arrived at his house, opposite the mouth of Tellequo river,[74] compleating a twenty-two days [29] course of continual fatigues, hardships, and anxieties.[75]

FRENCH CHAPTER V

OUR ENTERTAINMENT from these people was as good as the country could afford, consisting of roast, boiled, and fried meats of several kinds, and very good Indian bread, baked in a very curious manner. After making a fire on the hearth-stone, about the size of a large dish, they sweep the embers off, laying a loaf smooth on it; this they cover with a sort of deep dish, and renew the fire upon the whole, under which the bread bakes to as great perfection as in any European oven.

We crossed the river next morning, with some Indians that had been visiting in that neighbourhood, and went to Tommotly, taking Fort Loudon in the way, to examine the ruins.[76]

We were received at Tommotly in a very kind manner by Ostenaco,[77] the commander in chief, who told me, he had already given [30] me up for lost, as the gang I parted with at the Great Island had returned about ten days before, and that my servant was then actually preparing for his return, with the news of my death.

After smoaking and talking some time, I delivered a letter from Colonel Stephen, and another from Captain M'Neil,[78] with some presents from each, which were gratefully accepted by Ostenaco and his consort. He gave me a

Figure 18. Timberlake describes a process of baking bread on a hearthstone with the loaf covered by a shallow bowl similar to this one. (Frank McClung Museum collection)

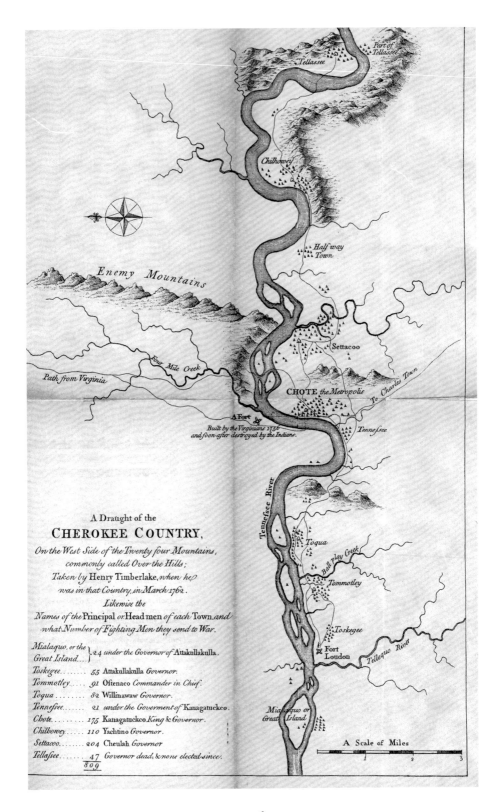

Part of
Tellassee

Tellassee

Chilhowey

Half way
Town

Enemy Mountains

Four Mile Creek

Settacoo

Path from Virginia

CHOTE the Metropolis

To Charles Town

▲ Fort
Built by the Virginians 1756
and soon after destroyed by the Indians.

Tennessee

Tennessee River

Toqua

Ball play Creek

Tommotley

A Draught of the
CHEROKEE COUNTRY,

*On the West Side of the Twenty four Mountains,
commonly called Over the Hills;
Taken by* Henry Timberlake, *when he
was in that Country, in March* 1762.

*Likewise the
Names of the* Principal *or* Head men *of each Town, and
what Number of* Fighting Men *they send to War.*

Toskegee

Mialaquo, or the } 24 *under the Governor of* Attakullakulla.
Great Island...

Fort
Loudon

Tellequo Ring

Toskegee........ 55 Attakullakulla *Governor.*

Tommotley...... 91 Ostenaco *Commander in Chief.*

Toqua......... 82 Willinawaw *Governor.*

Tennessee....... 21 *under the Goverment of* Kanagatuckco.

Chote......... 175 Kanagatuckco *King & Governor.*

Chilhowey...... 110 Yachtino *Governor.*

Settacoo....... 204 Cheulah *Governor*

Tellassee....... 47 *Governor dead, & none elected since.*
   ———
   809

Mialaquo or
Great Island

A Scale of Miles

1   2   3

general invitation to his house, while I resided in the country; and my companions found no difficulty in getting the same entertainment, among an hospitable, tho' savage people, who always pay a great regard to any one taken notice of by their chiefs.

Some days after, the headmen of each town were assembled in the townhouse of Chote, the metropolis of the country, to hear the articles of peace read, whither the interpreter and I accompanied Ostenaco. [31]

The town-house,[79] in which are transacted all public business and diversions, is raised with wood, and covered over with earth, and has all the appearance of a small mountain at a little distance. It is built in the form of a sugar loaf, and large enough to contain 500 persons, but extremely dark, having, besides the door, which is so narrow that but one at a time can pass, and that after much winding and turning, but one small aperture to let the smoak out, which is so ill contrived, that most of it settles in the roof of the house. Within it has the appearance of an ancient amphitheatre, the seats being raised one above another, leaving an area in the middle, in the center of which stands the fire; the seats of the head warriors are nearest it.

They all seemed highly satisfied with the articles. The peace-pipe was smoaked, and Ostenaco made an harangue to the following effect: [32]

"The bloody tommahawke, so long lifted against our brethren the English, must now be buried deep, deep in the ground, never to be raised again;[80] and

(facing) *Figure 19. Timberlake's map of the Cherokee Country includes the first published spelling of Tennessee as it is today.*

(below) *Figure 20. Artist's rendering of the Chota townhouse based on the archaeological record and historical descriptions. (From* Tellico Archaeology *by Jefferson Chapman)*

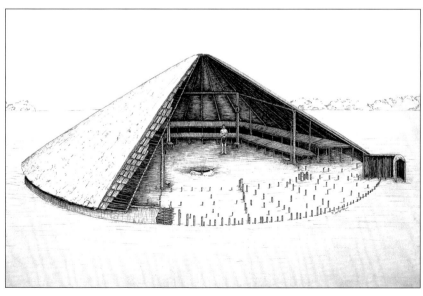

whoever shall act contrary to any of these articles, must expect a punishment equal to his offence.[81] Should a strict observance of them be neglected, a war must necessarily follow, and a second peace may not be so easily obtained. I therefore once more recommend to you, to take particular care of your behaviour towards the English, whom we must now look upon as ourselves; they have the French and Spaniards to fight, and we enough of our own colour, without medling with either nation. I [33] desire likewise, that the white warrior, who has ventured himself here with us, may be well used and respected by all, wherever he goes amongst us."

The harrangue being finished, several pipes were presented me by the headsmen, to take a whiff. This ceremony I could have waved, as smoaking was always very disagreeable to me; but as it was a token of their amity, and they might be offended if I did not comply, I put on the best face I was able, though I dared not even wipe the end of the pipe that came out of their mouths; which, considering their paint and dirtiness, are not of the most ragoutant, as the French term it.

After smoaking, the eatables were produced, consisting chiefly of wild meat; such as venison, bear, and buffalo; tho' I cannot much commend their cookery, every thing being greatly overdone: there were likewise potatoes, pumpkins, homminy, boiled corn, beans, and pease, served up in small flat baskets, made [34] of split canes, which were distributed amongst the croud; and water, which, except the spirituous liquor brought by the Europeans, is their only drink, was handed about in small goards. What contributed greatly to render this feast disgusting, was eating without knives and forks, and being obliged to grope from dish to dish in the dark. After the feast there was a dance, but I was already so fatigued with the ceremonies I had gone through, that I retired to Kanagatucko's hot-house;[82] but was prevented taking any repose by the smoke, with which I was almost suffocated, and the croud of Indians that came and sat on the bed-side; which indeed was not much calculated for repose to any but Indians, or those that had passed an apprenticeship to their ways, as I had done: it was composed of a few boards, spread with bear-skins, without any other covering; the house being so hot, that I could not endure the weight of my own blanket. [35]

Some hours after I got up to go away, but met Ostenaco, followed by two or three Indians, with an invitation from the headman of Settico,[83] to visit him the next day.

I set out with Ostenaco and my interpreter in the morning, and marched towards Settico, till we were met by a messenger, about half a mile from the town, who came to stop us till every thing was prepared for our reception: from this place I could take a view of the town where I observed two stand of colours flying, one at the top, and the other at the door of the town-house; they were as large as a sheet, and white. Lest therefore I should take them for French, they took great care to me, that their custom was to hoist red colours as an emblem of war; but white, as a token of peace. By this time we were joined by another messenger, who desired us to move forward.

About 100 yards from the town-house we were received by a body of between three and [36] four hundred Indians, ten or twelve of which were entirely naked, except a piece of cloth about their middle, and painted all over in a hideous manner, six of them with eagles tails in their hands, which they shook and flourished as they advanced, danced in a very uncommon figure, singing in concert with some drums of their own make, and those of the late unfortunate Capt. Damere;[84] with several other instruments, uncouth beyond description. Cheulah, the headman of the town, led the procession, painted blood-red, except his face, which was half black, holding an old rusty broadsword in his right hand, and an eagle's tail in his left. As they approached, Cheulah, singling himself out from the rest, cut two or three capers, as a signal to the other eagle-tails, who instantly followed his example. This violent exercise, accompanied by the band of musick, and a loud yell from the mob, lasted about a minute, when the headman waving his sword over my head, struck it into the ground, about two inches from my left foot; then directing himself to [37] me, made a short discourse (which my interpreter told me was only to bid me a hearty welcome) and presented me with a string of beads. We

Figure 21. The Warriors of AniKituhwa help maintain Cherokee traditions, including some dances witnessed by Henry Timberlake. At the Capitol Building, Colonial Williamsburg, 2006. (Photo by Barbara R. Duncan)

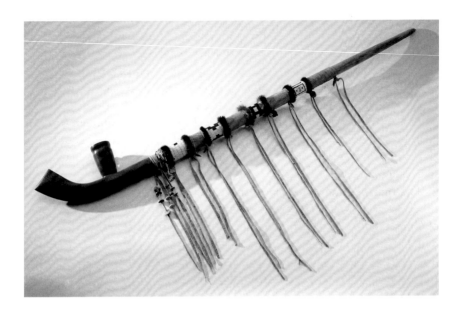

(above) *Figure 22. Timberlake described a large ceremonial pipe similar to this 21st century recreation by Joel Queen (Eastern Band Cherokee), with porcupine quillwork by Helen Smoker Martin (Eastern Band Cherokee) and Brad McMillan (Delaware). (Museum of the Cherokee Indian collection)*

(right) *Figure 23. At the town of Settico, Timberlake was offered more than 180 pipes to smoke in friendship with the men of the village. 18th-century Cherokee steatite pipe bowls. (Museum of the Cherokee Indian collection)*

then proceeded to the door, where Cheulah, and one of the beloved men, taking me by each arm, led me in, and seated me in one of the first seats; it was so dark that nothing was perceptible till a fresh supply of canes were brought, which being burnt in the middle of the house answers both purposes of fuel and candle. I then discovered about five hundred faces; and Cheulah addressing me a second time, made a speech much to the same effect as the former, congratulating me on my safe arrival thro' the numerous parties of the northern Indians, that generally haunt the way I came. He then made some professions of friendship, concluding with giving me another string of beads, as a token of it. He had scarce finished, when four of those who had exhibited at the procession made their second appearance, painted milk-white, their eagle-tails in one hand and small goards with beads in them in the other, which they rat- *[38]* tled in time to the musick. During this dance the peace-pipe was prepared; the bowl of it was of red stone, curiously cut with a knife, it being very soft, tho' extremely pretty when polished. Some of these are of black stone, and some of the same earth they make their pots with, but beautifully diversified. The stem is about three feet long, finely adorned with porcupine quills, dyed feathers, deers hair, and such like gaudy trifles.

After I had performed my part with this, I was almost suffocated with the pipes presented me on every hand, which I dared not to decline. They might amount to about 170 or 180; which made me so sick, that I could not stir for several hours.

The Indians entertained me with another dance, at which I was detained till about seven o'clock next morning, when I was conducted to the house of Chucatah,[85] then second in command, to take some refreshment. Here I found a white woman, named Mary Hughes,[86] *[39]* who told me she had been prisoner there near a twelvemonth, and that there still remained among the Indians near thirty white prisoners more, in a very miserable condition for want of cloaths, the winter being particularly severe; and their misery was not a little heightened by the usage they received from the Indians. I ordered her to come to me to Ostenaco's, with her miserable companions, where I would distribute some shirts and blankets I had brought with me amongst them, which she did some days after.

After a short nap, I arose and went to the town-house, where I found the letter for them to the Governor of South Carolina,[87] which signified their desire of living in peace with the English, as long as the sun shone, or grass grew, and desired that a trade might be opened between them. These wrote, I sealed them up, with some wampum and beads in the inside.[88] I was the same day invited to Chilhowey, *[40]* where I was received and treated much in the same manner as at Settico. I wrote some letters; and one that Yachtino[89] the headman had brought from Col. Stephen was interpreted to them which seemed to give them great satisfaction. I found here a white man, who, notwithstanding the war, lived many years among them; he told me that the lower towns had been greatly distressed when attacked by Colonel Montgomery;[90] being obliged to live many months upon horse-flesh,[91] and roots out of the woods, occasioned partly by the numbers drove among them, and the badness of the crops that year.

Returning home with Ostenaco the next day, being the 2d of January 1762, I enquired whether he thought I should receive any more invitations? He told me he believed not, because the towns to which I had already been invited, having been our most inveterate enemies during the war, had done this, as an acknowledgement and reparation of their fault.[92] *[41]*

I had now leisure to complete taking the courses of the river, from which, as I have already mentioned, I was deterred by the Indians, as likewise to make remarks upon the country and inhabitants.[93]

○○○○○○○○○○○○○○○○○○○○○○○○○○○○○○○○

THE COUNTRY being situated between thirty-two and thirty-four degrees north latitude, and eighty-seven degrees thirty minutes west longitude from London, as near as can be calculated, is temperate, inclining to heat during the summer-season, and so remarkably fertile that the women alone do all the laborious tasks of agriculture, the soil requiring only a little stirring with a hoe, to produce whatever is required of it; yielding vast quantities of pease, beans, potatoes, cabbages, Indian corn, pumpions, melons, and tobacco, not to mention a number of other vegetables imported from Europe, not so generally known amongst them, which flourish as much, or more here, than in their native climate; and, by the daily experience of the goodness of the soil, we *[42]* may conclude, that, with due care, all European plants might succeed in the same manner.[94]

Before the arrival of the Europeans, the natives were not so well provided, maize, melons, and tobacco, being the only things they bestow culture upon, and perhaps seldom on the latter. The meadows or savannahs produce excellent grass; being watered by abundance of fine rivers, and brooks well stored with fish, otters and beavers; having as yet no nets, the Indians catch the fish with lines, spears, or dams; which last, as it seems particular to the natives of America, I shall trouble the reader with a description of. Building two walls obliquely down the river from either shore, just as they are near joining, a passage is left to a deep well or reservoir; the Indians then scaring the fish down the river, close the mouth of the reservoir with a large bush, or bundle made on purpose, and it is no difficult matter to take them with baskets[95] when inclosed within so small a compass. *[43]*

North America, being one continual forest, admits of no scarcity of timber for every use: there are oaks of several sorts, birch, ash, pines, and a number of other trees, many of [70] which are unknown in Europe, but already described by many authors. The woods likewise abound with fruits and flowers, to which the Indians pay little regard. Of the fruits there are some of an excellent flavour, particularly several sorts of grapes, which, with proper culture, would probably afford an excellent wine. There are likewise plumbs, cherries, and berries of several kinds, something different from those of Europe; but their peaches and pears grow only by culture:[96] add to these several kinds of roots, and medicinal plants, particularly the plant so esteemed by the Chinese, and by them called gingsang, and a root which never fails curing the most inveterate venereal disease, which, however, they never had occasion for, for that distemper, before the arrival of Europeans among them. There are likewise an incredible number of buffaloes, bears, deer, panthers, wolves, foxes, *[44]* racoons, and opossums. The buffaloes, and most of the rest, have been so often described, and are so well known, that a description of them

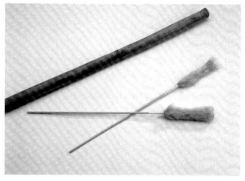

(left) *Figure 24. Metal tools such as this iron hoe were an important part of the deerskin trade. (Frank McClung Museum collection)*

(right) *Figure 25. Cherokee blowguns were used to hunt small game. Blowguns were made from river cane, hollowed and then straightened over an open fire. Darts are made from thistledown tied onto locust shafts. (Museum of the Cherokee Indian collection)*

would be but tedious; the opossum, however, deserves some attention, as I have never seen it properly described. It is about the size of a large cat, short and thick, and of a silver colour. It brings forth its young, contrary to all other animals, at the teat, from whence, when of a certain size, and able to walk, it drops off, and goes into a false belly, designed by providence in its dam for its reception, which, at the approach of danger, will, notwithstanding this additional load, climb rocks and trees with great agility for its security.

There are a vast number of lesser sort of game, such as rabbits, squirrels of several sorts, and many other animals, beside turkeys, geese, ducks of several kinds, partridges, pheasants, and an infinity of other birds, pursued only by the children, who, at eight or ten years old, are very expert at killing with a sar- *[45]* bacan, or hollow cane,[97] through which they blow a small dart, whose weakness obliges them to shoot at the eye of the larger sort of prey, which they seldom miss.

There are likewise a great number of reptiles, particularly the copper-snake, whose bite is very difficult to cure, and the rattle-snake, once the terror of Europeans, now no longer apprehended, the bite being so easily cured; but neither this, nor any other species, will attempt biting unless disturbed or trod upon; neither are there any animals in America mischievous unless attacked. The flesh of the rattle-snake is extremely good; being once obliged to eat one through want of provisions, I have eat several since thro' choice.

Of insects, the flying stag is almost the only one worthy of notice; it is about the shape of a beetle, but has very large beautiful branching horns, like those of a stag, from whence it took its name. *[46]*

The Indians have now a numerous breed of horses, as also hogs, and other of our animals, but neither cows nor sheep; both these, however, might be supplied by prisoners among them have procured both butter and cheese; and the fine long shag on its back could supply all the purposes of wool.[98]

The mountains contain very rich mines of gold,[99] silver, lead, and copper, as may be evinced by several accidentally found out by the Indians, and the lumps of valuable ore washed down by several of the streams, a bag of which sold in Virginia at a considerable price; and by the many salt springs, it is probable there are many mines of that likewise, as well as of other minerals. The fountains too may have many virtues, that require more skilful persons than the Cherokees or myself to find out.

They have many beautiful stones of different colours, many of which, I am apt to be- *[47]* lieve, are of great value;[100] but their superstition has always prevented their disposing of them to the traders, who have made many attempts to that purpose; but as they use them in their conjuring ceremonies, they believe their parting with them, or bringing them from home, would prejudice their health or affairs. Among others, there is one in the possession of a conjurer, remarkable for its brilliancy and beauty, but more so for the extraordinary manner in which it was found. It grew, if we may credit the Indians, on the head of a monstrous serpent, whose retreat was, by its brilliancy, discovered; but a great number of snakes attending him, he being, as I suppose by his diadem, of a superior rank among the serpents, made it dangerous to attack him. Many were the attempts made by the Indians, but all frustrated, till a fellow, more bold than the rest, casing himself in leather, impenetrable to the bite of the serpent or his guards, and watching a convenient oportunity, surprised and killed him, tearing this jewel from his head, which the conjurer has kept hid for many *[48]* years, in some place unknown to all but two women, who have been offered large presents to betray it, but steadily refused, lest some signal judgment or mischance should follow. That such a stone exists, I believe, having seen many of great beauty; but I cannot think it would answer all the encomiums the Indians bestow upon it. The conjurer, I suppose, hatched the account of its discovery; I have however given it to the reader, as a specimen of an Indian story, many of which are much more surprising.[101]

FRENCH CHAPTER VII

The Cherokees are of a middle stature, of an olive colour, tho' generally painted, and their skins stained with gun-powder, pricked into it in very pretty figures.[102] The hair of their head is shaved, tho' many of the old people have it plucked out by the roots, except a patch on the hinder part of the head, about twice the bigness of a crown-piece, which is ornamented with beads, feathers, wampum, stained deers hair, and such like baubles. The ears are slit and stretched to an enormous size, *[49]* putting the person who undergoes the operation to incredible pain, being unable to lie on either side for near forty days. To remedy this, they generally slit but one at a time; so soon as the patient can bear it, they are wound round with wire to expand them, and are adorned with silver pendants and rings,[103] which they likewise wear at the nose. This custom does not belong originally to the Cherokees, but taken by them from the Shawnese, or other northern nations.

They that can afford it wear a collar of wampum, which are beads cut out of clamshells, a silver breast-plate, and bracelets on their arms and wrists of the same metal, a bit of cloth over their private parts, a shirt of the English make, a sort of cloth-boots, and mockasons which are shoes of a make peculiar to the Americans, ornamented with porcupine-quills; a large mantle or match-coat thrown over all compleats their dress at home; but when they go to war they leave their trinkets behind, and the mere necessaries serve them. *[50]*

Figure 26. Based on the list of gifts for Cherokee warriors in 1759 from the papers of General Jeffrey Amherst, Cherokee men's clothing included a linen trade shirt, match coat of stroud cloth with bed lace, breechclout of saved list stroud, and side-seam leggings of stroud trade cloth with silk ribbon and beaded decoration. Reproduction by Robert Scott Stephenson. (Museum of the Cherokee Indian collection)

Figure 27. Brass springs were used by Cherokees in the 18th century to pluck hair and eyebrows for aesthetic appeal. (Museum of the Cherokee Indian collection)

Figure 28. Based on descriptions ca. 1760, Cherokee women's clothing included a shirt made of linen or calico, a wraparound skirt, and side-seam leggings made of wool stroud trade cloth and decorated with silk ribbons and beads. Cherokee women also wore linen waistcoats decorated with beads and shells and calico linen or cotton petticoats. Reproduction by Robert Scott Stephenson. (Museum of the Cherokee Indian collection)

Figure 29. 18th-century pipe tomahawk reproduction by Daniel Begay. (Museum of the Cherokee Indian collection)

The women wear the hair of their head, which is so long that it generally reaches to the middle of their legs, and sometimes to the ground, club'd, and ornamented with ribbons of various colours;[104] but, except their eyebrows, pluck it from all the other parts of the body, especially the looser part of the sex. The rest of their dress is now become very much like the European; and, indeed, that of the men is greatly altered. The old people still remember and praise the ancient days, before they were acquainted with the whites, when they had but little dress, except a bit of skin about their middles, mockasons, a mantle of buffalo skin for the winter, and a lighter one of feathers for the summer. The women, particularly the half-breed, are remarkably well featured; and both men and women are streight and well-built, with small hands and feet.[105]

The warlike arms used by the Cherokees are guns, bows and arrows, darts, scalp- *[51]* ping-knives, and tommahawkes, which are hatchets; the hammer-part of which being made hollow, and a small hole running from thence along the shank, terminated by a small brass-tube for the mouth, makes a compleat pipe. There are various ways of making these, according to the country or fancy of the purchaser, being all made by the Europeans; some have a long spear at top, and some different conveniencies on each side. This is one of their most useful pieces of field-furniture, serving all the offices of hatchet, pipe, and sword; neither are the Indians less expert at throwing it than using it near, but will kill at a considerable distance.

They are of a very gentle and amicable disposition to those they think their friends, but as implacable in their enmity, their revenge being only compleated in the entire destruction of their enemies. They were pretty hospitable to all white strangers, till the Europeans encouraged them to scalp; but the great reward offered has led them often since to com- *[52]* mit as great barbarities on us, as they formerly only treated their most inveterate enemies with. They are very hardy, bearing heat, cold, hunger and thirst, in a surprizing manner; and yet no people are given to more excess in eating and drinking, when it is conveniently in their power: the follies, nay mischief, they commit when inebriated, are entirely laid to the liquor; and no one will revenge any injury (murder excepted) received from one who is no more himself: they are not less addicted to gaming than drinking, and will even lose the shirt off their back, rather than give over play, when luck runs against them.[106]

They are extremely proud, despising the lower class of Europeans; and in some athletick diversions I once was present at, they refused to match or hold conference with any but officers.

Here, however, the vulgar notion of the Indians uncommon activity was contradicted [53] by three officers of the Virginia regiment, the slowest of which could outrun the swiftest of about 700 Indians that were in the place: but had the race exceeded two or three hundred yards, the Indians would then have acquired the advantage, by being able to keep the same pace a long time together; and running being likewise more general among them, a body of them would always greatly exceed an equal number of our troops.

They are particularly careful of the super-annuated, but are not so till of a great age; of which Ostenaco's mother is an instance. Ostenaco is about sixty years of age, and the youngest of four; yet his mother still continues her laborious tasks, and has yet strength enough to carry 200 weight of wood on

Figure 30. Earrings were worn by both men and women. Men sometimes slit and stretched their earlobes to accommodate more jewelry. (Frank McClung Museum collection)

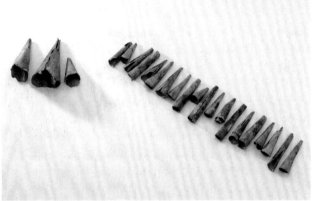

(above) Figure 31. Scrap metal, particularly brass, was often fashioned into jewelry, such as this twisted brass bracelet. (Frank McClung Museum collection)

(left) Figure 32. Brass cones were sometimes attached to clothing to create sound during dances. Mid-18th century. (Frank McClung Museum collection)

(left) Figure 33. Trade silver was highly prized as a status symbol and used in a variety of forms including armbands. Cherokee silver armband. 18th century. (Collection of Tommy Beutell)

(below) Figure 34. This shell gorget made from a marine mollusk shows a continuation of centuries old trade networks with the Gulf coast that continued into the historic period. (Frank McClung Museum collection)

Figure 35. This silver gorget is designed similarly to the precontact shell gorgets. The swan engraving may be purely decorative, or it may have had an affiliation or recognition meaning that has been lost. A swan's wing was the symbol of authority of the Beloved Woman. (Frank McClung Museum collection)

Figure 36. Brass from kettles was sometimes hammered into thinner sheets and fashioned into ornaments such as these tubular beads. (Frank McClung Museum collection)

Figure 37. Cherokee brass neck collar and arm bands, 18th century. (Collection of Tommy Beutell)

her back near a couple of miles. I am apt to think some of them, by their own computation, are near 150 years old.[107]

They have many of them a good uncultivated genius, are fond of speaking well, as that *[54]* paves the way to power in their councils; and I doubt not but the reader will find some beauties in the harangues I have given him, which I assure him are entirely genuine. Their language is not unpleasant, but vastly aspirated, and the accents so many and various, you would often imagine them singing in their common discourse.[108] As the ideas of the Cherokees are so few, I cannot say much for the copiousness of their language.[109]

They seldom turn their eyes on the person they speak of, or address themselves to, and are always suspicious when people's eyes are fixed upon them. They speak so low, except in council, that they are often obliged to repeat what they were saying; yet should a person talk to any of them above their common pitch, they would immediately ask him, if he thought they were deaf?

They have likewise a sort of loose poetry, as the war-songs, love-songs, &c. Of the latter many contain no more than that the young man loves the young woman, and will be uneasy, according to their own expression, if he does not obtain her. Of the former I shall present the following specimen, without the original in Cherokee, on account of the expletive syllables, merely introduced for the music, and not the sense, just like the toldederols of many old English songs.

A TRANSLATION of the W A R - S O N G.
Caw waw noo dee, &c.

WHERE'ER the earth's enlighten'd by the sun,
Moon shines by night, grass grows, or waters run,
Be't known that we are going, like men, afar,
In hostile fields to wage destructive war;
Like men we go, to meet our country's foes,
Who, Woman-like, shall fly our dreaded blows;
Yes, as a woman, who beholds a snake,
In gaudy horror, glisten thro' the brake,
Starts trembling back, and stares with wild surprize,
Or pale thro' fear, unconscious, panting, flies.[110]
Just so these foes, more tim'rous than the hind,
Shall leave their arms and only cloaths behind; *[56]*
Pinch'd by each blast, by ev'ry thicket torn,
Run back to their own nation, now its scorn:
Or in the winter, when the barren wood
Denies their gnawing entrails nature's food,
Let them sit down, from friends and country far,

And wish, with tears, they ne'er had come to war.[111]
We'll leave our clubs, dew'd with their country show'rs,
And, if they dare to bring them back to our's,
Their painted scalps shall be a step to fame,
And grace our own and glorious country's name.
Or if we warriors spare the yielding foe,
Torments at home the wretch must undergo.[112] [57]
But when we go, who knows which shall return,
When growing dangers rise with each new morn?
Farewel, ye little ones, ye tender wives,
For you alone we would conserve our lives!
But cease to mourn, 'tis unavailing pain,
If not fore-doom'd, we soon shall meet again.
But, O ye friends! in case your comrades fall,
Think that on you our deaths for vengeance call
With uprais'd tommahawkes pursue our blood,
And stain, with hostile streams, the conscious wood,
That pointing enemies may never tell
The boasted place where we, their victims, fell.[113] [58]

Both the ideas and verse are very loose in the original, and they are set to as loose a music, many composing both tunes and song off hand, according to the occasion; tho' some tunes, especially those taken from the northern Indians, are extremely pretty, and very like the Scotch.

FRENCH CHAPTER VIII

THE INDIANS being all soldiers, mechanism can make but little progress; besides this, they labour under the disadvantage of having neither proper tools, or persons to teach the use of those they have: Thus, for want of saws, they are obliged to cut a large tree on each side, with great labour, to make a very clumsy board; whereas a pair of sawyers would divide the same tree into eight or ten in much less time: considering this disadvantage, their modern houses are tolerably well built. A number of thick posts is fixed in the ground, according to the plan and dimensions of the house, which rarely exceeds sixteen feet in breadth, on account of the roofing, but often extend to sixty or seventy in length, beside the [59] little hot-house. Between each of these posts is placed a smaller one, and the whole wattled with twigs like a basket, which is then covered with clay very smooth, and sometimes white-washed. Instead of tiles, they cover them with narrow boards. Some of these houses are two story high, tolerably pretty and capacious; but most of them very inconvenient for want of chimneys, a small hole being all the vent assigned in many for the smoak to get out at.

Their canoes are the next work of any consequence; they are generally made of a large pine or poplar, from thirty to forty feet long, and about two broad, with flat bottoms and sides, and both ends alike; the Indians hollow them now with the tools they get from the Europeans, but formerly did it by fire: they are capable of carrying about fifteen or twenty men, are very light, and can by the Indians, so great is their skill in managing them, be forced up a very strong current, *[60]* particularly the bark canoes; but these are seldom used but by the northern Indians.[114]

They have of late many tools among them, and, with a little instruction, would soon become proficients in the use of them, being great imitators of any thing they see done; and the curious manner in which they dress skins, point arrows, make earthen vessels, and basket-work, are proofs of their ingenuity, possessing them a long time before the arrival of Europeans among them. Their method of pointing arrows is as follows: Cutting a bit of thin brass, copper, bone, or scales of a particular fish, into a point with two beards, or some into an acute triangle, they split a little of their arrow, which is generally of reeds; into this they put the point, winding some deers sinew round the arrow, and through a little hole they make in the head; then they moisten the sinew with their spittle, which, when dry, remains fast glewed, nor ever

Figure 38. Eleven paired summer and winter houses matching the descriptions of Henry Timberlake were found during the archaeological investigations at Chota in the 1970s. (Frank McClung Museum collection)

Figure 39. Cut brass arrow points, 18th century. These arrow points were cut from brass trade kettles that had worn out, according to Timberlake's description. Copper salts preserved parts of the cane shafts and deer sinew used to tie the point to the shaft. (Frank McClung Museum collection and Sequoyah Birthplace Museum collection)

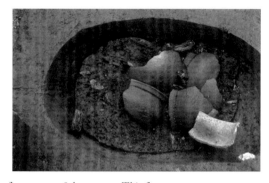

(left) *Figure 40. Cherokee Overhills pottery fragment, 18th century. This fragment comes from a cooking pot. Stamped patterns were not common in Overhill pottery but did exist. They were more characteristic of Cherokee pottery in the Middle Towns. (Frank McClung Museum collection)*

(right) *Figure 41. Pottery shards fill a refuse pit at the 18th-century townsite of Chota. (Frank McClung Museum collection)*

untwists. Their bows are of several sorts of wood, dipped in bears oil, and seasoned *[61]* before the fire, and a twisted bear's gut for the string.

They have two sorts of clay, red and white, with both which they make excellent vessels, some of which will stand the greatest heat. They have now learnt to sew, and the men as well as women, excepting shirts, make all their own cloaths; the women, likewise, make very pretty belts, and collars of beads and wampum, also belts and garters of worsted. In arts, however, as in war, they are greatly excelled by their northern neighbours.[115]

Their chief trade is with those Europeans with whom they are in alliance, in hides, furs, &c. which they barter by the pound, for all other goods; by that means supplying the deficiency of money. But no proportion is kept to their value; what cost two shillings in England, and what cost two pence, are often sold for the same price; besides that, no attention is paid to the goodness, and a knife of the best temper and workmanship will only sell for the *[62]* same price as an ordinary one. The reason of this is, that, in the beginning

(left) *Figure 42. Two thimbles. 18th century. These metal thimbles include the organic twine originally used to attach them. (Frank McClung Museum collection)*

(above) *Figure 43. Iron scissors. 18th century. (Frank McClung Museum collection)*

of the commerce, the Indians finding *[Williams ommitted 'finding'] themselves greatly imposed upon, fixed a price on each article, according to their own judgment; powder, balls, and several other goods, are by this means set so low, that few people would bring them, but that the Indians refuse to trade with any person who has not brought a proportionable quantity, and the traders are cautious of losing a trade in which 5 or 600 per cent. in many articles fully recompences their loss in these.

As to religion, every one is at liberty to think for himself; whence flows a diversity of opinions amongst those that do think, but the major part do not give themselves that trouble. They generally concur, however, in the belief of one superior Being, who made them, and governs all things, and are therefore never discontent at any misfortune, because they say, the Man above would have it so. They believe in a reward and punishment, as may be evinced by their answer to Mr. Martin[116] *[63]* who, having preached scripture till both his audience and he were heartily tired, was told at last, that they knew very well, that, if they were good, they should go up; if bad, down; that he could tell no more; that he had long plagued them with what they no ways understood, and that they desired him to depart the country. This, probably, was at the instigation of their conjurers, to whom these people pay a profound regard; as christianity was entirely opposite, and would soon dispossess the people of their implicit belief in their juggling art, which the professors have brought to so great perfection as to deceive Europeans, much more an ignorant race, whose ideas will naturally augment the extraordinary of any thing the least above their comprehension, or out of the common tract. After this I need not say that in every particular they are extremely superstitious, that and ignorance going always hand in hand.

They have few religious ceremonies, or stated times of general worship: the green *[64]* corn dance[117] seems to be the principal, which is, as I have been told, performed in a very solemn manner, in a large square before the town-house door: the motion here is very slow, and the song in which they offer thanks to God for the corn he has sent them, far from unpleasing. There is no kind of rites or ceremonies at marriage, courtship and all being, as I have already observed, concluded in half an hour, without any other celebration, and it is as little binding as ceremonious; for though many last till death, especially when there are children, it is common for a person to change three or four times a-year. Notwithstanding this, the Indian women gave lately a proof of fidelity, not to be equalled by politer ladies, bound by all the sacred ties of marriage.

Many of the soldiers in the garrison of Fort Loudoun, having Indian wives, these brought them a daily supply of provisions, though blocked up, in order to be starved to a surrender, by their own countrymen; and *[65]* they persisted in this, notwithstanding the express orders of Willinawaw, who, sensible of the retardment this occasioned, threatened death to those who would assist their enemy; but they laughing at his threats, boldly told him, they would succour their husbands every day, and were sure, that, if he killed them, their relations would make his death atone for theirs. Willinawaw was too sensible of this to put his threats into execution, so that the garrison subsisted a long time on the provisions brought to them in this manner.

When they part, the children go with, and are provided for, by the mother. As soon as a child is born, which is generally without help, it is dipped into cold water and washed, which is repeated every morning for two years afterward, by which the children acquire such strength, that no ricketty or deformed are found amongst them. When the woman recovers, which is at latest in three days, she carries it herself to the river to wash it; but though three days is the longest time of their *[66]* illness, a great number or them are not so many hours; nay, I have known a woman delivered at the side of a river, wash her child, and come home with it in one hand, and a goard full of water in the other.

They seldom bury their dead, but throw them into the river;[118] yet if any white man will bury them, he is generally rewarded with a blanket, besides what he takes from the corpse, the dead having commonly their guns, tommahawkes, powder, lead, silver ware, wampum, and a little tobacco, buried with them; and as the persons who brings the corpse to the place of burial, immediately leave it, he is at liberty to dispose of all as he pleases, but must take care never to be found out, as nothing belonging to the dead is to be kept, but every thing at his decease destroyed, except these articles, which are destined to accompany him to the other world.[119] It is reckoned, therefore, the worst of thefts; yet there is no punishment for this, or any other crime, mur*[67]*der excepted, which is more properly revenged than punished.

This custom was probably introduced to prevent avarice, and, by preventing hereditary acquisitions, make merit the sole means of acquiring power, honour, and riches. The inventor, however, had too great a knowledge of the human mind, and our propensity to possess, not to see that a superior passion must intercede; he therefore wisely made it a religious ceremony, that superstition, the strongest passion of the ignorant, might check avarice, and keep it in the bounds he had prescribed. It is not known from whence it came, but it is of great antiquity, and not only general over all North America, but in many parts of Asia. On this account the wives generally have separate property, that no inconveniency may arise from death or separation.

The Indians have a particular method of relieving the poor, which I shall rank among the most laudable of their religious ceremonies, *[68]* most of the rest consisting purely in the vain ceremonies, and superstitious romances of their conjurors. When any of their people are hungry, as they term it, or in distress, orders are issued out by the headmen for a war-dance, at which all the fighting men and warriors assemble; but here, contrary to all their other dances, one only dances at a time, who, after hopping and capering for near a minute, with a tommahawke in his hand, gives a small hoop, at which signal the music stops till he relates the manner of taking his first scalp, and concludes his narration, by throwing on a large skin spread for that purpose, a string of wampum, piece of plate, wire, paint, lead, or any thing he can most conveniently spare; after which the music strikes up, and he proceeds in the same manner through all his warlike actions: then another takes his place, and the ceremony lasts till all the warriors and fighting men have related their exploits. The stock thus raised, after paying the musicians, is divided among the poor. The same ceremony is made use of to recompence any ex- *[69]* traordinary merit. This is touching vanity in a tender part, and is an admirable method of making even imperfections conduce to the good of society.

Their government, if I may call it government, which has neither laws or power to support it, is a mixed aristocracy and democracy, the chiefs being chose according to their merit in war or policy at home; these lead the warriors that chuse to go, for there is no laws or compulsion on those that refuse to follow, or punishment to those that forsake their chief: he strives, therefore, to inspire them with a sort of enthusiasm, by the war-song, as the ancient bards did once in Britain. These chiefs, or headmen, likewise compose the assemblies of the nation, into which the warwomen are admitted. The reader will not be a little surprised to find the story of Amazons not so great a fable as we imagined, many of the Indian women being as famous in war, as powerful in the council. *[70]*

The rest of the people are divided into two military classes, warriors and fighting men, which last are the plebeians, who have not distinguished themselves enough to be admitted into the rank of warriors. There are some other honorary titles among them, conferred in reward of great actions; the first of which is Outacity, or Man-killer;[120] and the second Colona, or the Raven.[121] Old warriors likewise, or war-women, who can no longer go to war, but have distinguished themselves in their younger days, have the title of Beloved. This is the only title females can enjoy; but it abundantly recompences them, by the power they acquire by it, which is so great, that they can, by the wave of a swan's wing, deliver a wretch condemned by the council, and already tied to the stake.[122]

Their common names are given them by their parents; but this they can either change, or take another when they think proper; so that some of them have near half a dozen, which the English generally increase, by giving [71] an English one, from some circumstance in their lives or disposition, as the Little Carpenter to Attakullakulla, from his excelling in building houses; Judd's friend, or corruptly the Judge, to Ostenaco, for saving a man of that name from the fury of his countrymen; or sometimes a translation of his Cherokee name, as Pigeon to Woey,[123] that being the signification of the word. The Over-hill settlement is by these two chiefs divided into two factions, between whom there is often great animosity, and the two leaders are sure to oppose one another in every measure taken. Attakullakulla has done but little in war to recommend him, but has often signalized himself by his policy, and negotiations at home. Ostenaco has a tolerable share of both; but policy and art are the greatest steps to power. Attakullakulla has a large faction with this alone, while Oconnestoto, sir-named the Great Warrior, famous for having, in all his expeditions, taken such prudent measures as never to have lost a man, has not so much power, and Ostenaco could never have obtained the su- [72] periority, if he had not a great reputation in both.[124]

On my arrival in the Cherokee country, I found the nation much attached to the French, who have the prudence, by familiar politeness (which costs but little, and often does a great deal) and conforming themselves to their ways and temper, to conciliate the inclinations of almost all the Indians they are acquainted with, while the pride of our officers often disgusts them; nay, they did not scruple to own to me, that it was the trade alone that induced them to make peace with us and not any preference to the French, whom they loved a great deal better. As however they might expect to hasten the opening of the trade by telling me this, I should have paid but little regard to it, had not my own observations confirmed me, that it was not only their general opinion, but the policy of most of their head-men; except Attakullakulla, who conserves his attachment inviolably to the English. [73]

I shall be accused, perhaps, for mentioning policy among so barbarous a nation; but tho' I own their views are not so clear and refined as those of European statesmen, their alliance with the French seems equal, proportioning the lights of savages and Europeans, to our most masterly strokes of policy; and yet we cannot be surprized at it, when we consider that merit alone creates their ministers, and not the prejudices of party, which often create ours.[125]

The English are now so nigh, and encroached daily so far upon them, that they not only felt the bad effects of it in their hunting grounds, which were spoiled, but had all the reason in the world to apprehend being swallowed up, by so potent neighbours, or driven from the country, inhabited by their fathers, in which they were born, and brought up, in fine, their native soil, for which all men have a particular tenderness and affection. The French lay farther off, and were not so powerful; from them therefore they had less to [74] fear. The keeping these foreigners then more upon a footing, as a check upon one another, was providing for their own safety, and that of all America, since they foresaw, or the French took care to shew them, that, should they be driven out, the English would in time extend themselves over all North America. The Indians cannot, from the woods of America, see the true state of Europe: report is all they have to judge by, and that often comes from persons too interested to give a just account. France's circumstances were not in such a flourishing condition as was represented; the French were conquered, and a war carried into the heart of the Cherokee country; many of their towns were sacked and plundered without a possibility of relieving them, as they lay straggled on a large extent of ground, many miles from one another; it was then their interests, or rather they were compelled to ask for peace and trade, without which they could no longer flourish. [75]

Were arts introduced, and the Cherokees contracted into a fortified settlement, governed by laws, and remoter from the English, they might become formidable; but hunting must be then laid more aside and tame cattle supply the deficiency of the wild, as the greater the number of hunters, the more prey would be required; and the more a place is haunted by men, the less it is resorted to by game. Means might be taken, would the Cherokees follow them, to render the nation considerable; but who would seek to live by labour, who can live by amusement? The sole occupations of an Indian life, are hunting, and warring abroad, and lazying at home. Want is said to be the mother of industry, but their wants are supplied at an easier rate.[126]

Some days after my reception at Chilhowey, I had an opportunity of seeing some more of their diversions. Two letters I received from some officers at the Great Island occasioned a great assembly at Chote, where I was conducted to read them; but the Indians finding no- [76] thing that regarded them, the greater part resolved to amuse themselves at a game they call nettecawaw;[127] which I can give no other description of, than that each player having a pole about ten feet long, with several marks or divisions, one of them bowls a round stone, with one flat side, and the other convex,[128] on which the players all dart their poles after it, and the nearest counts according to the vicinity of the bowl to the marks on his pole.

As I was informed there was to be a physic-dance at night, curiosity led me to the townhouse, to see the preparation. A vessel of their own make, that might contain twenty gallons (there being a great many to take the medicine)

Figure 44. Timberlake described Cherokee chunkey stones as flat on one side and convex on the other. This example was found in the fire hearth in the Chota town house. (Frank McClung Museum collection)

Figure 45. Depiction of a chunkey game as described by Henry Timberlake, by Artist H. Tom Hall. Created for National Geographic's Ancient Cities *by Gene S. Stuart (1988:45). (Courtesy National Geographic Society)*

was set on the fire, round which stood several goards filled with river-water, which was poured into the pot; this done, there arose one of the beloved women, who, opening a deer-skin filled with various roots and herbs, took out a small handful of something like fine salt; part of which she threw on the headman's seat, and part into the fire close to the pot; she *[77]* then took out the wing of a swan, and after flourishing it over the pot, stood fixed for near a minute, muttering something to herself; then taking a shrub-like laurel (which I supposed was the physic) she threw it into the pot, and returned to her former seat. As no more ceremony seemed to be going forward, I took a walk till the Indians assembled to take it. At my return I found the house quite full: they danced near an hour round the pot, till one of them, with a small goard that might hold about a gill,[129] took some of the physic, and drank it, after which all the rest took in turn.[130] One of their headmen presented me

(above) *Figure 46. Feather cape. White goose feathers simulate swan feathers, fastened to a netting of hand-twined hemp. Ties are hand-twisted dogbane. Made by Deborah Harding. (Collection of Barbara R. Duncan)*

(right) *Figure 47. Conch shell dipper used for serving the Black Drink. Acquired through intertribal trading networks from the Gulf of Mexico. Mid–18th century. (Frank McClung Museum collection)*

with some and in a manner compelled me to drink, though I would have willingly declined. It was however much more palatable than I expected, having a strong taste of sassafras: the Indian who presented it, told me it was taken to wash away their sins; so that this is a spiritual medicine, and might be ranked among their religious ceremonies. They are very solicitous about its success; the conjurer, for several mornings before it is *[78]* drank, makes a dreadful howling, yelling, and hallowing, from the top of the town-house, to frighten away apparitions and evil spirits. According to our ideas of evil spirits, such hideous noises would by sympathy call up such horrible beings; but I am apt to think with the Indians, that such noises are sufficient to frighten any being away but themselves.

I was almost every night at some dance, or diversion; the war-dance,[131] however, gave me the greatest satisfaction, as in that I had an opportunity of learning their methods of war, and a history of their warlike actions, many of which are both amusing and instructive.

I was not a little pleased likewise with their ball-plays (in which they shew

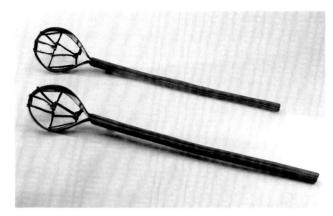

Figure 48. Cherokee stickball sticks used today are very similar to those used at the time of Timberlake's visit. Sticks made from white oak. (Museum of the Cherokee Indian collection)

great dexterity) especially when the women played, who pulled one another about, to the no small amusement of an European spectator. *[79]*

They are likewise very dexterous at pantomime dances; several of which I have seen performed that were very diverting. In one of these, two men, dressed in bear-skins, came in, stalking and pawing about with all the motions of real bears: two hunters followed them, who in dumb shew acted in all respects as they would do in the wood: after many attempts to shoot them, the hunters fire; one of the bears is killed, and the other wounded; but, as they attempt to cut his throat, he rises up again, and the scuffle between the huntsmen and the wounded bear generally affords the company a great deal of diversion.

The taking the pigeons at roost was another that pleased me exceedingly; and these, with my walking and observations, furnished me with amusement for some time; but the season not always permitting my going abroad, and as I had so little to do at home, I soon grew tired of the country. The Indian senate indeed would sometimes employ me in reading and writing letters for them; of which I generally *[80]* acquitted myself to their satisfaction, by adding what I thought would be acceptable, and retrenching whatever might displease.

FRENCH CHAPTER IX

ON THE 17TH, a party came home from hunting on Holston's River, bringing with them an eagle's tail, which was celebrated at night by a grand war-dance, and the person who killed it had the second war-title of Colona conferred upon him, besides the bounty gathered at the war-dance, in wampum, skins, &c. to the amount of thirty pounds; the tail of an eagle being held in the greatest esteem, as they sometimes are given with the wampum in their treaties, and none of their warlike ceremonies can be performed without them.

This Indian acquainted the headman of a current report in the English camp, that a large body of English were to march next spring through the Cherokees country, against the French. There was little probability or possibility in such a report, yet it was received with some degree of belief; every thing of *[81]* news, every flying rumour, is swallowed here by the populace. The least probability is exaggerated into a fact, and an Indian from our camp, who scarce understands four or five words of a conversation between two common soldiers, who often know as little of the state of affairs as the Indians themselves, turn all the rest of it to something he suspects, and imagines he has heard what was never once mentioned; and this, when he returns to his own country, is passed about as a certainty. From hence flows the continual mistakes the Indians unavoidably make in their councils; they must act according to intelligence, and it requires a great penetration indeed to discern the truth, when blended with so much falsity: thus they are often obliged to act according to the report of a mistaken or lying Indian, who are all but too much adicted to this vice, which proved a continual fund of uneasiness to me all the time I remained in their country. *[82]*

On the 26th of January, advices were received from the Great Island, that some Cherokees had been killed by the northern Indians, who had been encouraged, and much caressed, by the commanding officer. This piece of news seemed greatly to displease them; they suspended however their judgment, till further intelligence. I began to be very uneasy for the return of an express I had sent out on my arrival, who was to come back by the Great Island, and was the only person who could give me any accounts I could rely on, as I was sensible the Indian one was infinitely exaggerated. We were yet talking of this, when the *News Hallow* was given from the top of Tommotly townhouse; whereupon Ostenaco rose from the table, and went immediately to the town-house, where he staid till day. On asking him next morning, What news? he seemed very unwilling to tell me, and went out of the house, seemingly very much displeased. I then made the same question to several other Indians, whose different stories convinced me it was something they endeavoured to conceal. *[83]*

I was under some apprehension at this unusual incivility. It was no wonder I was alarmed; had the English given any encouragement to these northern savages, nay, had the French faction persuaded their countrymen of our countenancing them in the slaughter, the meanest of the deceased's relations had it in his power to sacrifice me to their manes, and would certainly have done it, since, in default of kindred, their revenge falls on any of the same country that unfortunately comes within their reach;[132] and nothing could be a protection to an hostage, when capitulating could not save the garrison of Fort Loudoun: a body of Indians pursued them, and breaking through the articles, and all the laws of war and humanity, surprised and butchered them.[133] Disguising, however, my uneasiness, I seemingly took to some diversions, while I sent M'Cormack to pry into the true cause of such a change; he following my host, found no difficulty in shuffling amongst the crowd into the townhouse, where Ostenaco made the following speech. *[84]*

We have had some bad talks lately from the Great Island, which I hope nevertheless are not true, as I should be very sorry that the peace, so lately concluded with our brethren the English, should be broke in so short a time: we must not judge as yet of what we have heard from the Great Island. If Bench the express does not return soon, I myself will raise a party, and go to the Great Island where I shall get certain information of all that has happened."

This speech was received with shouts of applause, and the assembly betook themselves to dancing.

On the 28th,[134] I was invited to a grand eagle's tail dance,[135] at which about 600 persons of both sexes were assembled. About midnight, in the heat of their diversion, news was brought of the death of one of their principal men, killed at the Great Island by the northern Indians. This put a sudden stop to their diversion, and nothing was heard but threats of *[85]* vengeance. I easily concluded that this could only proceed from the confirmation of the ill news already received. I tried as much as laid in my power to mollify their anger, by telling them, that, if any accident had happened to their people, it was neither by consent or approbation of the English; that tho' the northern Indians were our allies as well as they, I was certain more favour would be shewn them than their enemies, as Capt. M'Neil, who commanded the fort, was a good, humane, brave officer, and had always shewn so much friendship for their nation, as to leave no room to doubt of his protection to any of their people who should be under his care. This satisfied them so well, that some proposed dancing again; but as it was late, they agreed to give over their diversion for that night.

On the 4th of February, an account came in almost contradictory to this. An Indian woman from Holston's River was the messenger, who related, that the northern Indians had turned their arms against the English, and *[86]* were then actually building a breast-work within a quarter of a mile of Fort Robinson; that, whilst one half were employed in carrying on the work, the other observed the motions of our people; but this lie was even too gross for Indians to digest; tho' the next day, another who came in confirmed it, and moreover affirmed the enemy's fortifications to be already breast-high.

The 15th[136] was the day appointed for the return of the Little Carpenter; and his not arriving began to give his friends a great deal of uneasiness. Ostenaco bore likewise his share in it as his brother was of the party. Here is a lesson to Europe; two Indian chiefs, whom we call barbarians, rivals of power, heads of two opposite factions, warm in opposing one another, as their interest continually clash; yet these have no farther animosity, no family quarrels or resentment, and the brother of the chief who had gained the superiority is a volunteer under his rival's command. *[87]*

For my part, I was no less anxious about the express. I dispatched my servant out to meet him, and bring me the particulars of what had been transacted at the Great Island; he returned in about five or six days, with the letters the express had been charged with, leaving him to make out the rest of the journey as his fatigue would permit. Among others was a letter from Capt. M'Neil, informing me, that a party of about seventy northern Indians came to Fort Robinson a short time after I had left it, who told him, that they came from Pittsburg, with a pass from the commanding officer, to join us against the Cherokees, not knowing that we had already concluded a peace. They seemed very much dissatisfied at coming so far to no purpose, and demanded if any Cherokees were near? They were answered, that a party were out a hunting; but, if they would be looked upon as friends to the English, they must not meddle with them, while under the protection of the commanding officer. The Indians, however paying but little regard to this admonition, went immediately in pursuit of *[88]* them, and finding them a few hours after, as in no apprehension of any enemy, they fired on them before they discovered themselves, killing one, and wounding another, who however made his escape to the fort. His countrymen all did the same, without returning the fire, as few of their guns were loaded, and they inferior in number. Their enemies pursued them to the fort, but could never see them after, as Capt. M'Neil took great care to keep them asunder. Finding therefore no more likelihood of scalping, the northern Indians marched away from the fort.

This was the same party I encamped with the first night after my departure from the Great Island, and were surprised at the same place, where they had still continued.

He farther informed me, that I should probably find Fort Robinson, and all the posts on the communication, evacuated, as the regiment was to be broke. *[89]*[137]

I made this letter public, with which they seemed tolerably well satisfied, particularly when I feigned the wounded Indian was under the care of an English surgeon, who would not fail to cure him in a little time.

FRENCH CHAPTER X

○○○○○○○○○○○○○○○○○○○○○○○○○○○○○○○○○○○○

I NOW BEGAN to be very desirous of returning, and acquainted Ostenaco of my anxiety, desiring him to appoint fifteen or twenty headmen, agreeable to the orders I had received from Col. Stephen, as likewise to collect all the white persons and negroes, to be sent conformable to the articles of peace, to Fort Prince-George.[138] He replied, that, as soon as the white prisoners returned from hunting, where they then were with their masters (the white people becoming slaves, and the property of those that take them) he would set about the performance. Some time after this, when all the prisoners were come in, I again attacked Ostenaco; but then his horses could not be found, and there was a necessity of having one or two to carry my baggage and his own. I then waited till the horses were found; but when *[90]* I supposed all things ready for our departure, I was greatly surprised to find it delayed. Ostenaco told me, that one of the Carpenter's party, which was on its return home, had come in the night before, and reported, that the Carolinians had renewed the war before they had well concluded a peace. The Indian had, according to custom, a long account of it; but tho' I shewed the improbability of such a story, Ostenaco refused to set out before the Carpenter arrived, which was not till the 23d following. He brought in the same report, but owned he did not believe it, as it was told him by a person who he thought wanted to raise some disturbance.

I now began to be very pressing with Ostenaco, threatening if he would not set out immediately, to return without him. This however would have been my last resource, as was for the space of 140 miles ignorant of every step of the way. I at last prevailed on him; but on the 10th of March, while we were again preparing for our departure, the *Death [91] Hallow* was heard from the top of Tommotly town-house. This was to give notice of the return of a party commanded by Willinawaw, who went to war towards the Shawnese country some time after my arrival. After so many disappointments, I began to think I should never get away, as I supposed this affair would keep me, as others had done, two or three days, and till some new accident should intervene to detain me longer. About eleven o'clock the Indians, about forty in number, appeared within sight of the town; as they approached, I observed four scalps, painted red on the flesh-side, hanging on a pole, and carried in front of the line, by

Figure 49. Snaffle bit. Circa 1760. (Frank McClung Museum collection)

Figure 50. Horseshoe. 18th century. (Frank McClung Museum collection)

the second in command, while Willinawaw brought up the rear. When near the town-house, the whole marched round it three times, singing the war-song, and at intervals giving the *Death Hallow*; after which, sticking the pole just by the door, for the crowd to gaze on, they went in to relate in what manner they had gained them. Curiosity prompted me to follow them into the town-house; where, *[92]* after smoking a quarter of an hour in silence, the chief gave the following account of their campaign.

"After we left Tommotly, which was about the middle of January, we travelled near 400 miles before we saw the least sign of the enemy; at last, one evening, near the river Ohio, we heard the report of several guns, whereupon I sent out several scouts to discover who they were, and if possible where they encamped, that we might attack them early next morning; about dark the scouts returned, and informed us they were a party of Shawnese, hunting buffaloes; that they had watched them to the river-side, where, taking to their canoes, they had paddled across the river; and seeing a great many fires on the other side, where our scouts directed our sight, we concluded it to be a large encampment; we thereupon began to consult, whether it would be more advisable to cross the river over night, or early next morning: it was *[93]* decided in favour of the former, notwithstanding its snowing excessively hard, lest we should be discovered. We accordingly stripped ourselves, tying our guns to our backs, with the buts upwards, to which we hung our ammunition, to prevent its getting wet; we then took water, and swam near half a mile to the other side, where we huddled together to keep ourselves* [Williams omits 'ourselves'] warm, intending to pass the remainder of the night in that manner, and to fall on the enemy at daybreak; but as it continued snowing the whole time, it proved so cold, that we could endure it no longer than a little past midnight, when we resolved to surround the enemy's camp, giving the first fire, and, without charging again, run on them with our tommahawkes, which we had tucked in our belts for that purpose, should there be occasion. We accordingly surrounded them; but when the signal was given for firing, scarce one fourth of our guns went off, wet with the snow, notwithstanding all the precautions we had ta- *[94]* ken to preserve them dry: we then rushed in; but, before we came to a close engagement, the enemy returned our fire; as, it was at random, not being able to see us before we were upon them, on account of the darkness of the night, and the thickness of the bushes, we received no damage. They had not time to charge again, but fought us with the buts of their guns, tommahawkes, and firebrands. In the beginning of the battle we took two prisoners, who were continually calling out to their countrymen to fight strong, and they would soon conquer us; this made them fight much bolder, till the persons who had the prisoners in custody put a stop to it, by sinking a tommahawke in each of their skulls, on which their countrymen took to flight, and left every thing behind them. As soon as it was day, we examined the field, where we found two more of the enemy dead, one of which was a French warrior, which, with the prisoners we had killed, are the four scalps we have brought in. We lost only *[95]* one man, the poor brave Raven of Togua,[139] who ran rashly before us in the midst of the enemy. We took what things we could conveniently bring with us, and destroyed the rest."

Having finished his account of the expedition, out of his shot-pouch he pulled a piece of paper, wrapped up in a bit of birch-bark, which he had taken out of the Frenchman's pocket, and gave it to me to look at, asking if I did not think it was his commission?[140] I replied in the negative, telling him it was only some private marks of his own, which I did not understand. It appears to me to have been his journal,[141] every seventh line being longer than the others, to denote the Sunday; the death's head, and other marks, relate to what happened on the several days; but having filled his paper long before his death, he had supplied it by interlining with a pin. These are my conjectures, I have however annexed it here from the ori- *[96]* ginal, still in my possession, that each reader may make his own.

About one o'clock the baggage and all things being ready, Ostenaco took leave of his friends, tho' this ceremony is unusual among them, and we began our march sooner than I expected. Passing thro' Toqua, we saw several Indians weeping for the death of their relations, killed in the late battle. In an hour's time we arrived at Chote, where we found a great number of headmen assembled to give us a talk, containing instructions to my Indian conductors, to remind the English of their promises of friendship, and to press the Governor of Virginia to open a trade; for the Indians to behave well to the inhabitants when they arrived, as that was the only way to keep the chain of friendship bright; that we should keep a good look-out, as the enemy were very numerous on the path. What occasioned this precaution, and probably Ostenaco's delaying his departure so long, was, the defeat of a party of about thirty Indians, who went out to war some time before, the same way *[97]* that we were to go,[142] eight of whom had been killed or taken. They attributed this loss to the want of arrows, the northern Indians having poured several vollies of arrows, and done great execution, before the Cherokees could charge again, after the first fire. This was especially disadvantageous to the Cherokees, as both parties met unexpectedly on the top of a mountain, which they were both crossing, and engaged so close, that the northern Indians availed themselves of this advantage, and the superiority of their numbers.

Two pieces of cannon[143] were fired when we had got about 200 yards from the town-house, after which Ostenaco sung the war-song, in which was a

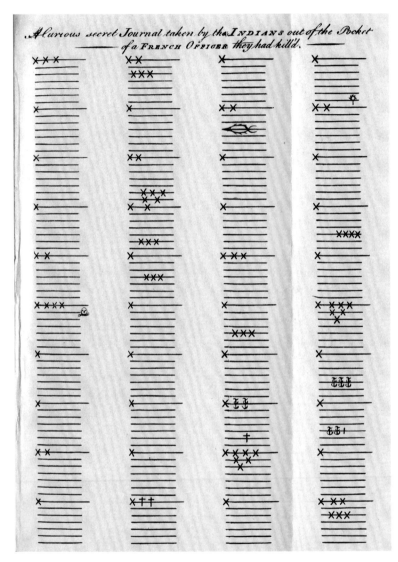

Figure 51. A mysterious journal taken from the body of a Frenchman killed by Cherokees on the Ohio River; it was given to Timberlake by Willinawaw on March 10, 1762. Although its meaning was not understood by Timberlake or the Cherokees, it is obviously a pocket calendar designating "holy days of obligation" for a forty-week period beginning September 27, 1761 and ending July 3, 1762.

prayer for our safety thro' the intended journey; this he bellowed out loud enough to be heard at a mile's distance. We did not march above three miles before we encamped, in order to give time to some Indians who were to accompany us, but had not yet joined us, which they did in the evening, about fourteen or fifteen in number. Next *[98]* morning, the 11th of March, we rose tolerably early, marching to Little River, about twenty miles from the nation, where we encamped.

At this place had formerly been an Indian town, called Elajoy; and I am surprised how the natives should ever abandon so beautiful and fertile a spot. Were it in a more polished country, it would make the finest situation for a gentleman's seat I ever saw.[144]

We marched the next day to Broad River, which we crossed about four o'clock in the afternoon, without much difficulty, by reason of the lowness of the waters; but the river, which is here 700 yards over, runs with great rapidity, and the banks extremely steep on either side. We encamped directly, and were all employed in making a large fire to dry ourselves, as most of us had got very wet.

Before sun-set I perceived a considerable number of Indians passing at the same place, whom I at first imagined to be enemies; but the *[99]* arrival of some of them shewed them to be Cherokees, who kept continually dropping in, so that I was greatly surprised next morning at their numbers. I demanded where they were going? to which they replied, To Virginia; that the headsmen had thought proper to send a reinforcement, thinking it unsafe for so small a body to march, through a country so much frequented by the enemy, where, if I met with any accident, the blame would fall upon them. I thanked them; but at the same time told them peremptorily to go back, and give themselves no further trouble on my account; that I had no occasion for them; and that it would be impossible for so large a body to subsist when passed the hunting grounds, as the people on the frontiers of Virginia had been so impoverished by the late war, they would not be able to supply us with provisions. This made no impression on them, and they marched on without saying another word, and persisted in going, notwithstanding all the efforts Ostenaco and I could make to prevent them. Indeed I was more earnest to have them return, as I *[100]* found it was the scent of presents, more than the desire of escorting me, that was the real motive of all this good-will.

We left the camp the next day, about 165 in number, and marched without any extraordinary occurrence till the 15th, about mid-day, when we heard our scouts on the left (for we always kept on both flanks) fire pretty quick after one another, and in less than a minute seventeen or eighteen buffaloes ran in amongst us, before we discovered them, so that several of us had like to have been run over, especially the women, who with some difficulty sheltered themselves behind the trees. Most of the men fired, but, firing at random,

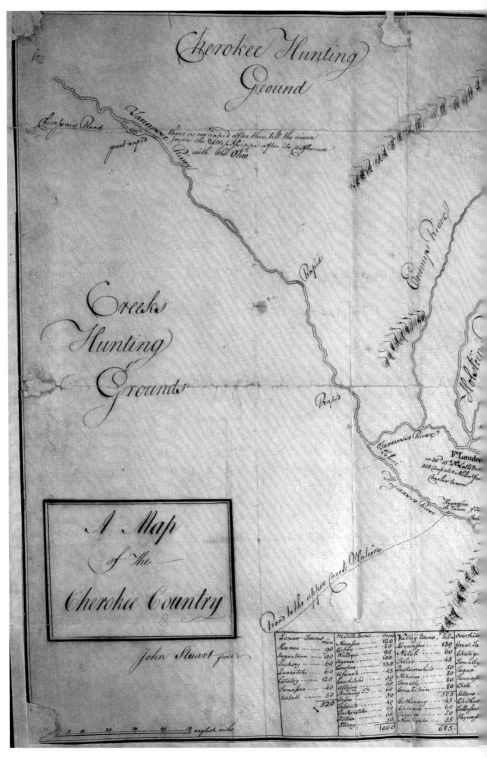

Figure 52. After the capitulation of Fort Loudoun, Captain John Stuart made his escape to Virginia along the same route later followed by Timberlake and Ostenaco. Stuart produced this map of his escape route in 1764. (Courtesy of the British Library)

Virginia Part.

Augusta County

Abandoned Plantation

North Carolina Part

Long Island

into the Settlements to Virginia

Etatoy
Quaratchi

Hunting
Ground

N

W ———— E

S

Savannah River

520
1000
685
715
2920

one only was killed, tho' several more wounded. Our scouts likewise killed another, and brought in the best parts of the meat, all which was cooked overnight for our departure next morning.[145]

After passing a very disagreeable night on account of the rain, which, as the evening had been clear, I had taken no precaution to shelter my- *[101]* self against. We had as disagreeable a march, it proved very rainy, and were again obliged to encamp to a great disadvantage for the convenience of good water.

FRENCH CHAPTER XI

ON THE 17th, about two o'clock in the afternoon, we met an Indian who left the Great Island some time after me, with a party of ten or twelve, destined to Williamsburg, who, after he had eat, drank, and smoaked, told us the party that he belonged to had been attacked two days before; that two of them had been killed, two or three taken, and the rest dispersed; that he had reason to believe there were a great many of the enemy upon the path, as he had seen a great many tracks and other signs.

On this intelligence, Ostenaco ordered all his men to fresh prime their guns, and those that had bows and arrows to put them in readiness, sending out some scouts, and desiring all to keep a good look-out. After these dispositions we parted with the fugitive Indian, and continued our route. At night our scouts came in, and in- *[102]* formed us, that they had seen some old tracks, and a piece of an old red waistcoat, dropped by the enemy, to inform us they were thereabouts. We made large fires to dry ourselves, while Ostenaco, and four or five others, took out and waved their eagles tails, then turning towards the place where the tracks had been discovered, gave the war-hoop several times extremely loud. This was to let the enemy know, if within hearing, and disposed for an engagement, where he and his party lay. This however Ostenaco probably would not have done, had he not confided in the number of his party, being greatly superior to what commonly go to make war on one another. Before the Indians went to sleep, he gave them a strong caution, and instructions how to act in case they were attacked.

We decamped pretty early next morning, in order, if possible, to reach the Great Island that day; but the scouts had not been out an hour before some returned with an account of fresh tracks and other signs of the enemy. I really expected a skirmish with the northern Indians, as they *[103]* might probably imagine some Cherokees would return with me when I left their country; and it was probable the party I had received an account of, and had given so many checks to the Cherokees since, were still waiting.

As we marched very slow, on account of receiving intelligence from our scouts, which they brought in every two or three hours, we encamped short of the Great Island about seven or eight miles.

The next morning we were in no great hurry to decamp, as we intended to go no farther than the Great Island that day. By this retardment each man had time to put his arms in proper order. We set out about eleven o'clock, and, after four or five miles march, Ostenaco desired me to go before, to see if any of the enemy were there. The northern Indians being at peace with us, was urged as a sufficient protection, tho', at setting out, they seemed a little apprehensive of my falling into such desperadoes hands, or rather of their losing their share of the *[104]* presents. I was to tell the enemy, If I met them, that the Cherokees were but few in number, and but indifferently armed; after which Sumpter and I were furnished with horses, and went forward pretty briskly, till we reached Holston's River, the crossing-place of which was within a mile of Fort Robinson. We had not forded above half-way over, when we heard the report of a gun, which made us conclude that our suspicions of the enemy's being there were but too justly grounded; we rode gently towards the fort to make our observations; but no enemy appearing, on entering the clear ground about the fort, and perceiving some smoak from one of the chimnies, we rode within an hundred yards of it, and hallowed, but nobody appearing, we went to the gate, and gave another hoop, which, to my great surprise, instead of the enemy, brought a white man out of one of the houses, whom I immediately recollected to be M'Lamore the interpreter,[146] that accompanied the discomfited party of Cherokees, I lately mentioned, to Virginia, *[105]* and he was soon followed by the man who had fired the gun.

I returned to the party, highly satisfied at my good fortune, in not being obliged to displease the Indians, by breaking thro' so disagreeable and dangerous a commission, who had already crossed the river when I joined them.

We found in the fort eleven or twelve hundred weight of flour, left by the garrison when they evacuated the place, which abundantly recompensed the Indians for all their fatigues.

We remained here all next day to rest ourselves, and mend our mockasons, tho' such fine weather was scarce to be lost, considering the very bad we had experienced most of the way from the Cherokee country; this made me extremely anxious to be going forward, but the Indians seldom hurry themselves when they were to leave such good cheer, after having passed most of the way without bread. I was in- *[106]* formed by M'Lamore, that the flour had been left for want of horses to carry it away, as well as the goods I had observed in one of the store-houses, belonging to a private trader; that the northern Indians, after defeating the small party to which he belonged, and taking him and two more prisoners, came to the fort, where, notwithstanding our alliance with them, they destroyed a great quantity of the flour and goods, and carried a great quantity more away, as well as the man that had the care of them; but that, after some days march, all the prisoners found means to make their escape: that they two returned to the fort, one proposing to wait my coming, and return with me to Virginia, and M'Lamore to go back to the Cherokee country.

I next day intreated Ostenaco to order his men to get ready for the march, as the weather was fine, and it would be agreeable travelling; but notwithstanding all he or I could say, not a man of them would stir; their excuse was, that one of their horses was lost, and the owner out *[107]* in search of him. We waited his return till night, when he came, but no horse was to be found. I was very much mortified at this accident, as I was anxious to know what was become of my camp-equipage, cloaths, &c. I had left at Fort Attakul-lakulla.[147]

On the 22d, we rose early in the morning, to make a good day's march, but the horse was not found till near twelve o'clock: I then thought our immediate departure certain, but was again disappointed; the person who had the care of the goods, missing a piece of broad-cloth, charged the Indians with the theft, and a general search was made to no purpose. Ostenaco then ordered all within the fort, while he and the conjuror went into the house from whence it was stole, to beg the devil's advice about recovering it. The conjuror might perhaps have saved himself that trouble, for tho' I am at a loss to guess in what manner, I am inclined to believe he had as great a hand in the loss as in the recovery of it. I desired him to trouble himself no farther about it, chus- *[108]* ing rather to pay for it, than be detained any longer; but all I could say could not divert him from his conjuring, which however furnished me with a few more of their oddities.

After staying some time, the conjuror sallied out blindfolded, and groped about, till he came to the skirts of the woods, where, pulling off the blind, he went straight forwards, a considerable way, and returned in about five minutes with the broad-cloth on his shoulders. I observed his cheek tied up with a bit of twine, which, when untied, bled very much. I gave the conjuror two yards as a reward for playing the fool, and we marched forward, encamping about ten miles from the fort.

We called in our way at Fort Attakullakulla, which was likewise evacuated, looked for my cloaths, &c. but they were all stolen and carried off by the soldiers, except a small trunk, with a few trifles, I found afterwards at New River. *[109]*

Some time after, we met Capt. Israel Christian[148] going with a cargo of goods, to trade in the Cherokee country. I here endeavoured to send back the greatest part of the Indians; but notwithstanding all the persuasions the Captain and I could make use of, not a man of them would return, till the

Captain promised the same presents to those that would go back as would be given to those that went forward, not doubting but that he would be reimbursed, as the charge of victualling of them would be entirely saved; but as this expence fell entirely upon me, as will appear in the sequel, it was rather taking the burthen off me than off the public. I am heartily sorry, however, this gentleman has suffered, as well as myself, for his good intentions, and more so, that it is not in my power to discharge the public debt, and reimburse him. But even by this we could only reduce our number to about seventy-two.

We called at Fort Lewis,[149] where we found William Shorey the interpreter,[150] who, by order of Col. Stephen, had waited our coming, to ac- *[110]* company the Indians to Williamsburg.[151] I received here between seventy and eighty pounds that was due to me, which came very opportunely to defray our expenses to Williamsburg; where we arrived in about eleven days after our departure from Fort Lewis.[152]

FRENCH CHAPTER XII

○○○○○○○○○○○○○○○○○○○○○○○○○○○○○○○○○

ON MY ARRIVAL, I waited on the Governor, who seemed somewhat displeased with the number of Indians that had forced themselves upon me.[153] Orders however were issued out for their accommodation, and a few days after a council was called, at which Ostenaco, and some of the principal Indians, attended.[154] After the usual ceremonies, and mutual promises of friendship, the Indians were dismissed, and presents ordered them to the amount of 125£ currency; 12£ 10 s. for Ostenaco, the same sum to be sent back to King Kanagatucko, and the rest to be divided among the party, who seemed much displeased when it came to be divided, being, as they said, like nothing among them. I was apprehensive of some bad consequence should they return dissatisfied, and therefore ad-*[111]*vanced pretty considerably out of my own pocket to content them.[155]

A few days before they were to depart for their own country, Mr. Horrocks,[156] invited Ostenaco and myself to sup with him at the College, where, amongst other curiosities, he shewed him the picture of his present Majesty.[157] The chief viewed it a long time with particular attention; then turning to me, "Long," said he "have I wished to see the king my father; this is his resemblance, but I am determined to see himself; I am now near the sea, and never will depart from it till I have obtained my desires." He asked the Governor next day, who, tho' he at first refused, on Ostenaco's insisting so strongly upon it, gave his consent.[158] He then desired, as I had been with him so long, that I might accompany him to England: this I was to do at my own expence;

Figure 53. At Colonial Williamsburg and in England, the Cherokees found themselves in a strange environment, as this painting by Robert Griffing entitled At the Castle, *suggests. (Courtesy Robert Griffing and Paramount Press)*

but the Governor told me he would recommend me to the minister of state, which he did in as strong terms as I could desire.[159] *[112]*

I was then upon the point of entering into a very advantageous commerce, which I quitted to please the Indians, and preserve them ours, yet wavering to the French interest. I prepared every thing necessary for my voyage; but this was not my only expence, the Indians having no money, expect the person who travels with them to treat them with whatever they take a fancy to.

We set out for Hampton[160] about the begining of May, where we were to embark; but contrary winds, and other delays, retarded us till the 15th, during which time it generally cost me between 15 and 20 s. per day.

Figure 54. King George III in his twenties. Engraving after an original painting by Allan Ramsay. (Collection of Duane King). See also Color Plate 13 in this volume for the official coronation portrait by Ramsay.

We had very fine weather during the whole voyage, yet both the Indians[161] and myself were sea-sick all the way. We parted with a convoy we had under our care off Newfoundland, in a very thick fog, notwithstanding all the efforts Capt. Blake could make, by ringing bells, and firing every quarter of an hour, to keep them together, tho'I afterwards heard him se- *[113]* verely accused in England of taking this opportunity to leave his charge.[162]

We had the misfortune here to lose the interpreter Shorey, who was much regretted by us all, but especially by the Indians, as he was a thorough master of their language. He had lingered some time in a consumption, caught in passing a small river, for, being drunk, his Indian spouse plunged him in to sober him, but was unable to draw him out, and had not some Indians come to her assistance he must have been drowned. This was an effectual means of sobering him, but by it he contracted the malady that carried him off.

During our voyage the Indians conceived very advantageous ideas of our naval force; the Captain having chased and brought too about sixteen sail, found them all to be English or neutral vessels, on which the Cherokees concluded the French and Spaniards were certainly afraid to put to sea. [114]

On the 16th of June we arrived at Plymouth, where, before we went on shore, the Indians had their desire of seeing a large man of war gratified, by being carried on board the *Revenge*,[163] a seventy-four gun ship, with which they were equally pleased and surprised.

While in the boat that took us to shore, Ostenaco, painted in a very frightful manner sung a solemn dirge with a very loud voice to return God thanks for his safe arrival. The loudness and uncouthness of his singing, and the oddity of his person, drew a vast crowd of boats, filled with spectators, from all the ships in the harbour; and the landing-place was so thronged, that it was almost impossible to get to the inn, where we took post for London.

We stopped at Exeter, where the Indians were shewed the cathedral, but, contrary to my expectation, were as little struck as if they had been natives of the place. They were much better pleased the next day with Lord Pembroke's

Figure 55. The Cherokees visited Exeter Cathedral on June 17, 1762 but apparently were unimpressed with its grandeur.

WILTON HOUSE the Seat of the EARL of PEMBROKE

Figure 56. At the Wilton House (the Seat of the Earl of Pembroke) on July 17, 1762, the Cherokees were impressed with the building but were frightened by a statue of Hercules, according to Timberlake. This depiction was published in 1771. (Collection of Duane King)

seat at Wilton,[164] till they saw the statue *[115]* of Hercules with his club up-lifted,[165] which they thought so dreadful that they begged immediately to be gone.[166]

We arrived the next day in London,[167] without any other accident than the breaking down of the chaise in which the Indians were, but happily none of them were hurt.[168]

Capt. Blake waited on Lord Egremont,[169] to acquaint him with our arrival.[170] We were immediately sent for,[171] and, after some few questions, dismissed. Lodgings were ordered, and taken by Mr. N—— Caccanthropos.[172] We were again sent for by Lord Egremont,[173] but more to gratify the curiosity of some of his friends than about business.[174] I however took this opportunity of slipping my letter of recommendation into his Lordship's hands, which he read, and assured me he would shew it to the King that day;[175] telling me to let the Indians or myself want for nothing; that as I was a perfect stranger, he had ordered Mr. Caccanthropos to provide whatever we desired. *[116]*

My first care was to equip the Indians. I attended Mr. Caccanthropos, to order all after the mode of their own country.[176]

As several days passed before I had any further orders, the Indians became extremely anxious to see the King. "What is the reason," said they, "that we are not admitted to see the Great King our Father, after coming so far for that purpose?" I was obliged to reply, "That his Majesty was indisposed,[177] and

Figure 57. Suffolk Street. Lodgings for the Cherokee delegation were taken at the Quin home on Suffolk Street. The outward appearance of the buildings has changed little since the Cherokee visit. (1829 lithograph courtesy of the British Museum)

Figure 58. The Coronation of George III in Westminster Abbey, September 22, 1761. (Collection of Duane King)

BAGNIGGE WELLS, *near* Battle Bridge, Islington.

Figure 59. Bagnigge Wells. The Cherokees tasted the waters and had breakfast at Bagnigge Wells on July 27, 1762. (Courtesy of the British Museum)

WHITE CONDUIT HOUSE IN THE LAST CENTURY. *1788*

Figure 60. At the White Conduit House, "the concourse of people to see the Cherokees was inconceivable." On July17, during the Cherokee visit, pickpockets had a field day in the crowd. A prodigious number of watches and other valuables were reported stolen. (Courtesy of the British Museum)

could not be waited on till perfectly recovered," which in some measure pacified them.[178] We were taken not long after to court;[179] but I was only asked a few questions, of which I gave the interpretation to the Indians that might be most favourably received.[180]

The uncommon appearance of the Cherokees[181] began to draw after them great crowds of people of all ranks;[182] at which they were so much displeased, that home became irksome to them, and they were forever teizing me to take them to some public diversion.[183] Their favou- [117] rite was Sadler's-Wells;[184] the activity of the performers, and the machinery of the pantomime, agreeing best with their notions of diversion.[185] They were likewise very fond of Ranelagh,[186] which, from its form they compared to their town-house;[187] but they were better pleased with Vauxhall,[188] tho' it was always against my inclination I accompanied them there,[189] on account of the ungovernable curiosity of the people,[190] who often intruded on them, and induced them to drink more than sufficient.[191] Once, in particular, one of the young Indians got extremely intoxicated, and committed several irregularities, that ought rather to be attributed to those that enticed them, than to the simple Indians who drank only to please them.[192]

I cannot indeed cite sobriety as their characteristic; but this I can say, these excesses never happened at home. A bottle of wine, a bowl of punch, and a little cyder, being the ordinary consumption of the three Indians, Sumpter,

Figure 61. Sadler's Wells was a favorite of the Cherokees because the entertainment there conformed so closely to their own notions of diversion. The Cherokees were at Sadler's Wells on July 2, 3, 24, and 30, and August 11, 1762. (Courtesy of the British Museum)

Engrav'd for the Universal Magazin 1750 for I. Hinton at the Kings Arms in S.t Pauls Church Yard, London.

A Perspective View of RANELAGH HOUSE and Garden.

Figure 62. The Cherokees compared the rotunda at Ranelagh to the townhouse at Chota. They visited Ranelagh on July 5, 1762. (Collection of Duane King)

Figure 63. Timberlake was reluctant to take the Cherokees to Vauxhall because of the ungovernable curiosity of the public. The Cherokees first visited Vauxhall Pleasure Gardens during the week before July 6, and returned to Vauxhall on July 9, 16, 21, 23, and 29, 1762. (Collection of John Low)

Figure 64. *"Austenaco, Great Warriour, / Commander in Chief of the Cherokee Nation." Above image: "Engraved for the Royal Magazine." Painter & engraver unstated. In* Royal Magazine, *vol. VII, facing p. 16, issue for July, 1762. (Collection of William Sturtevant)*

Engraved for the Royal Magazine.

AUSTENACO, Great Warriour, Commander in Chief of the Cherokee Nation.

and myself; and as we were seldom at home, it could not put the nation to a great expence.[193] If the bills given in for these articles were to *[118]* the greatest degree excessive, let them that charged them answer who consumed them; I only know that no more was ever drank by us.[194]

This was not the only thing laid to my charge; I was accused of receiving money for admission to see the Indians.[195] The sheep was accused by the wolf of rapine, who carried his point. He was a thorough-paced under-courtier; the sheep, a raw Virginian, who, ignorant of little arts, innocently believed

Habit of Cunne Shote a Cherokee Chief.

Cunne Shote Chef des Chiroquois.

others as honest as himself, and could never believe such impudence existed, as to accuse another of crimes his conscience assured him he was sole actor of. I was so prepossessed with these opinions, that I can scarce as yet, however severely I have felt it, believe that some men have no ideas of conscience, and esteem it the prejudices of education, and a narrow mind; and that blasting an innocent person's character, whenever it answered their ends, or that robbing the nation was no crime, when they could escape punishment. *[119]*

It was a long time before I knew any thing of these money-taking works.

The following accident was what brought it to light. Finding myself entirely confined by the continual crowds of visitors, I resolved to lessen the number, by ordering the servants to admit none but people of fashion.[196] This was what would have been at once agreeable to the Indians, and raised their ideas of the English nation. So far from these orders being complied with, the whole rabble of the town was ushered in the next day. Not a little mortified, I complained to Lord Egremont, who, already perhaps prepossessed against me, only told me coldly, that he would speak of it to Mr. Caccanthropos. At my return, tho' I found the house full of people, I said nothing more.

Some days after, Sumpter, who had contracted some genteel acquaintance, some of whom he was bringing to see the Indians, was stopped by the servant, Mr. Caccanthropos's relation, who refused to admit them without money. The young man, who had faced all dangers for the [120] service of his country in the war, who had been so highly instrumental in saving us from the dangers that threatened us in going to their country, and had accompanied us ever since, received that affront from an insolent servant; but not being able to bear the insult, he took a warrior's satisfaction, and knocked him down. A blunt Virginian soldier cannot know the laws of England, as little can he bear an insult from so mean a quarter.

The servant informed his kinsman, who came next day open-mouthed, threatening Sumpter with the crown-office. He next gave me such scurrilous language, that I was perfectly at a loss how to retort it adequately; I had subject enough, but being accustomed to gentlemen's company, I could scarce understand his dialect: piqued, however, at the stinging truths I told him, he threatened me with confinement also, assaying to intimidate me from publishing them, by reminding me that he was a justice of the peace. Happily I reflected on the disparity of his years and strength to mine; my hands had [121] near disgraced me, by striking a person I so much every way despised.[197] He dared not, however, put his threats into execution; his only vengeance for affronting me, was ordering the people of the house to feed us for the future on ox-cheek, cow-heel, and such like dainties, fit entertainment for Indians accustomed to only the choicest parts of the beast, and very fit to raise their opinion of England. I however understanding Lord Egremont's orders in a different light, took care to provide whatever was requisite for the Indians, avoiding at the same time all appearance of extravagance.

Sumpter's company were not the only persons to whom admittance was refused; the same servant had even the impudence to stop Lady T-r-l-y.[198] Her Ladyship sent immediately for Mrs. Quin,[199] the gentlewoman of the house, to enquire if I encouraged the servants in taking money for seeing the Indians. Mrs. Quin set her Ladyship to rights in that particular; but still whatever exactions these fellows made, the public generally laid to me. I was cleared, how- [122] ever, by Cacanthropos himself, who once attempted to stop Mr.

OUTACITE,
King of the Cherokees.

AUSTENACO, Great Warriour,
Commander in Chief of the Cherokee Nation.

Figure 66. "Outacite, / King of the Cherokees." Painter & engraver unstated. In Court Magazine, *vol. 1, No. XI, August, 1762, facing p. 491. (Collection of Duane King)*

Figure 67. "Austenaco, Great Warriour, / Commander in Chief of the Cherokee Nation." At top: "Engraved for the British Magazine." Painter & engraver unstated. In British Magazine, *vol. III, facing p. 378 (July, 1762). (Collection of Duane King)*

Montague;[200] and his fear and confusion on finding whom he had offended in some measure revenged me.

Soon after these disturbances, orders were given by Lord Egremont, that no person whatever should be admitted, without an order from himself, or Mr. Wood,[201] under Secretary of State: but instead of the throngs decreasing by this order, it rather increased; and I really believe few persons have more friends than Mr. Wood, if he knew but half of those that were ushered in under that name; nay, grown bolder by that sanction, they pressed into the Indians dressing room,[202] which gave them the highest disgust, these people having a particular aversion to being stared at while dressing or eating; on which last occasion, if I was irksome myself, judge what a crowd of strangers must be.[203] They were so disgusted, that they grew extremely shy of being seen,[204] so that I had the greatest difficulty in procuring Lord C-t-f-d[205] a sight of

Figure 68. The Times Plate I *by William Hogarth, published September 7, 1762. Hogarth in this rendering satirized the abolishment of hanging signs, British politics, and the carnival-like atmosphere that surrounded the Cherokee visit. The scantily clad native with the caption "Live from America" represents a Cherokee. (Museum of the Cherokee Indian collection)*

them; on which, being a little angry, I was afterwards in- *[123]* formed his Lordship had been offended at something I am yet a stranger to. It ever was against my inclination to give offence to even the lowest class of mankind, much less to Lord C-t-f-d.

I was not only, however, accused of receiving money at our lodgings, but at the public places we frequented.[206] To this I answer, so far from making by them, it generally cost me pretty considerable to the servants, besides coach-hire; for tho' one was allowed us, we could command it no oftener than Mr. Cacanthropos was pleased to do us that favour; and this expence was entirely out of my own pocket, without any prospect of reimbursement.

As to the charge laid against me, the proprietors are still alive, and any

Figure 69. English tea pot patterned after a Chinese import. Circa 1760–1770. (Collection of Duane King)

Figure 70. Chinese tea bowl and saucer. Mid–18th century. (Museum of the Cherokee Indian collection)

Figure 71. Tankard of silver-plated brass with wooden base, monogrammed with initials TW. Mid–18th century. (Museum of the Cherokee Indian collection)

Figure 72. Small wine glass circa 1760. (Museum of the Cherokee Indian collection)

person that entertains the smallest doubt, may, and would oblige me, by enquiring of themselves, whether I ever demanded or took directly or indirectly any money or consideration whatever from them. *[124]*[207]

But let us now return to the Indians. Some time before they left England, they were admitted to a conference with his Majesty at St. James's.[208] Ostenaco's speech on that occasion contained nothing more than protestations of

Figure 73. Page from a song book published in 1762. The song was popularized at Vauxhall. (Museum of the Cherokee Indian collection)

Figure 74. Copy of 18th-century violin. During one visit to Vauxhall Gardens, there were no fewer than 10,000 people there to see the Cherokees. Escaping to the orchestra pit, the Cherokee delegation tested several instruments, including a violin. (Collection of Duane King)

Figure 75. Wooden flute, late 18th century. The Cherokee delegation attended live musical performances, including several at Vauxhall, in which instruments like this one were played. Flutes with six holes and one key were the most popular flutes used in England during the second half of the eighteenth century. The name Florio on this flute is probably not the maker's name but an endorsement by Pietro Grassi Florio (b. 1730), a popular Italian flautist who came to London about 1760 and was appointed first flute in the Opera. (Museum of the Cherokee Indian collection)

Figure 76. Eyeglasses. Late 18th century. The optician's bill according to Timberlake was "fifty odd pounds in these costly play-things for the Cherokees." (Museum of the Cherokee Indian collection)

Figure 77. St. James's Palace. 18th-century engraving. The Cherokee delegation met with King George III in the Drawing Room of St. James's Palace on Thursday, July 8, 1762. On Friday August 6, they bid farewell to the King in the courtyard of St. James's Palace. (Courtesy of the British Museum)

friendship, faithful alliance, &c.[209] To which an answer was afterwards given in writing, to be interpreted in their own country,[210] as I was not conversant enough in their language to translate it; though I understood whatever they said, especially the speech, which I gave word for word to his Majesty, as Shorey had likewise explained it before his death, except the last part, which was so much in my favour that I was obliged to suppress it, and was in some confusion in finding wherewith to supply it; till I at last told his Majesty, that it was only in some manner a repetition of that part of his discourse.

They were struck with the youth, person, and grandeur of his Majesty, and conceived as great an opinion of his affability as of his power, the greatness of which may be seen *[125]* on my telling them in what manner to behave; for finding Ostenaco preparing his pipe to smoak with his Majesty, according to the Indian custom of declaring friendship, I told him he must neither offer to shake hands or smoak with the King, as it was an honour for the greatest of our nation to kiss his hand. You are in the right, says he, for he commands over all next to the Man above, and no-body is his equal.[211] Their ideas were likewise greatly increased by the number of ships in the river, and the war-ren at Woolwich, which I did not fail to set out to the greatest advantage, intimating that our Sovereign had many such ports and arsenals round the kingdom.[212]

FRENCH CHAPTER XIII (LISTED AS XV)

SOME DAYS BEFORE the Indians set out on their return to their own coun-try Lord Egremont sent for me, and informed me that the Indians were to be landed at Charles Town; but this was so contrary to their inclination, that Os-tenaco positively declared, that, unless he was to land in Virginia, he would not stir *[126]* a step from London.[213] His Lordship then desired me to tell them that they should land at Virginia, but at the same time gave me to un-derstand, that the ship being to be stationed at Charles Town,[214] they must absolutely be landed there. I informed his Lordship that it was entirely out of my power to accompany them there, having scarce five shillings remain-ing out of the 130 pounds I had received, the best part of which I laid out for the Indians use, rather than apply to Mr. Cacanthropos;[215] that I was ready to obey his Lordship, if he would please to order me wherewith to defray my ex-pences from Charles Town to Virginia. My Lord replied, that no more could be advanced; that if I refused to accompany them, others must be found that would.[216]

Sumpter was immediately sent for by Mr. Wood; but he refused the em-ploy till he had obtained my approbation; nay, I was obliged to use the most persuasive arguments to determine him to go; so that it was then in my power (had I been the man I was represented) to have made what terms I pleased, since the *[127]* Indians would not have gone without one of us, and Sumpter had too much honour to accompany them to my prejudice. I scorned so low an action; but told Sumpter, that tho' I had only asked my expences, which might amount to about twenty or twenty-five pounds, there was a difference between his going and mine; that he must make the voyage in the view of ad-vantage, whereas I had sought none in it, except returning to my native coun-try.[217] The terms agreed on were fifty pounds in hand, and a hundred on his arrival;[218] and it was even in his power to insist on more.[219]

Had I really had the money, I should not have troubled the government, or deserted the Indians; but to be landed in a strange country without money, and far from my friends, did not seem very eligible. I was extremely rejoiced at the young man's advantage; yet could not but think it hard to be left in England for so small, so reasonable a demand, as no other business than the Indian affairs had brought me there, when seven times the sum *[128]* was granted to another.[220] Lord Egremont indeed had informed me that the King, in consideration of my services in the Cherokee country, had ordered me a Lieutenancy in an old regiment which I should receive from Sir Jeffery Amherst in North America,[221] and positively assured me I should never be reduced to half pay; so that, had I been in my own country, I had reason to be satisfied; but I had no money to carry me there.

The Indians soon re-imbarked in the same vessel that brought them, and left England about the 25th of August;[222] so that I was now entirely at my own expence without money or friends.[223] I continually solicited Lord Egremont for money sufficient to defray my passage to Virginia, during which my circumstances were continually growing worse. I disclosed my distressed situation to a Gentleman with whom I had contracted an intimacy, who advised me to present a petition to the King assuring me at the same time, that he would speak to a Nobleman of his acquaintance to *[129]* second it. I went to the Park next morning with a petition that my friend approved, but was very irresolute whether to deliver it or not; my necessities, however, at last determined me.

Some days after I was sent for by Mr. Wood, who, after a short reverie, told me, that Lord Egremont had ordered a hundred pounds, *if that would do.* I knew from whence these orders came; but, as he industriously avoided mentioning the petition, I only answered that it would. I was since informed, that two hundred pounds were ordered me; but even one had been sufficient, had I received it at one payment; but getting it at different times, before I had paid my debts, and received it all, I was again run short.

Upon applying to the treasury for this money, I was asked by Mr. M-t-n[224] if I was not the person that accompanied the Cherokees to England? On answering in the affirmative, he *[130]* desired me to revise Mr. Cacanthropos's accounts, exclaiming against their extravagance. On looking over them, I did not find them quite so extravagant as I expected, being only overcharged by about 150 pounds; but what I mean by overcharging, is what the Indians never had; for I cannot be so sensible of what was overcharged by other means. The Indians being remarkable for their skill in mathematics, but unfortunate in not having sufflcient workmen among them, he had wisely stocked the whole nation with instruments. Mr. W——[225] the optician's bill being to the amount, as near as I can remember, of fifty odd pounds in these costly playthings for the Cherokees; but as neither they nor I had ever seen or heard of such instruments, although I was desired to order all things they might have occasion for, as best judge of what was necessary, I am inclined to think they

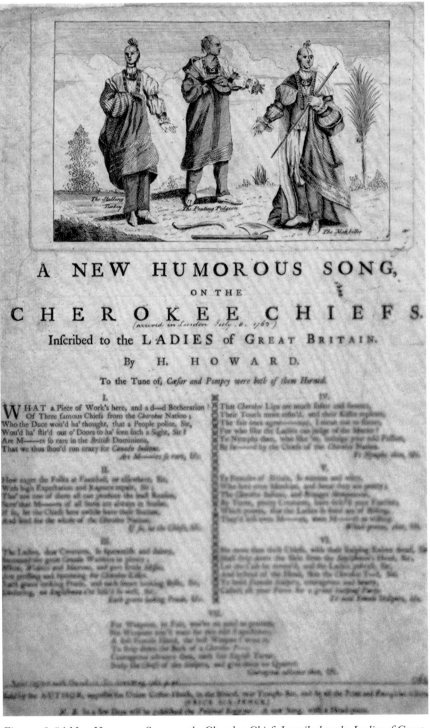

Figure 78. "A New Humorous Song, on the Cherokee Chiefs Inscribed to the Ladies of Great Britain." By H. Howard. The masthead identifies the three Cherokees as The Stalking Turkey, The Pouting Pidgeon, and The Mankiller. (Courtesy of the British Museum)

were turned to a much better purpose.[226] There was another bill from Mr. L—d for stocks and stockings, to the amount of forty odd pounds. Wampum, I suppose, is become so scarce among the In- *[131]* dians, that they are resolved to adopt the English custom of stocks. It is a little unconscionable to have forty pounds worth in change; but then Mr. Cacanthropos can easily account for that. These people wear a great deal of vermilion, and are naturally not over cleanly, so of consequence their stocks would very soon be dirty; besides they cannot be expected to wear so long as everlasting wampum. Very true! very provident, Sir! And I suppose you presume too the bushes would tear a great many stockings; but if I can judge of Indians, they are a great deal wiser than to be fine in stockings among the briars, at the expence of their legs, which good leggons keep unscratched, and a great deal warmer. This does not however, dear Sir, prevent my admiring your provident views; they are absolutely too striking ever to admit of that.

Five yards of superfine dove-coloured cloth, at a guinea a yard, was charged at the woolen-draper's. Ah! dear Sir, you were short sighted here; two yards and three-quarters make a *[132]* match-coat and leggons, five yards will not make two; a coarser cloth would have suited Indians, and another colour would have pleased them much better; for I am much mistaken if these are not the only Indians that ever wore other than their favourite colours of red and blue; but the laceman's bill will clear up this affair. Let me see! Vellum lace broad and narrow: Was it for button holes for a Cherokee mantle? Sure Ostenaco never once had the ridiculous fancy of putting useless, and solely ornamental, buttons upon a matchcoat; where the duce then were the button-holes placed? But I may, I believe, give a history of that affair, without being master of an uncommon penetration. A certain *Man-Killer*[227] wanting a holiday suit to appear in, at the installation of some royal and noble knights of the garter—but here some critic, a pretended judge of Indian affairs, will perhaps say, that Indians have no such installations, and that they would never become the laughing-stock of their countrymen, by being swathed up in English cloaths. Well, sharp-eyed critic, good cloaths will never want *[133]* wearers; it is a pity good things should be lost, and the gentleman that provided them must absolutely be obliged to wear them himself, since the Indians will not. What goodness! Condescend to wear the Indians refusals! *O tempora! O mores!* The washerwoman's bill, with many others, I had already paid; but as it had not paid toll *en passant*, it found its way into the treasury, with an encrease of five or six pounds, being just as much again as the contents of the bill; so summing up the gentleman's profits on what was really received, I imagined it to be about *cent. per cent.*

Mr. Martin[228] desired me to take the accounts home to revise at my leisure, which I soon after returned with alterations, little to the honour of the original accomptant, however great his skill in figures. But as his character has been sufficiently known in several late affairs,[229] I shall spend no more of my time, or the reader's patience, in quoting numerable instances of the same dye. I shall only mention the injury done to Mr. Quin, whose house was so spoiled *[134]* by the rabble that came to see the Indians, that he was at a great expence to put it to rights; but instead of Mr. Cacanthropos's allowing out of the immense profits of the show, wherewith to repair the damage, he got him to sign a receipt in full, and then curtailed and perquisited three pounds.[230]

FRENCH CHAPTER XIV (LISTED AS XVI)

BUT IT is now time to return to my own misfortunes. After paying the debts I had contracted, my finances were, as I have already hinted, so low, that I had not wherewith to defray my passage. I made no doubt of getting credit for a part till my arrival. At the Virginia Coffee-house I found a Captain of my acquaintance, bound to Virginia, into whose hands I deposited ten guineas to secure my passage; but the ship, thro' some unaccountable delays, did not quit her moorings till December, when the Captain told me she would go round to Portsmouth, which place he thought would be more convenient for me to embark at.[231] I readily acquiesced with this, as I thought my passage would be long enough without any ad- *[135]* dition. But before I arrived at Portsmouth, my money ran so short, that I was forced to borrow of the landlord, to pay the last stage. I had staid here nine or ten days, in expectation of the ship, when a letter arrived from the Captain, to desire me to return immediately to London, or repair to Deal, as his employers had sent him orders not to touch at Portsmouth, but to proceed immediately to sea. I was thunderstruck. The tavern-keeper had just sent in his bill for payment, the instant I received this letter. I was obliged to deposit cloaths and other effects to the amount of forty pounds, and borrow ten guineas to return.

As soon as I arrived at London, I sent my servant to enquire if the ship had fallen down the river, who shortly after returned with information that she had. I then went to Gravesend, where my money running short again, I had recourse to the landlady. I sent to the office, to know if such a ship had cleared, and was agreeably informed there had not. After expecting the ship four or five days, I sent my *[136]* servant to London, to procure some money on my watch, with orders to inquire after the ship at every place between London and Gravesend. On his return the next day he informed me the ship, with several more, were frozen up at Deptford. I now began to be under the greatest uneasiness about my return to Virginia, fate seeming determined to detain me where misfortunes daily increased. I sent to the Captain for the ten guineas I had advanced for my passage, since I found it impossible to go with him, and returned to London, where my first concern was, to enquire at the war-office whether there had lately arrived any returns from Sir Jeffery Amherst? I was informed there had, and, on turning over the books, found my-self appointed Lieutenant in the forty-second or Royal Highland regiment of foot, with several months subsistence due to me,[232] which I received soon after from Mr. Drummond, the agent, to whom I made known my circum-stances, intreating him to lend me fifty pounds more, without which I found it impossible to get out of England. He [137] obligingly told me, that if I could get any gentleman to accept a bill payable in four months, he would willingly advance that sum. I applied to a gentleman in the city, who was kind enough to accept the bill.

I agreed with a Captain of a ship bound to Virginia, about the middle of March, and paid him thirty-two guineas for my wife's passage and my own; for I had married, or rather made a young lady a companion of my mis-fortunes some time before; but her father having refused his consent to our union, had the barbarity to deny us the least assistance, nay, refused me even ten guineas that I found deficient, after paying my debts, and laying in what was necessary.[233] All affairs being seemingly settled, I went to Billingsgate overnight to save expences, by going in a Gravesend boat the next day, but was prevented by a bailiff, who, as soon as I was up, arrested me, at the suit of a person, who, not making any demand upon me, in my confusion I forgot, or rather did not know where to find. [138]

I was carried immediately to Wood-Street Compter,[234] where I wrote to a friend for money to discharge it but being disappointed, I was obliged to pay away the little I had reserved for my expences, so that I had but two shil-lings left. We now embarked for Gravesend; but before we had got two miles down the river, the boat ran foul of a ship's hawser, by which we were almost overset. We staid a considerable time, to no purpose, to get her clear, but were obliged at last to go ashore and return to Billingsgate, where we staid all night, and next morning, for want of money to discharge our reckoning, I was forced to sell a gold seal that cost me four guineas, for only eleven shillings.

I then embarked in another boat, and got within four miles of Gravesend without any further interruption; but the tide being spent here, we were obliged to walk to Gravesend on foot, where the ship came down, and an-chored next morning. [139]

The Captain informed me, that two gentlemen and a lady, passengers in the ship, would be glad that we should all dine together. This I readily con-sented to, but begged a couple of guineas that I had been deficient in my old reckoning at the White-Hart. Unwilling to borrow any more from the Cap-tain, I sent my servant with a pair of new crimson velvet breeches that cost me three guineas, who returned with thirteen shillings that he had raised on them. Being now on board, I thought myself secure from all further demands or impediments; but we no sooner arrived in the Downs than my servant left me, and demanded four guineas for the time he had served me; a gentleman that was going ashore did me the favour to pay him the money he demanded.

This detail may seem very dry to a reader; but this must effectually convince the public, that had I made money of the Indians, nay, partook of the great sums that were clandestinely made by them, I should not have been *[140]* so soon reduced to the necessities I underwent.

After some difficulties in getting out, we had a very good passage to Virginia. I staid there but just long enough to settle my affairs, and then set out for New York to wait on Sir Jeffery Amherst for my commission; but to save the expences of going by land, I embarked in an old worn-eaten sloop that belonged to a gentleman at New York, who had been obliged to send a Captain to bring her home, her former one having deserted her in that ruinous condition. She had, however, tolerable pumps and sails, and three good hands besides the Captain.

The first day the wind was very fair, and gave us hopes it would continue so the whole passage, but shifting next day to the northwest quarter, we experienced a perfect hurricane, in which the vessel made water so fast, that the men were constantly at the pumps to clear her. The sea ran so high, and the vessel *[141]* was so old and crazy, that I expected each wave would dash her to pieces; the third day we shewed a little sail, though it continued blowing very fresh till evening, when it became pretty fair; yet she still made water at a prodigious rate, and extremely fatigued the men. We saw land next day, but were becalmed till the morning after, when a fresh gale springing up fair, we went at the rate of eight knots an hour till four in the afternoon, when a pilot came on board; the Captain told him that he must run the vessel quite to New York that night, as he had no cable to bring her to an anchor. Had I known this circumstance before, which even the pilot was astonished at, I should not, I believe, have trusted so much to fair weather. We arrived, however, safe in New York.

I waited next morning on Sir Jeffery Amherst, who gave me my commission, with orders immediately to join my regiment, which was then on its way to Pittsburg. I dined with his Excellency next day; after which he *[142]* told me to wait on Col. Reid, and not be in a hurry to join my regiment. A packet it seems had arrived from England the same day I received my commission, which, I suppose, brought a list of the officers to be reduced on half pay, and on waiting on Col. Reid, I found I was of the number. I related Lord Egremont's assurances to the contrary, and produced this his Lordship's Letter to Sir Jeffery Amherst in my favour.

"*Sir,*   *Whitehall, July 23, 1762.*
"*Mr. Fauquier, Lieutenant Governor of Virginia, having represented the long and very useful services, particularly in the Cherokee country, of Mr. Timberlake, and having strongly recommended him to some mark of his Majesty's royal favour, and Mr. Timberlake having accompanied some chiefs of the Cherokee nation to London, where he has constantly attended*

them, and has conducted himself entirely to the King's satisfaction: I am to acquaint you that his Majesty, in consid- [143] *eration of the above services of Mr. Timberlake, has been pleased to command me to signify to you his royal pleasure, that you should appoint him to the first Lieutenancy in an old regiment, which shall become vacant in North America, after you receive this letter. I am, &c.*

(Signed)
EGREMONT"

The Colonel, on perusing it, was of the same opinion, that certainly his Lordship never intended me to be reduced. I went again to wait on the General; but being denied admission, I immediately inquired for a vessel bound to Virginia, and having at last found one, returned home after spending between twenty and thirty guineas to no purpose; for had it been this Lordship's intention to have had me reduced, I could have been no more in a young regiment, without sending me to New York, in North America, for a commission. *[144]*

I remained at home till January 1764, when the General Assembly of the colony met for the dispatch of public business, whither I repaired to petition for my expences from the Cherokee country to Williamsburg; which, however, were greatly superior to the accounts I gave in, lest they should judge any of them unreasonable. While my money lasted the Indians wanted for nothing, and I am still considerably indebted on their account.

I gained a majority, and a committee was appointed to look into my accounts,[235] who told me it was to be paid by the council, out of the money for contingent charges, and not by the colony. After waiting a considerable time, at a very great expence, whilst urgent business required my presence elsewhere, I at last got the favour of Mr. Walthoe, Clerk of the Council, to undertake presenting my petition and accounts to the Governor and Council, in my absence, which he did at the next meeting, and soon after sent me the following letter. *[145]*

"Sir   *Williamsburg, Feb. 3, 1764*

 "*It would have afforded me a very sensible pleasure, had I been enabled by the resolution of the Council to have returned a satisfactory answer to your letter of the 26th of last month. In compliance with your request, I the last day of the sessions presented to the board your account, and the opinion of the committee to which it was referred. It was maturely considered and debated, and, extremely contrary to my hopes, disapproved of and rejected; for this reason principally, that you went, as they were persuaded, not by any order, to the Cherokee nation but in pursuit of your own profit or pleasure,* * * * * * * * *, *&c.*

(Signed)
N. Walthoe.*"[236]

I was quite astonished to find, on the receipt of this letter, that these gentlemen imagined I had made a party of pleasure to a savage country, in the winter season; or that I went in the view of profit, with a stock of twenty pounds worth *[146]* of goods, most of which I distributed amongst the necessitous prisoners. Had I intended profit, I should certainly have taken the safest way, and a sufficient quantity of goods to have recompenced me for all my fatigues and danger, as I surely did not expect presents in the Cherokee country.

I went to convince the Indians of our sincerity, to know the navigation, and to serve my country. Let others take care how they precipitate themselves to serve so ungrateful a——.[237] But the reader, by this time, is too well acquainted with the particulars of my journey, to pass judgment with these gentlemen. I have already shewn, that my expences and losses, during that unfortunate jaunt, was upwards of an hundred pounds in ready money, besides what I gave them in presents at their return to their own country, and what I am still indebted for on their account.

It was objected, that I was not ordered. I own it. Do they know Col. Stephen? Did he ever order any officer on such a service? Is my *[147]* service of less merit, because I offered myself to do what, tho' necessary, he could not well command? Does the brave volunteer, who desires to mount the breach, merit less than the coward, whose officer compels him to it? No, certainly. We should praise and countenance such forwardness; yet for this same reason have I been refused my expences. Can any one think Col. Stephen would command any officer amongst a savage and unsettled enemy, whose hands were still reeking, as I may say, with the blood of Demeré and the garrison of Fort Loudoun, massacred after they had capitulated, and were marching home according to agreement, who have no laws, and are both judges and executors of their revenge?

I had no written orders. I never doubted they would be called in question, tho' verbal. But here are some extracts of two of Col. Stephen's letters to me, while in the Cherokee country, that may clear up this particular. In one dated Fort Lewis, January 30, 1762, he says,

"Give my compliments to your best friends, *[148]* and I should have been extremely glad to have heard that Judd's Friend (i.e. Ostenaco) had received the small present I sent him from the Great Island. I know no reason which will prevent you and Judd's Friend taking your own time to come in, and should be glad to see you, &c."

In another, dated Fort Lewis, February 14, 1762, he says, "The Governor is extremely pleased with Judd's Friend's favours to you, and the kindness of all the Cherokees, and I think it is the better how soon the chiefs come in with you."

I was to bring some chiefs in then: this has likewise been disputed?

But if I had no written orders, those given to Shorey will prove my verbal ones. The original, among my other papers, is in Mr. Walthoe's hands: but the substance, as near as I can recollect, was as follows: "William Shorey, you are to wait at Fort Lewis for the *[149]* coming of Mr. Timberlake, and accompany Judd's Friend in quality of interpreter to Williamsburg. I can rely more upon you than on M'Cormack. Pray put the country to as little expence as possible."

Through these continual series of ill fortunes I got so much in debt, that I was obliged to sell my paternal estate and negroes. My friends advised me to return to London, promising to send me their tobacco, and I to make returns in such goods as would best suit the country, of which I was a tolerable judge. I communicated this project to many of my acquaintances, who gave me great encouragement and promises of assistance. Mr. Trueheart, a gentleman of Hanover county, so much approved it, that he proposed himself a partner in the undertaking, as a voyage to England might be the means of recovering his health then much on the decline. I did not hesitate to accept the proposals of a person of fortune, who could advance money to carry it into execution. We accordingly begun our preparations for the voyage, which were al- *[150]* ready in some degree of readiness, when walking one day in Mr. Trueheart's fields, I perceived five Indians coming toward's the house, in company with one of Mr. Trueheart's sons, whom, upon a nearer view, I recollected to be some of my Cherokee acquaintance. I enquired of Mr. Trueheart where he found them? He told me at Warwick, enquiring for me, and overjoyed when he offered to conduct them to his father's house, where I was, since they had feared being obliged to go a great way to seek me.

After eating and smoking, according to custom, the headman told me he had orders to find me out, even should I be as far off as New-York, to accompany them to Williamsburg, being sent with a talk to the Governor, about business of the greatest consequence, and the headman hoped I was too much their friend to refuse them that favour. I replied, that the behaviour of the Cherokees to me, while in their country, obliged me to return what lay in my power while they were in mine; that I *[151]* would never refuse anything that could be of any advantage to them, but do every thing to serve them. After resting a couple of days, we set out, and in two more arrived at Williamsburg. They waited next morning on the Governor to disclose their business, which the headman afterwards told me, was to demand a passage to England, as encroachments were daily made upon them, notwithstanding the proclamation issued by the King to the contrary; that their hunting grounds, their only support, would be soon entirely ruined by the English; that frequent complaints had been made to the Governors to no purpose, they therefore resolved to seek redress in England. Next day a council met on the occasion, and an answer promised the day following. As I had some particular business with the Governor, I waited on him the morning the Indians were to have their answer. The chief of what the Governor said concerning them was, that they should have applied to Capt. Stuart, at Charles Town,[238] he being superintendent for Indian affairs; that if the white people encroached, he saw no way to prevent it, *[152]* but by repelling them by force. I no sooner left the Governor than the Indians came to wait on him. I am unacquainted with what passed during this interval; but the interpreter came just after to my lodgings, and told me their demand was refused; that the headman, who was then down at the Capitol, intended to go to New-York for a passage; on which I rode down there, to take my leave of them. The interpreter then told me, that the headman intreated me to take them to England, as he understood by Mr. Trueheart's people that I was going over. I replied, that however willing to do the Cherokees any favour, it was utterly out of my power to do that, as their passage would be a great expence, and my finances ran so low, I could scarce defray my own. I should then have objected the Governor's orders to the contrary, if any such had ever been given; but I am apt to think they came in a private letter to England many months afterwards. I strove to shuffle the refusal on Mr. Trueheart, hinting that he was a person of fortune, and had it in his power; on which they returned back with me, and applied to him. *[153]*

On my return, I acquainted Mr. Trueheart with the whole affair, who, moved by their intreaties and a sense of the injustice done to these unfortunate people, who daily see their possessions taken away, yet dare not oppose it, for fear of engaging in a war with so puissant an enemy, contrary to my expectation, agreed to bring them over. One of them died before we set out, but we proceeded with the other four to York Town. We were already embarked, and weighing anchor, when Mr. Trueheart finding the cabin much lumbered, resolved to take his passage in another vessel. We were scarce out of York River, when the wind shifted directly contrary, and in a little time blew so hard, that we were obliged to let go another anchor, the vessel having dragged the first a considerable way. We got to sea in a day or two after, and proceeded on our voyage to Bristol. The day we made land, one of the Indians, brother to Chucatah the headman, died suddenly. We saw a ship lying off Lundy, which we found, on speaking with, to be the same Mr. Trueheart was on board, and that his *[154]* son had died on the passage. In a day or two after our arrival, we set out for London, where the day after we arrived I went, as Mr. Trueheart knew nothing of the town, to acquaint Lord H——[239] of the Indians arrival; but his Lordship was not at home. I called again next day, but received the same answer. I went some time after to the office, and acquainted one of the Under-Secretaries with their business, who told me, as well as I can remember, that his Lordship would have nothing to do with them, as they did not come over by authority; at which Mr. Trueheart and the Indians were greatly displeased: that gentleman, then, to lessen the expences as much as possible, took a cheap lodging in Long's-Court[240], Leicester-Fields, for himself and the Indians, where, after a short illness, he died on the 6th of November.

This was a great loss to me, and likely to be severely felt by the Indians, who must have perished, had I not taken care of them, and promised payment for their board, &c. I ne- *[155]* ver indeed doubted but when Lord H—— should be informed with the true situation of affairs, he would readily reimburse me; I sent him a letter for that purpose, but received no answer. The Indians began to be very uneasy at so long a confinement, as my circumstances would not permit their going so often to public diversions as they should have done. They, therefore, begged to come and live with me.

I some time after, the better to accommodate them, took a house, and gave my note for their board, which came to £29: 13: 6. I wrote again to Lord H——, and received a verbal answer at the office, from Mr. St-h-e,[241] which was, that his Lordship took very ill my troubling him with those letters: that since I had brought the Indians here, I should take them back, or he would take such measures as I should not like. I replied, something hastily, that I had not brought the Indians, neither would I carry them back: that his Lordship might take what measures *[156]* he pleased; which I suppose offended a courtier accustomed to more deceitful language. I am a soldier, and above cringing or bearing tamely an injury.

But should these people commence a war, and scalp every encroacher, or even others, to revenge the ill treatment they received while coming in a peaceable manner to seek redress before they had recourse to arms, let the public judge who must answer it; I must, however, lay great part of the blame on Mr. Cocoanthropos, who, possessing the ear of Lord H——, made such an unfavourable report of me, that either his Lordship believed, or pretended to believe them impostors, or Indians brought over for a shew. They were known by several gentlemen in London to be of power in their own country; and had not the government been convinced of that, I scarce think they would have sent them home at all. As to his other suspicion, even when I had been so great a loser, without hopes of redress, I might have justified making a shew of them; *[157]* but they were quite private; few knew there were such people in London. Nay, I did not enough disabuse the public when that impostor, who had taken the name of Chucatah, was detected; so the public, without further examination, imagined Chucatah himself to be the impostor. What contributed greatly to raise this report, was, that three Mohock[242] Indians were, after making the tour of England and Ireland, made a shew of in the Strand, and immediately confounded by the public with the Cherokees, and I accused of making a shew all over England of Indians who never stirred out of London. Had I showed them, I should not have been under such anxiety to have them sent away; I should have wished their stay, or been able to have sent them back without any inconveniency in raising the necessary money for that purpose: but as it was entirely out of my power, I was advised to put in an advertisement for a public contribution; I first, however, resolved to present a petition to the Board of Trade,[243] in answer to which Lord H-h told me, that it no way *[158]* concerned them, but Lord H-, to whom I must again apply.[244] On a sec-

Figure 79. Unidentified soldier. Copper plate engraving printed on wove about the time of the Timberlake visit to England. Artist, subject, and original publication unknown. (Collection of Duane King)

ond application, Lord H——[245] agreed I should be paid for the time they remained in London, and that he would take care to have them sent home. I was allowed two guineas a week for the month they stayed afterwards in town; but from Mr. Trueheart's death, what in cloaths, paint, trinkets, coach-hire, and other expences, including the bill from their late lodgings (for which I was arrested, and put to a considerable expence) and the time they had lived with me, I had expended near seventy pounds, which I must enevitably lose, as Lord H—— has absolutely refused to reimburse me.[246]

About the beginning of March 1765, by the desire of Mr. Montague,[247] I accompanied the Indians on board the Madeira packet, in which they returned to their own country,[248] leaving me immersed in debts not my own, and plunged into difficulties thro' my zeal to serve both them and my country, from which the selling of twenty pounds a year out of my *[159]* commission has rather allayed than extricated me. The Indians expressed the highest gratitude and grief for my misfortunes; all the recompence they could offer, was an asylum in their country, which I declined; since their murmurs, and some unguarded expressions they dropt, convinced me they would not fail at their return to spirit up their countrymen, to vindicate their right by force of arms, which would infallibly again have been laid to my charge, and I perhaps be reputed a traitor to my country. My circumstances, however, are now so much on the decline, that when I can satisfy my creditors, I must retire to the Cherokee, or some other hospitable country,[249] where unobserved I and my wife may breathe upon the little that yet remains.[250]

FINIS.

[160]

Appendix A

Visual Representations of the
CHEROKEE KINGS IN LONDON, 1762

William C. Sturtevant

National Museum of Natural History, Smithsonian Institution

BY UNKNOWN PAINTER & ENGRAVER:

Engravings

1. *The Three Cherokees, came over from the head of the River Savanna to London, 1762. / Their interpreter that was Poisoned*

Plus details on the individuals shown. Sold in Marys Buildings, Covent Garden, according to Act, by G. Bickham. Full lengths. Image 8½ × 11¼".

Copies: Museum of the Cherokee Indian (sold to them by William Reese & Co., 1995); Glenbow Alberta Institute, Calgary (B.65.40.6); Colonial Williamsburg; and, according to Fundaburk, *Southeast Indians* (p. 114), British Museum, New York Public Library (not located in Prints or Rare Books, nor in their catalogs of these two, 28 December 1995), and University of Georgia Libraries.

Copy: British Museum, Prints and Drawings, 1862-10-11-662; quite yellowed, upper right corner missing (doesn't affect image), otherwise fairly good condition (seen by WCS, 22 April 1996).

Reproduced: Swan, *Portraits*, no. 144 (from National Anthropological Archives, NAA neg. 1063-h-i): Fundaburk, *Southeast Indians*, no. 119; and Time-Life Books, *Tribes of the Southern Woodland*, p. 66.

Derivative:

[Bust, after "Outacite or Man-Killer" in the above]

2 Cherokee Chief [sic], 4.7 cm high, in "Frontispeice [*sic*] to the Celebrated Lecture on Heads," engraving, 31 × 23.5 cm, in "George Stevens's Celebrated lecture on heads; Which has been exhibited Upwards of Two Hundred and Fifty successive Nights, to crowded audiences, and met with the most universal Applause. . . . The Seventh Edition. With an entire new Frontispiece, representing all the various Heads, &c. Printed for J. Pridden, at the Feathers in Fleet-street, near Fleet Bridge, 1766. Price only Six-pence."

Described on p. 2 of the text: "N° 2. This is the head of a CHEROKEE CHIEF, called Sachem - Swampum - Scalpo - Tomakauk;—He was a great hero, warrior, and mankiller-Lately."

Copy: British Library, shelf mark 1484m35 (seen by WCS, 3 March 1999).

85

By Sir Joshua Reynolds:

2. *Syacust Ukah, Cherokee Chief*

Inscribed at right "Scyacust Ukah 1762." Oils, 47½ × 35". In Gilcrease Museum, Tulsa, Oklahoma. No entry in Witt Library Index, Courtauld Institute, London.

Reproduced: *Journal of Cherokee Studies* 2, no. 3 (1977), cover (color).

3. *Outacite, Chief of the Cherokees*

Location of original unknown. The gorget shown in the busts (below, 3.1–3.3) is silver and has a width of 10.8 cm. It survives in the Royal Ontario Museum, Toronto, as HD6313 (see W. C. Sturtevant, gen. ed., *Handbook of North American Indians*, vol. 4: W. E. Washburn, *History of Indian-White Relations* [1988], p. 9, fig. 3). It is well shown except for the omission of the inscription along the lower edge: "LOYAL CHIEF OUTACITE CHEROKEE WARRIOR."

Engravings after (3) (no entries in Witt Library Index)

3.1. *Outacite, / Chief of the Cherokees.* "Reynolds Pinxt." Engraver unstated. Bust, right profile. Image 4 ½ × 4". Frontispiece of vol. 2 of [Pierre F. X. de] Charlevoix, *A voyage to North-America* . . . (Dublin, 1766), only in this edition.

Copy (of print): WCS collection.

3.2. *Outacite, / Chief of the Cherokees.* Painter and engraver unstated. Bust, right profile. Very close copy of 3.1. In Samuel G. Drake, *Biography and History of the Indians* . . . (1851), bk. 4, opposite p. 373; impression from same block is in "3d. ed." (1834); not in the 1833 ed.

Reproduced: Fundaburk, *Southeast Indians*, no. 121 (from Bureau of American Ethnology, NAA neg. 1063-h-3). DHK collection.

3.3. *Outacite, / King of the Cherokees.* Painter and engraver unstated. Bust, left profile. Close copy of 3.1, but laterally reversed. In *Court Magazine*, 1, no. 11 (August 1762), facing p. [491]. No printing on verso, no watermark. Plate mark 7 × 4⅜", image (without caption) 5¹⁄₁₆ × 4⅛".

Original: Beinecke Library, Yale University, Z17/2981/1762 (seen by WCS, 19 December 95). Slightly yellowed, with faint water stain lower left corner (doesn't interfere with image).

Copy of print: New York Public Library, Rare Books, Indian Portraits Scrapbook, no. 101, call no. *KW (seen by WCS, 28 December 95). A clear impression, somewhat yellowed but otherwise in good condition. (Librarian entered the source, from WCS, on the typed table of contents for the scrapbook.) DHK collection (acquired September 1999).

3.4. *Outacite: The Cherokee Chief.* Painter and engraver unstated. Full length, head in right profile. Image 8¼ × 4⅞". Bust is closely related to 3.1; rest of body and tomahawk on ground probably influenced by Four Kings mezzotints.

Copy: Amon Carter Museum of Western Art, Fort Worth, Texas (274.68) (from Collection of Robin Bethell, Toronto).

3.5. *Skiagusta Ostinaco, the Cherokee King.* Painter and engraver unstated. Full length, head in left profile. Close copy of 3.4, laterally reversed. Image 6 × 3¾".

Copy: Museum of the Fur Trade, Chadron, Nebraska.

Reproduced: Time-Life Books, *Tribes of the Southern Woodlands*, p. 82.

3.6. *Outacite / oder / Menschentodter, / Konig der Cherokesen.* Possibly after 3(?), image not yet compared. 6⅝ × 3⅜".

Copy: Fitzwilliam Museum, University of Cambridge (P. 205-1951) (seen by WCS in 1968, not located in 1995–96).

4. *Austenaco, Great Warriour*

Artist and location of original unknown; unless Fundaburk, *Southeast Indians*, p. 114, under no. 122, is in error in saying that "engraving from *Royal Magazine* [4.1 here] [is] after Reynolds." No entry in Witt Library Index.

Engravings after (4):

4.1. *Austenaco, Great Warriour, / Commander in Chief of the Cherokee Nation.* Above image: "Engraved for the Royal Magazine." Painter and engraver unstated. In *Royal Magazine*, vol. 7 (July 1762), facing p. 16. Full length. Page size 8¼ × 4⅞", plate mark 7 × 4⅛", image 5⅜ × 3½".

Copies: Beinecke Library, Yale University (in copy of *Royal Magazine*), rather yellowed and slightly foxed (but better impression than the one reproduced by Fundaburk—latter reproduction compared by WCS, 19 December 95); British Museum, Prints and Drawings 1862-10-11-661, yellowed, but quite good condition except for a small rubbed area on lower left (doesn't affect image)—comparison with Fundaburk reproduction suggests this may be the one photographed for Bureau of American Ethnology, NAA neg. 1863-g (seen 22 April 1996).

Reproduced: Fundaburk, *Southeast Indians*, no. 122 (Bureau of American Ethnology, NAA neg. 1063-g); H. Honour, *The New Golden Land* (New York: Pantheon Books, 1975), p. 126 (with the Four Kings); Williams, *Memoirs*, frontispiece. WCS collection.

4.2. *Austenaco, Great Warriour, / Commander in Chief of the Cherokee Nation.* At top: "Engraved for the British Magazine." Painter and engraver unstated. In *British Magazine*, vol. 3 (July 1762), facing p. 378. Full length, standing, head slightly turned to his right. Holds staff in right hand; tomahawk by his left foot. Otherwise a version, laterally reversed, of 4.1. Plate mark ca. 7 × 4⅜"; frame ³⁄₁₆ × 3⅝"; figure 5⅞". No watermark.

Copy: Beinecke Library, Yale University, in *British Magazine*, Z17 297d (seen by WCS, 19 December 1995). Fine condition, no foxing, but tightly bound so doubtful whether a photo would show whole image undistorted.

Copy: Bodleian Library, Oxford, in *British Magazine*, Hope Adds 1160(3).

Copy: collection of Gerald Schroedl.

Copy: DHK collection (acquired Berkshire, England, 19 January 2005).

5. *Cunne Shote*

Oils, 28 × 35" (35 × 28[?]). Bust, half-length. In Gilcrease Museum, Tulsa, Oklahoma. *Note*: In files of Witt Library, Courtauld Institute, London, is a large photograph of this marked "Bromhead, Cutts & Co., London, 1924"; Witt Library Index (queried by WCS, 23 April 1996) indicates that he was an art dealer and publisher in London in existence at least from 1920 to 1924.

Reproduced: Fundaburk, *Southeast Indians*, no. 120; Time-Life Books, *Tribes of the Southern Woodlands*, p.16 (color); *Journal of Cherokee Studies* 1, no. 1 (1976), cover (color).

Engravings after (5):

5.1. *Cunne Shote, the Indian Chief, a great warrior of the / Cherokee Nation. / Sold at the Golden head, in Queen Square, Ormond Street.* In ink, probably eighteenth-century hand, beneath image. Mezzotint. Proof impression, pulled before caption set. Bottom edge is irregular, clearly meant to be cut off. An extremely close copy of (5) (compared by WCS with copy of Fundaburk, *Southeast Indians*, no. 120). Somewhat earlier state than 5.2 (e.g., lacks white lines in sky for clouds; no significant difference in ethnographic details). Plate mark 14 × 10", print area 12½ to 12¾ × 9¹⁵⁄₁₆".

   Copy: New York Public Library, Prints Collection, filed under McArdell, James, with call number MEVG, JCS 50 (seen by WCS, 28 December 1995). This example has some rubbed areas on right shoulder, on outer edge of right upper sleeve, on edging of robe, in two spots by his hand, and across lower edge of image approximately where later cut off.

5.2. [*Cunne Shote, the Indian Chief . . . Pr. 2s. 6d.*] [London, 1762]. Proof before lettering. Title from Smith. "F. Parsons pinxt. Js. McArdell fecit." Smith, *British Mezzotint Portraits*, vol. 2, p. 854.—information from John Carter Brown Library (JCB), Providence, Rhode Island, card catalog of engravers. Example is JCB call no. En762.P267c (seen by WCS, 10 October 1996): mezzotint, in excellent condition. The proof copy in the New York Public Library is in a somewhat later state than 5.1. Comparison of photos by WCS shows this one is cut off at bottom about where 5.1 is marked; cloud patterns added, white highlight on forehead added, white lines in feather on head and in palm tree at left strengthened (although these differences—except for the cropping at the bottom—may be due to better inking in this example). Sheet 34.6 × 26.4 cm (13⅞ × 10⅜"), plate mark 25.2 cm (10 or 9¹⁵⁄₁₆") wide, runs off bottom of sheet.

5.3. *Cunne Shote, the Indian Chief, / A great Warrior of the Cherokee Nation. / Sold at the Golden Head, in Queen Square, Ormond Street.* Painter and engraver not stated. Same plate as 5.1, in slightly later state. Paper 13⅞ × 9⅞", image 12⅛ × 9⅞".

   Copy: New York Public Library, Prints Collection, in same folder as 5.1, with same call number (seen by WCS, 28 December 1995). Good condition.

5.4. *Cunne Shote, the Indian Chief, / A great Warrior of the Cherokee Nation. / Was in England in 1762. / Sold at the Golden Head, in Queen Square, Ormond Street. / Pr. 2s/ 6d.* Beneath image: "F. Parsons pinxt. Js. McArdell fecit." Height 13⅞", sub. 12⅛", width 9⅞" (according to Smith, *British Mezzotint Portraits*, vol. 2, p. 854).

Copies: Harvard Peabody Museum, Bushnell Collection (Bureau of American Ethnology, NAA neg. 997); Yale University Art Gallery (1946.9.817); Joslyn Art Museum, Prince Maximilian Collection; Albany Institute of History and Art; Glenbow Alberta Institute, Calgary, Canada (P.65.40.7); British Museum, Prints and Drawings 1851-3-8-591, fairly good condition, with note in pencil beneath: "CS. Vol. II. 854 No. 50" (a reference to Smith, *British Mezzotint Portraits*), image 12⅛ × 10", including caption 13¾ × 10".

Reproduced: Swan, *Prints of the American Indian*, no. 136.

Parsons, *Cunne Shote*, mezzotint, 13 ¾ × 9⅞", 349 × 241 mm [London, ca. 1762]. Sale of Siebert Collection, Part II, Sothebys sale 7356, 28 October 1999, item 579, p. 39.

5.5. *Cunne Shote, the Indian Chief, / A great Warrior of the Cherokee Nation. / Printed for Robt. Sayer, Map & Printseller, near Sergeants Inn Fleet Street.* Image 31 × 26 cm.

Copy: Museum für Volkerkunde, Gottingen (seen by WCS, 15 July 1988, but not compared with any of the above; equation based on title). Badly hand-colored, with red robe, except for fine copper-colored face and hands. In old frame. On back, wood slats with glued-on label in Blumenbach's hand, 6 × 10.3 cm: "Der Kup ferrothen Hautfarbe wegen nach dem Leben coloriert in Philadelphia, von warnach ich es von Dr Ad. Seybert zum Geschenk erhaltaen. J. Fr. Blbach" [The copper-red skin color colored after life in Philadelphia, whence WCS obtained it as a gift from Dr. Ad. Seybert. Johann Friedrich Blumenbach].

6. Cunne Shote

Location unknown. Source behind 6.1—unless (as seems probable) the latter is based on 5.4, with body added by Jefferys.

Engravings after (6):

6.1. *Habit of Cunne Shote a Cherokee Chief. / Cunne Shote Chef des Chiroquois.* "207." Full length. 24.7 × 20.3 cm. From Thomas Jefferys, *A collection of the dresses . . .*, vol. 4 (1772), where (p. 27) it is said to be "from a metzotinto print scraped by MacArdell, from a painting of Mr. Parsons." WCS collection.

6.2. *Cunne Shote. / Chef des Chiroquois / d'apres Parson / Paris chez Duf os rue St. Victor A.P.D.R.* Colored engraving. Full length. 11 × 8⅝".

Copy: De Renne Library, University of Georgia.

Reproduced: Fundaburk, *Southeast Indians*, no. 123.

BY S. WALE:

7. *Cunne Shote, the Indian Chief*

1762. Drawing in colored crayons 4¾" × 3". Location unknown. Bought by David
I. Bushnell Jr. in July 1924, from Maggs Bros., London, for £5/5/-, according to
letter in Box 2, Special Collections Division, Earl Gregg Swem Library, College
of William & Mary (WCS notes, 12 March 1984). Not listed in the standard
typed catalog by Whatmough of the Bushnell Collection of paintings and
drawings in Harvard Peabody Museum.

8. Two satirical engravings

Reproduced by Stephens and Hawkins, *Catalogue of Prints and Drawings in the
British Museum* (1883):

No. 3868 (pp. 84–85): "A new humorous song, on the Cherokee Chiefs Inscribed
to the Ladies of Great Britain. By H. Howard."

No. 3877 (pp. 93–94): "Without Within To the King of the Cherokees."

Also of No. 3874 (pp. 89–90) on Catawba subject but without ethnographic
illustrations, copies at New York Public Library.

REFERENCES

Books and Catalogues

Cotton, William. *A Catalogue of the portraits painted by Sir Joshua Reynolds*, Knt.,
   P.R.A. Compiled from his autograph memorandum books and from printed
   catalogues, etc. London: Longman, Brown, Green, Longmans, and Roberts,
   1857. vii + [82] pp.
   [Entries arranged alphabetically by name of sitter, with dates in separate
   column. No entries for 1762–1763, few for 1761 and 1764. No entries under
   Outacite, Scyacuste, Cherokee, or Austenaco. Anna Wells Rutledge told WCS,
   in letter dated 6 August 1984, that Reynolds's notebooks for the period, including
   July 1762, are not known, according to Ellis Waterhouse.]
Editors of Time-Life Books. *Tribes of the Southern Woodlands*. Alexandria, Va.: Time-
   Life Books, 1994.
Foreman, Carolyn. *Indians Abroad, 1493–1939*. Norman: University of Oklahoma,
   1943. Chapter 7.
Forster, John. *The Life and Adventures of Oliver Goldsmith: A Biography in Four Books*.
   London: Bradbury & Evans and Chapman & Hall, 1848. 704 pp.
   [British Library, 1202.d.12, p. 252: anecdote re: Cherokees in London]
Fundaburk, Emma Lila. *Southeast Indians: Life Portraits, A Catalogue of Pictures, 1564–
   1860*. Birmingham, Ala.: Birmingham Printing Company, 1958.
Hamilton, Edward. *The Engraved Works of Sir Joshua Reynolds: A Catalogue Raisonné
   of the Engravings Made after His Paintings from 1755–1822* . . . New enlarged ed.
   Amsterdam, 1973.
   [National Portrait Gallery, N40.1/.R463H2/1973]
Hunnisett, Basil. *A Dictionary of British Steel Engravers*. Leighton-Sea, England: F.
   Lewis, 1980.
   [National Museum of American Art, NE628.3/.H84X]

———. *An Illustrated Dictionary of British Steel Engravings.* 1989.
  [National Portrait Gallery, RefgNE625.H86.1989X] Aldershot, England:
  Scolar Press; Brookfield, Vt., U.S.A.: Gower, 1989.

———. *Steel Engraved Book Illustrations in England.* 1980.
  [National Museum of American Art, NE6283/.H86/1980x8] Boston: D.R.
  Godine, 1980.

Mannings, David. *Sir Joshua Reynolds: A Complete Catalogue of His Painting.* The
  subject pictures catalogued by Martin Postle. New Haven: Yale University Press
  for the Paul Mellon Centre for Studies in British Art, 2000.

Postle, Martin. *Sir Joshua Reynolds: The Subject Pictures.* New York: Cambridge
  University Press, 1994 .

Reynolds, Joshua. *Discourses on Art.* Edited by Robert R. Wark. New Haven: Yale
  University Press for the Paul Mellon Centre for Studies in British Art, 1975.
  [P. 137 mention of face painting of Cherokee man, evidently related to his
  portrait of 1762 visitors]

Smith, John Chaloner. *British Mezzotint Portraits; being a descriptive catalogue . . .
  arranged according to the engravers . . . .* 4 vols. London: Henry Sotheran, 1883.
  [Index in vol. 4(?); only vol. 2 examined by WCS at New York Public Library,
  Prints Collection, 28 December 1995. "See Forster's 'Life of Goldsmith' for
  anecdote of one of them [i.e., the Cherokees] embracing him" (vol. 2, p. 854).
  National Museum of American History, 1926 edition, NPG fNE/1815/.R96]

Stephens, Frederic George, and Edward Hawkins. *Catalogue of Prints and Drawings
  in the British Museum.* Division I: Political and Personal Satires. Vol. 4: *A.D. 1761
  to c. A.D. 1770.* London, 1883.
  [Copy in New York Public Library, Print Collection. Arranged
  chronologically; July–October 1762 searched by WCS, 28 December 1995]

Swan, Bradford. *Prints of the American Indian in Boston Prints and Printmakers
  1670–1775.* Boston: Colonial Society of Massachusetts, 1971.
  [For details re: derivation from Four Kings of Canada and Cunne Shote
  portrait]

Waterhouse, Ellis Kirkham. *Reynolds.* London: Kegan Paul . . . , 1941 [Not seen.]
  National Museum of American Art:N40.1/.R463W3r; 2d edition: N40.1/.
  R463W3

———. *Dictionary of British Eighteenth Century Painters.* Woodbridge, England:
  Antique Collectors Club, 1981.
  [Brief entry on Francis Parsons.]

Periodicals

The British Magazine or Monthly Repository for Gentlemen & Ladies. Vol. 3. London:
  Printed for J. Fletcher, Jan.–Dec. 1762; paginated (1)–672, plus index.
  See index under "Cherokee Nation, account of," p. 377. On pp. 377–378 are
  three paragraphs with the title "An Account of the Cherokee Nation." Facing
  p. 378: engraving of Austenaco. The Beinecke Library, Yale University, has
  original copy (Z17 297d), seen by WCS, 19 December 95, but too tightly bound
  to photograph adequately (no copying permitted). Not in Library of Congress.
  New York Public Library has vol. 2 only. Copy in the British Library (Main
  Reading Room) damaged (evidently in World War II bombing) and replaced
  in 1971 by a microfilm of copy in Bodleian Library (special permission from
  Preservation Section needed to see the original in British Library; information

from visit of WCS, 23 April 1996); in March 1999, British Library had no (obvious) record of existence of the damaged copy and referred me to the microfilm alone. The shelf-mark in the Bodleian Library is Hope Adds 1160 (3).

Court Magazine (= *Court Magazine or Royal Chronicle*), vols. 1–2, Sept. 1761–Feb. 1763; then it became *The Court & City Magazine*, then (as in Beinecke) *The Court, City & Country Magazine*).

OCLC wrongly lists originals in Western Carolina University, University of Pittsburgh, Clarion University of Pennsylvania; all three have only microfilms. Microfilm (1761–63) at SUNY Buffalo (May–September 1762) read by WCS for all references to Cherokees. Not listed in *Union List of Serials*; *British Union Catalogue of Periodicals* (1955) lists it only in British Museum (now British Library) and there evidently only vol. 2. Beinecke Library has originals for Sept. 1761–Nov. 1765; vol. 1 (9Z17/2981/1762) seen by WCS, 19 December 1995. See engraving 3.3 above.

Public Advertiser (= *Oracle and Public Advertiser*), London.

Microfilm for July–10 Aug. 1762 from Pennsylvania State University read by WCS for all references to Cherokees in London (only missing issue here is 1 Aug. 1762). Found ads for engraving of Outacite (to appear in the *Court Magazine*, no. 11) but no reproductions or other pictures.

The Royal Magazine or Gentleman's Monthly Companion, vol. 7. London: Printed . . . for J. Coote. Vol. 7, July–Dec. 1762; paginated 1–320 + index.

Index under "Cherokees," pp. 16, 73, 80. In original in Beinecke Library, Yale University, only p. 16 checked by WCS, 19–20 December 1995. This page (issue for July 1762) has descriptive paragraph and engraving of Austenaco (see 4.1 above). There is said to be another copy of the original periodical in the Library of Congress.

The St. James's Chronicle, or The British Evening-Post.

Microfilm of no. 205 (1–3 July 1762) through no. 223 (12 Aug. 1762) in Sterling Memorial Library, Yale University; read by WCS, 20 December 1995, for all references to Cherokees. No pictures, but according to no. 206, Saturday, 3 July, to Tuesday, 6 July, 1762, p. [3]: "The Cherokee Chiefs are sitting for their Pictures, to Mr. Reynolds." No copies in the Library of Congress or the New York Public Library.

London Social Calendar, 1762, Followed by a Map of Places
Visited by the Cherokees and Timberlake, 1762–1765

1762

Wednesday, June 16: Epreuve lands at Plymouth; Cherokees tour the *HMS Revenge*, go
   to an inn, hire chaise for London.

Thursday, June 17: Exeter Cathedral, Wilton House, and view statue of Hercules;
   talk to news reporter at Salisbury.

Friday, June 18: Arrive in London in the evening after a two-day, 230-mile trip from
   Plymouth.

Saturday, June 19: Captain Blake calls on Lord Egremont at Piccadilly; Egremont
   sends for and questions Cherokees.

Sunday, June 20: Nathan Carrington, a royal messenger, is assigned to the
   Cherokees, who settle into the Quin house on Suffolk Street.

Monday, June 21: Dinner at Egremont House at Piccadilly at 7:00 P.M. Other dinner
   guests accompany Cherokees home.

Wednesday, June 23: First public appearance during a walk in Kensington Gardens
   dressed in English fashion.

Thursday, June 24: "Cloaths" being made for the Cherokees in English fashion;
   equipage ordered.

Friday, June 25: Return to Kensington Gardens. They dine with Governor Ellis of
   Georgia.

Saturday, June 26: Visit Westminster Abbey to view the monuments and curiosities
   there.

Sunday, June 27: Oconastota arrives in Chota from New Orleans quite naked, as the
   French had nothing to give them.

Monday, June 28: Sir Joshua Reynolds lists the "King of the Cherokees" among
   sitters for June.

Tuesday, June 29: Cunne Shote sits for his picture with Mr. Francis Parsons at
   Queen's Square.

Wednesday, June 30: Cherokees go to the Tower of London to view the zoo and
   crown jewels.

Thursday, July 1: At 9:00 A.M. Ostenaco sits for Reynolds. Later they go to St. Paul's
   Cathedral, both houses of Parliament, and Westminster Abbey.

Friday, July 2: First visit to Sadler's Wells. Miss Wilkinson performs on muscial
   glasses; music and dancing.

Saturday, July 3: Ostenaco sits for Mr. Reynolds. Cherokees return to Sadler's Wells.

Sunday, July 4: Visited Vauxhall sometime this past week (possibly Wed., June 30)
   and had sumptuous entertainment.

Monday, July 5: Visit Ranelagh Gardens, compare rotunda to Chota townhouse.

Tuesday, July 6: Dine with the Lord Mayor at Mansion House?

Wednesday, July 7: British Chronicle approves of Cherokees' entertainment schedule.

Thursday, July 8: Spend one-and-a-half hours with King George III in drawing room of St. James Palace, led by Lord Eglinton.

Friday, July 9: At Dwarf's Tavern and at Vauxhall Gardens, Cherokees shake hands with hundreds of gentlemen.

Saturday, July 10: Cherokees are at Star and Garter at end of Five Rows Fields in Chelsea.

Sunday, July 11: At Dwarf's Tavern, Chelsea Fields, at 7 P.M. to drink tea and will return in a few days.

Monday, July 12: Jackson's *Oxford Journal* questions priorities in hosting Cherokees. Why not principles of Christian religion?

No date: Oliver Goldsmith joins crowd of people at Suffolk Street to see Indians. Is admitted after three-hour wait.

Wednesday, July 14: Cherokees again at Star and Garter to watch Mr. Johnson perform. No dogs allowed on grounds.

Thursday, July 15: Cherokees dine at Mansion House on wines, sweet meats, and fruits. Viewed by the crowds.

Friday, July 16: At Vauxhall Gardens this evening.

Saturday, July 17: The concourse of people to see the Cherokees at the White Conduit House is inconceivable. Pickpockets do well.

Sunday, July 18: Cherokees fear treachery when grenadiers fix bayonets in guard room. *St. James Chronicle*, July 22, 1762.

Monday, July 19: On the evening of the seventeenth, the Cherokees were at the Haymarket for Mr. Foote's oratorical course.

Tuesday, July 20: Mr. Foote's thirty-first performance was preceded by the comedy *The Minor*, which was performed for the Cherokees.

Wednesday, July 21: Cherokees return to Vauxhall this evening. Timberlake hesitant because of ungovernable British curiosity.

Thursday, July 22: John Montague, agent from Virginia, takes Cherokees on tour of lower Thames on an admiralty barge. See ships in stocks, etc.

Friday, July 23: Cherokees at the Dwarf's Tavern in afternoon and at Vauxhall Gardens in the evening.

Saturday, July 24: The Cherokees will return to Sadler's Wells at 5:00 P.M. for a variety program of music, dance, and gymnastics.

Sunday, July 25: Cherokees' activities not reported. May have taken a day off.

Monday, July 26: The *Public Advertiser* reports that Cherokees will be at Bagnigge Wells on the twenty-seventh and at Vauxhall on the twenty-ninth.

Tuesday, July 27: At Bagnigge Wells to taste the waters and have breakfast. Dine with the Earl of Macclesfield at Twickenham.

Wednesday, July 28: Cherokees go to New Theatre at the Haymarket for the Scots pastoral *A Gentle Shepherd.*

Thursday, July 29: At Marybone Gardens. A grand box prepared for the Cherokees' reception. Admission 6d.

Friday, July 30: At Vauxhall Gardens for last time. Ten thousand people turn out to see them. Party ends between 2 and 3 A.M.

Saturday, July 31: Cherokees at Springs Gardens at Vauxhall to hear Miss Davies play the harmonica for second day in a row.

Sunday, August 1: Timberlake writes letter to printer of the *Advertiser* defending the Cherokees from criticism in the press; published in *Advertiser*, August 4, 1762.

Monday, August 2: Mock appeal from bar owner claiming his wife made him "shew the Cherokees"; published in the *Advertiser* on August 5, 1762.

Tuesday, August 3: Ad in *London Chronicle:* King of Cherokees' likeness published today in *Royal Magazine* (July issue).

Wednesday, August 4: Evening Post reports that three men impersonating the Cherokees have been shown at many public places.

Thursday, August 5: The *Gazette* in mock ad: Cherokees will be present at the next pillory exhibition and at Newgate for the next public execution.

Friday, August 6: Cherokees take leave of King George III in courtyard of St. James Palace, with queen looking on.

Saturday, August 7: Egremont orders that the Cherokees not be taken to any more places of public entertainment.

Sunday, August 8: Duchess of Northumberland describes appearance of Cherokees on this date in her diary.

Monday, August 9: The *London Evening Post* contrasts the intemperance of Ostenaco with the sobriety in 1730 of Attakullakulla.

Tuesday, August 10: Destination of Cherokees is changed from Virginia to South Carolina.

Wednesday, August 11: At Sadler's Wells the Cherokee king invites Mr. Matthews, a wire dancer, to return to the Cherokee Nation with them.

Thursday, August 12: Cherokees join in public celebration of the birth of Prince George. Bonfires, illuminations, and huzzas.

Friday, August 13: Because of limited resources Timberlake decides not to return to South Carolina.

Saturday, August 14: No date: Pantomine called *The Witches or the Harlequin Cherokees* is written and opens at Drury Lane in November.

No date: Timberlake laments the damage to the Quin House caused by unruly spectators.

Monday, August 16: Lord Egremont takes his leave and gives Ostenaco official documents and parting gifts.

No date: H. Howard publishes humorous song ridiculing British women for their affection for the Cherokee chiefs.

No date: William Hogarth prepares *The Times*, plate 1, satirizing the Cherokee visit; published in the *Times*, September 7, 1762.

No date: Salmon's Wax Works plans a life-size diorama of the Cherokees, which is displayed for more than thirty years.

Friday, August 20: The Cherokees set out for Portsmouth, with Mr. Montague, Sumter, and Charles Bullin in a coach and six horses.

Saturday, August 21: The Cherokees visit the Winchester camp, dine with Lord Bruce, and see a play.

Sunday, August 22: Cherokees see five thousand French prisoners, visit Winchester College, and are entertained with fruit and wine.

Monday, August 23: Watch the Wiltshire militia exercise with an infinite variety of firings. Attend a comedy, *The Two Sophias.*

Tuesday, August 24: Board the *Epreuve* at 10:00 A.M. and immediately sail.

Places in London visited by the
Cherokees and Timberlake, 1762-176[5]

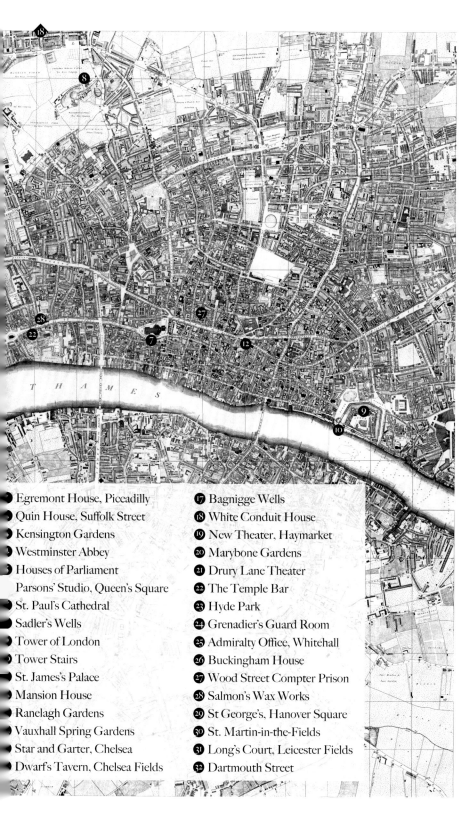

97

Notes

In these notes, annotations and descriptions provide additional information where the original *Memoirs* are lacking in sufficient detail, as well as commentary to allow the reader to better understand the context of Timberlake's writings. The notes follow the sequence of events described in the *Memoirs*, with additional editorial notes for ease of reading. The notes appended to Timberlake's text are indicated in this reprint, as in the original, by marks such as an asterisk (*) or a dagger (†), and by a (T). Timberlake's spellings and punctuation are left intact. Notes by Samuel Williams from the 1927 edition of the *Memoirs* are indicated by a (W). Explanations and notes of the present editor are indicated by a (K).

1. This number is close to that of the Cherokee population at the time of European contact. The Cherokees were spared the devastating effects of European diseases that decimated coastal tribes in the sixteenth and seventeenth centuries. The first major smallpox epidemic to reach the Cherokees occurred in 1738.
2. David Corkran, *The Cherokee Frontier: Conflict and Survival 1740–1762* (Norman: University of Oklahoma Press, 1962).
3. Charles Hudson and Paul E. Hoffman, *The Juan Pardo Expeditions: Explorations of the Carolinas and Tennessee, 1566–1568* (Scranton, Pa.: Smithsonian Institution Press, 1990).
4. Ibid.
5. Duane H. King, Ken Blankenship, and Barbara R. Duncan, *Emissaries of Peace: The 1762 Cherokee and British Delegations* (Cherokee, N.C.: Museum of the Cherokee Indian Press, 2006), vii. See also Duane King (ed.), *The Cherokee Indian Nation: A Troubled History* (Knoxville: University of Tennessee Press, 1979).
6. United Kingdom, Public Record Office, C.O. 5/400, fol. 384, South Carolina, Entry Book of Letters and Instructions, 1720–1740. Cited in William L. Anderson and James A. Lewis, *A Guide to Cherokee Documents in Foreign Archives* (Metuchen, N.J.: Scarecrow Press, 1983), 279.
7. John Phillip Reid, "A Perilous Rule: The Law of International Homicide," in Duane H. King (ed.), *The Cherokee Indian Nation*, 33–45.
8. Corkran, *The Cherokee Frontier*, 44.
9. The Virgina fort was built across the river from Chota on the west bank of Four Mile Creek. It was 105 feet square and completed in August 1756. It was

never garrisoned. See Corkran, *The Cherokee Frontier*, 82. The South Carolina fort was Fort Loudoun. See Louis DeVorsey, Jr. (ed.), *DeBrahm's Report of the General Survey in the Southern District of North America* (Columbia: University of South Carolina Press, 1971).

10. United Kingdom, Public Record Office, C.O. 5/59, fol. 101, Secretary of State: Original Correspondence, Military Dispatches: 1760, 2 July 1760. Montgomery's description of his second march into the Cherokee country.

11. The *London Gazette*, November 1760, p. 606, reported:
    > *The Little Carpenter gave everything he could command, to save capt. Stuart; and having left the Indians, under the pretense of going hunting, has conducted him to major Lewis, who was on the Holston River, with an advanced party of Virginians. Capt. Stuart, a doctor, and capt Stuart's servant, are all that are yet come in, escorted by the Little Carpenter, his brother, two young fellows, with three Indian women.* See also note 52.

12. United Kingdom, Public Record Office, C.O. 5/61, fol. 379, Secretary of State: Original Correspondence, Military Dispatches: 1761, copy of Colonel Grant's "Journal of the March against the Cherokees," 12 pages.

13. United Kingdom, Public Record Office, C.O. 5/62, fol. 13, Secretary of State: Original Correspondence, Military Dispatches: 1762, Governor Boone to Amherst, April 2, 1762, 3 pages.

14. Samuel Cole Williams, *The Memoirs of Lieut. Henry Timberlake* (Johnson City, Tenn: Watauga Press, 1927), 15. Hereafter cited as Williams, *Memoirs*.

15. "Henry Timberlake" in *Dictionary of American Biography* (New York: Charles Scribner and Sons, 1936), vol. 9, 553.

16. The Marriage Allegation of Henry Timberlake is in the Lambeth Palace Archives in London.

17. Williams, *Memoirs*, 40.

18. Ibid., 29.

19. "... *when they are injured by any other nation, as supposing one of their own nation to be killed, they send to demand satisfaction; but if this is refused, they make reprisals upon the first they can take of the nation that committed the injury. Thus their wars begin, which are very frequent; they are carried on with great rage, there not being any people in the world braver, or more dextrous in the use of their arms, and manner of fighting among woods and mountains, none more patient of labour, or swifter on foot.*" (*British Magazine*, vol. 3 [July 1762], 378)

20. Williams, *Memoirs*, 40.

21. Ibid., 41.

22. Jefferson Chapman, *Tellico Archaeology: 12,000 Years of Native American History* (Knoxville: Tennessee Valley Authority, 1985).

23. United Kingdom, Public Record Office, W.O. 34/37, fol. 269, Letters of the Governor of Virginia and the Commander in Chief, 1758–1763; Amherst to Lt. Governor Fauquier, 18 October 1762, acknowledges receipt orders to reward Timberlake. Timberlake is appointed a lieutenant in the Royal Highland Regiment.

24. The academic debate over the credibility of the legends of Prince Madoc was fueled, in part, by another three-member Cherokee delegation that journeyed to London in 1791. This group included a mixed-blood person named Mo-

ses Price, called Wasi in Cherokee, and two others: Kwantikiski (peach-eater) and Unatoy or Ama-edohi. The latter might be translated as "water walker." The experience of this delegation has been researched and reported by William Sturtevant in "The Cherokee Frontiers, the French Revolution, and William Augustus Bowles," in Duane H. King (ed.), *The Cherokee Indian Nation* (Knoxville: University of Tennessee Press, 1979), 61–91.

25. See Chapman, *Tellico Archaeology*.

26. United Kingdom, Public Record Office, T.1/633, Treasury Board Office: in Letters 1787, fol. 337: January 23, 1787, Dartmouth Street, Westminster, Memorial of Helena Teresa Timberlake Ostenaco to Lords of the Treasury, requesting assistance, 4 pages; fol. 338: July 20, 1786, Whitehall, Lord Amherst to George Younge, Amherst endorses assistance, 2 pages; fol. 339: July 21, 1786, War Office, George Younge to George Rose, Younge recommends assistance be given to Mrs. Timberlake, 2 pages.

27. In the original text, Timberlake renders the name here in Greek letters. Elsewhere he provides an English spelling, Caccanthropos, which can be translated "bad, difficult" /cacc-/ "man" /anthropos/. The pseudonym was devised by Timberlake to express strong contempt for his adversary without exposing himself to libel by revealing the man's identity. Caccanthropos is the only person in the *Memoirs* who is referred to by a pseudonym. In addition to the first rendering in Greek letters, in the next three citations the name is spelled Caccanthropos, in the following four references the name has only two c's (Cacanthropos), and in the last citation it is spelled Cocoanthropos. In the first reference in which name is given in English characters, it is listed as Mr. N—— Caccanthropos. The French translator clearly recognizes the name as a pseudonym, noting that it is "*composé de deux mots grecs; anthropos homme* (man), *et xaxos méchant* (evil)." Timberlake offers the Greek spelling kappa alpha chi omicron, whereas the French translator renders it chi alpha chi omicron sigma. On first reading it appears that the individual might be of Greek origin; however, his characterization by Timberlake is obviously too coincidental with the translation of his name, "bad man." In his *Memoirs* Timberlake gives few clues as to the identity of Caccanthropos. On one occasion when a physical altercation between the two nearly erupted, Timberlake speaks of his advantage because of the difference in their ages. Timberlake, who was then about twenty-six years old, seems to suggest that Caccanthropos was considerably older. On August 16, 1763, Timberlake wrote to Lord Egremont stating that he hoped that Carrington would be severely punished for overcharging the Cherokees' account by £200. It appears that the most likely candidate for Mr. Caccanthropos is Nathan Carrington, a royal messenger and an associate of Lord Egremont, Sir Charles Wyndham, 2nd Earl of Egremont (1710–63). Carrington may have been employed by the government as early as 1729. In 1730, he reported being robbed by a highwayman (United Kingdom, Public Record Office, State Papers SP 36/19, Part 1, fols. 54–57). In 1746, he was charged with escorting Jacobite prisoners from Scotland to London for trial. Timberlake found little sympathy among government officials for his charges against another government official. James Rivers, in particular, stated that he believed Timberlake to be in the wrong.

The Timberlake affair was not the most noteworthy controversy in which Carrington was involved. In 1763, the British government passed a new tax on cider. King George III personally defended the tax. The tax angered John Wilkes, an outspoken critic of the government. In his underground newspaper called *The North Briton*, no. 45, he attacked the tax and the king's speech. In November 1763, Carrington and three other Royal Messengers in Ordinary (John Money, James Watson, and Robert Blackmore), acting on a warrant issued by Lord Dunk Halifax, invaded the home of John Entick, a clerk, looking for this particular publication, which was considered to be treasonous. More than forty people were subsequently arrested under the warrant, including John Wilkes. In the 1765 trial that followed, Entick sued Carrington and others; Entick prevailed. The legal decision that the warrant was unlawful (constituting "unreasonable search and seizure") has become a cornerstone of Anglo-American legal thought. (K)

28. Samuel Cole Williams, in his 1927 publication of Timberlake's *Memoirs*, suggests that the family resided in Hanover County, the early records of which were destroyed during the Civil War. In *British Travelers Among the Southern Indians, 1660–1763* (Tulsa: University of Oklahoma Press, 1973), 14, J. Ralph Randoph follows Williams's supposition that Timberlake was from Hanover County. He also gives his birthdate as 1730 but does not provide a source. In January 1763, Henry Timberlake, on his marriage allegation now at Lambeth Palace Archives, gives his age as twenty-seven, suggesting a birth year of 1735. In March 1763, he returned to Virginia with his wife. On August 16, 1763, he wrote to Lord Egremont from the James River expressing surprise that Amherst gave him his commission at half pay and hoped that Carrington would be severely punished for overcharging the Cherokee Indians' account by £200. United Kingdom, Public Record Office, C.O. 5/1345, fol. 46, Virginia, Secretary of State: Original correspondence, 1762–1767. (K)

29. In 1730 Sir Alexander Cuming accompanied seven Cherokees to London; they signed a treaty with King George II pledging perpetual friendship and to fight all enemies of the crown, both foreign and domestic. When the French and Indian War broke out a quarter of a century later, the British invoked the treaty. The Cherokees were reluctant, however, to send warriors to the frontier unless the British took necessary steps to protect the exposed Overhill settlements from French attack.

In 1756, both Virginia and South Carolina built forts in the Overhill country. The Virginia fort was constructed by Colonel Andrew Lewis near Nine Mile Creek, which was opposite and slightly upstream from the capital of Chote. The fort was 105 feet on each side and never garrisoned. The South Carolina fort, called Fort Loudoun, was built downstream from Tommotley, which was the westernmost of the Cherokee towns at that time, and upstream from the mouth of the Tellico River. The fort was garrisoned by South Carolina militia. Convinced of British good will and protection, the Cherokees sent warriors to the Virginia frontier. The construction of the forts followed a downturn in the war by Virginia. In April 1756, the French and their Indian allies from the Ohio valley invaded the back settlements of Virginia in retaliation for Colonel Andrew Lewis's failed Sandy Creek expedition against the Shawnees earlier that year. In response, Governor Dinwiddie ordered the militia of the ten counties nearest to Winchester to go to the relief of Colonel George Washington at that place. Some of the coastal counties also sent volunteers for service on the frontier. Govenor Dinwiddie reported on May 10, 1756: "*About 100 of our Gentlemen are entered into an Association at their own Expence, properly accoutred on Horse Back, to go to our Frontier against the Enemy— a brave Example for the other People.*" R. A. Brock, *The Official Records of Robert Dinwiddie* ("*Dinwiddie Papers*") (1883), vol. 2, 411, 423, 439. The volunteers numbered about 150 when they reached the headquarters of Colonel George Washington. Ibid., 439. (K)

30. On May 24, 1756, Governor Dinwiddie noted: "*On the march of the militia they [the French and their Indian allies] dispersed and returned to their Fort on the Ohio, I fear to reinforce their numbers and return to pillage and murder.*" *Dinwiddie Papers*, vol. 2, 417. The French continued to make overtures to the Cherokees throughout this period. An intercepted letter from Duc de Mirapoix dated March 1, 1756, stated: "*The Cherokees who are very numerous and have never been conquered have entered into an alliance with the English and chose (in great form) King George as their King and father—they have offered me 1000 of their men to join me at the Ohio, provided I would take them in the Government's pay.*" United Kingdom, Public Record Office, C.o. 5/52, fol. 12, Secretary of State: Original Correspondence, 1756–1761, 11 pages. (K)

31. George Washington (February 22, 1732–December 14, 1797) was the commander of the First Virginia Militia Regiment (1752–1758). He was later the commander-in-chief of the Continental Army from 1775 to 1783. Washington served as the first president of the United States from 1789 to 1797. Washington's estimate of the Cherokees is given in his letter to the governor (September 1756): "*Those Indians who are serving [under Ostenaco] should be showed all possible respect, and the greatest care taken of them, as upon them much depends. It is a critical time; they are very humorsome, and their assistance very necessary. One false step might lose us all that, but even turn them against us.*" S. M. Hamilton (ed.), *Letters to Washington and Accompanying Papers* (Boston, 1898–1902), passim (hereafter cited as *Letters to Washington*); *Dinwiddie Papers*, vol. 2.

32. Governor Dinwiddie wrote to George Washington on August 19, 1756: "*Mr. Timberlake, if he inclines to serve as a Volunteer, must wait the Course of Preferment with the other young Gentlemen.*" *Dinwiddie Papers*, vol. 2, 482. (K)

33. William Byrd III, of "Westover" on the James River, colonel of the Second Virginia Regiment, and a member of the Council of State. Byrd (September 6, 1728–January 1, 1777) inherited his family land and continued his family's prestige as a member of the Virginia House of Burgesses, but chose to fight in the French and Indian War rather than devote time to politics. In 1756, he was appointed colonel of the Second Virginia Regiment. He was a notorious gambler, and he initiated what is said to be the first major horse race in North America. Byrd eventually fathered fifteen children by his first and second wives (Eliza Carter, d. 1760 and Mary Willing). In 1759, a British traveler wrote: "*The honourable colonel Byrd has a small place called Belvedere, upon a hill at the lower end of these (the James River) falls, as romantic and elegant as any thing I have ever seen. It is situated very high, and commands a fine prospect of the river,*

which is half a mile broad, forming cataracts." Andrew Burnaby, *Travels through the Middle Settlements in North-America in the Years 1759 and 1760 with Observations upon the State of the Colonies* (Ithaca, N.Y.: Cornell University Press, 1960). After he lost much of the family fortune gambling and through bad investments, William Byrd III parceled up the family estate and sold lots in a 1768 lottery. William Byrd III committed suicide on January 1, 1777. (K)

34. An ensign was the lowest-ranking officer in the British army. A subaltern was any officer in the British army lower than the rank of captain. A cornetcy was a commission beneath the rank of captain. (K)

35. Ray's Town is present-day Bedford, Pennsylvania. (K)

36. In late 1758, Brigadier General John Forbes (September 5, 1707–March 11, 1759) led the Forbes expedition that captured the French outpost at Fort Duquesne. He was born in Pittencrief, Fife, Scotland and was the son of an army officer. He intended to study medicine, but in his second year as a medical student, he decided to become a soldier. In 1735, he was commissioned as a lieutenant in the Royal Scots Dragoon Guards. He saw action in the War of the Austrian Succession. He later was a member of the Scots Greys and served under the Duke of Cumberland as acting quartermaster-general. In 1757, he was ordered to reinforce an attack on the French fortress of Louisburg in what is now Nova Scotia.

In December 1757, Forbes was promoted to brigadier general and assigned to capture Fort Duquesne, which guarded the vital forks of the Ohio River. General Edward Braddock had tried and failed to capture the fort in 1755. Braddock was mortally wounded in an ambush. Forbes chose Lieutenant Colonel George Washington, who had been a member of Braddock's campaign, to be his aide.

In the summer of 1758, Forbes began his campaign to capture Fort Duquesne. His plan was to complete a slow and methodical march to the fort, taking great pains to secure his lines of supply and communication with a string of forts along a newly constructed road from the Pennsylvania frontier. Rather than move on Fort Duquesne via Braddock's road, which began in western Maryland, Forbes began his march in eastern Pennsylvania. This decision led to major political infighting among the Pennsylvanians and Virginians in his expedition. Both colonies claimed the Ohio River country. Forbes was able to quell the dissent by agreeing to improve Braddock's original road but to travel the route through Pennsylvania, which was longer but required fewer river crossings. This route also gave the tactical advantage of forcing the French to divide their assets and defend both approaches.

With 7,000 regular and provincial troops, Forbes began his push from his main stores in Carlisle, Pennsylvania, into the trackless wilderness of western Pennsylvania. West of Raystown he cut a wagon road over the Allegheny Mountains, later known as Forbes' Road, and built a series of fortifications to serve as supply depots, including the fort at Raystown and Fort Ligonier.

Forbes authorized a reconnaissance in force. In the Battle of Fort Duquesne, during the night of September 13–14, 1758, the advance column under Major James Grant, was bloodily repulsed by French and Indian warriors who sallied from the fort. Subsequently, the French, who were hopelessly outnumbered, abandoned and razed Fort Duquesne before the British arrived. (K)

37. Fort Ligonier, one of the principal British forts, was built during the Forbes expedition in 1758. Even though it was not as essential to routes of heavy travel as Fort Bedford, it had been well built and stood in an excellent natural defensive location. It was built as the site of an Indian village called "Loyalhannon," which lay almost exactly halfway from Raystown. Work on this fort was begun September 4, 1758. The fort was later named Fort Ligonier in honor of Sir John Ligonier, commander-in-chief of the British army. By mid-October 1758, Colonel Washington and his Virginia regiment had joined the rapidly growing force there, but not until after the fort had already repulsed several severe attacks by the French and Indians on October 12. After a short rest, Forbes's expedition army struck out and reached Fort Duquesne on November 25, 1758.

   Ligonier had several features not duplicated elsewhere in Pennsylvania. It was located on a low plateau, and on its south, irregular cliffs rose from the creek, which made that part easy to defend. The north was also protected by a stream, with low cliffs in between. The inner fort also contained unique structures. The vulnerable east side consisted of walls seven feet high and ten feet thick. Defenders of this wall were protected by a row of seven-foot-long sharpened logs embedded in the front wall. Fort Ligonier had facilities for a considerable quantity of artillery. This post was defended twice, once in 1758 shortly after it was built and again in 1763, both times with success. Fort Ligonier was officially abandoned in 1765, after seven eventful years in history.

   During the 1960s, archaeologists found 35,000 artifacts, including hinges, spikes, and door handles. The original stone wall and stairwell to an underground powder magazine were also preserved. These discoveries aided in an accurate reconstruction of the fort, which can still be viewed today. (K)

38. Forbes occupied the charred remains of Fort Duquesne on November 25, 1758. He immediately ordered the construction of a new fortification to be named Fort Pitt, after the British secretary of state William Pitt the Elder. This site is the location of modern Pittsburgh, Pennsylvania. (K)

39. General Forbes was also seriously ill at the time and was carried on a litter. Forbes's health, which had been poor for much of the campaign, began a rapid decline during his occupation of Fort Pitt. On December 3, 1758, Forbes, now gravely ill, began the arduous journey back to Philadelphia, leaving Colonel Hugh Mercer in command. General Forbes died in Philadelphia on March 11, 1759. He was buried in Christ Churchyard in Philadelphia. (K)

40. The French abandoned the post rather than attempt to defend it against overwhelming numbers of British and American troops. (K)

41. As the capital of colonial Virginia, Williamsburg was, from 1699 to 1780, the political, cultural, and educational center of what was then the largest, most populous, and most influential of the American colonies. (K)

42. Byrd was appointed colonel of the Second Virginia Regiment in 1756, and Colonel Washington resigned as colonel of the First Virginia Regiment in 1758. (K)

43. Brigadier John Stanwix was born in England about 1690 and died at sea in December 1765. He joined the army in 1706 and worked his way up the ranks, became a captain of the grenadiers in 1739, major of marines in 1741, and lieutenant colonel in 1745. In January 1756, he was appointed colonel-commandant of the First Battalion of the Sixtieth or Royal American regiment. On his arrival in this country, he was given the command of the southern district. He was promoted to brigadier general on December 27, 1757. After his relief by General John Forbes in 1758, General Stanwix went to Albany, whence he was ordered to the Oneida carrying place, to secure that important position by the erection of a work that was called Fort Stanwix in his honor. In 1759, he returned to Pennsylvania, repaired the old fort at Pittsburgh, surmounted the works with cannon, and secured the good will of the Indians. On June 19, 1759, he was appointed major general, but he was relieved by General Robert Monckton on May 4, 1760, and became lieutenant general on January 19, 1761. After his return to England, he was appointed lieutenant governor of the Isle of Wight, became colonel of the Eighth Foot, and was a member of Parliament for Appleby. He was lost at sea while crossing from Dublin to Holyhead in *The Eagle* packet. (K)

44. In 1759 Fort Burd was constructed by the Pennsylvania Militia south of Pittsburgh on a hilltop overlooking the Monongahela River. The fort was used as a supply depot for the British army during the French and Indian War and to facilitate river transportation to Pittsburgh. The fort was square in shape, with curtain walls 97.5 feet in length. Its bastions had thirty-foot faces with sixteen-foot flanks. This stockade was surrounded by a ditch. Fort Burd was constructed on the same site as an even earlier Indian fortification known as Redstone Old Fort. It was named after James Burd (1723–1793), who moved with his family from Philadelphia to Lancaster County in 1752. (K)

45. Adam Stephen (ca. 1718–1791) was born in Scotland and attended the Universities of Aberdeen and Edinburgh, receiving a degree in surgery around 1746. He immigrated to America in 1748 and established a medical practice in Fredericksburg, Virginia. He joined the military in 1754 at the beginning of the French and Indian War and was a senior captain in Colonel Joshua Frey's regiment. He was promoted to major when Washington assumed command and was with Washington at Great Meadows. The following year, he was severely wounded in Braddock's defeat. He led an expedition of relief to South Carolina in 1757 and took command of the Virginia regiment sent to chastise the Cherokees after Colonel Byrd resigned. He commanded the Virginia regiment in Pontiac's War (1763). In 1770, he first acquired land along the Tuscarora Creek in present-day Berkeley County, where he later sold lots to develop the town of Martinsburg. In Lord Dunmore's War (1774) he was second to Governor Dinwiddie in command. He served in the Virginia Convention of 1775; the next year he was chosen brigadier general of the Revolutionary forces operating in New Jersey, and shortly thereafter was promoted to major general. He served in the General Assembly of Virginia (1780–85) and in the convention that ratified the Federal Constitution (1788). Perhaps his greatest contribution to America's future was his stirring speech at the Virginia Constitutional Convention of 1788, which influenced the Virginia dele-

gates to ratify the United States Constitution. This in turn led other states to ratify the Constitution at their state conventions. In 1789, Adam Stephen wrote an article for the *Virginia Gazette* entitled "Expostulations on the Potomack" to promote the location of the federal capital on the Potomac River. Adam Stephen died in Martinsburg on July 16, 1791, and was buried on his brother Robert Stephen's estate on "the monument lot" in the 600 block of South Queen Street in Martinsburg. According to Williams, Stephen "was of great stature and physical strength, and was held in awe by the Indians." His waistcoat worn during the French and Indian War, recently displayed in the "Price of Freedom" exhibit in the National Museum of American History, would suggest that he was a small individual by today's standards. (K)

46. Lt. Governor Fauquier wrote to Major General Robert Monckton on October 17, 1760, from Williamsburg that the Assembly of Virginia had passed a bill recalling all Virginian provincials under Monckton's command to place them under Colonel Byrd in defense of the southern frontiers against the Cherokees; he had sent orders to Colonel Stephen accordingly. United Kingdom, Public Record Office, W.O. 34/43: Amherst Papers, SR number 02886, Reel number 303, 1756 to April 1763, References: Lists and Indexes No. XXVIII, Supplementary Vol. 1, fols. 90–91. Hereafter cited as Amherst Papers. (K)

47. The Sayers family were among the early settlers of present-day Fincastle County, Virginia. Reuben Thwaites and Louise Phelps Kellogg, *Documentary History of Dunmore's War* (Madison, Wisc.: Historical Society of Wisconsin, 1905), 171; Lewis Preston Summers, *History of Southwest Virginia* (Richmond, Va.: J. L. Print Co., 1903), 46, 292. Williams, *Memoirs*, 33, suggests that John Sayers or Sears was an ensign along with Timberlake on the expedition of 1761. Virginia Act, 1762, in W. W. Hening, *Statutes of Virginia* (Richmond, Va., 1818–1823), 493. (K)

48. Portmantua is an English variant of portmanteau, a traveling case. (K)

49. About March 16, 1761, Colonel Stephen was ordered to assemble at Winchester those Provincials that had returned from Fort Pitt and to prepare to move southward. W.O. 34/37: Amherst Papers, SR 01751, Reel 300, July 1756 to November 1763, Lists and Indexes No. XXVIII, Supplementary vol. 1, p. 86; Andrew's List, pp. 387–392, fols. 52–53. Colonel Byrd wrote to Lt. Governor Fauquier on May 29, 1761, that Stephen's provincials from Winchester had joined him. He also declared the impossibility of advancing due to the lack of provisions, the need of cartridge paper, and the assumed intention to postpone or abandon the operation. He also asked for a leave to go to Philadelphia to see his wife, who was reported "dangerously ill." (fols. 76–78). (K)

Williams, *Memoirs*, 36, wrote: "*In October, 1760, the Virginia Assembly passed an act providing for the withdrawal of Virginia forces from the north and concentrating the strength of the entire regiment against the Cherokees.*" Letters to Washington, vol. 3, 211. "*Our last accounts from that Quarter was in a letter rec'd from Colo. Byrd, dated at Campbell's Aug't 10th. I cannot imagine he will proceed after he is informed that Fort Loudoun, the principal object of his Destination, is surrendered to the Savages.*" Captain Robert Stewart to Washington, October 1760, in ibid., 197. Williams, *Memoirs*, 36, further states: "*Col. Byrd camped at Stalnakres during the winter of 1760–61, and not at Long Island of Holston, as is fre-*

quently stated." It appears that Williams was in error on this point. In examining the correspondence from the period, there is no evidence that Colonel Byrd had reached Stalnakres before July 1761. On July 1, he wrote to Amherst to report his arrival at Fort Chiswell "yesterday at this our most advanced post," without any assistance from the contractors, stating his intention to advance with 500 men to Stalnakres and to leave Lieutenant Colonel Adam Stephen with the rest of the regiment at Fort Chiswell to escort provisions forward to Stalnakres later. W.O. 34/47: Amherst Papers, SR 01755, Reel 305, June 1757–Oct 1763, References: Lists and Indexes No. XXVIII, Supplementary vol.1, p. 86; Andrew's List, pp. 388–392, fols. 268–270.

On August 1, 1761, Colonel William Byrd wrote to Amherst from his camp at Stalnakres on the Holston River, reporting his arrival at Stalnakres on July 19, and being there detained by want of carriages and horses, his contact with the Little Carpenter heading a Cherokee delegation suing for peace; he complained of his "dispicable" situation, being unable to chastise the Indians and forbidden to treat with them, and asking permission to hand over command to Lt. Colonel Adam Stephen and to retire. Amherst Papers, fols. 271–274.

On September 7, 1761, Byrd complained bitterly to Amherst about the failure of contractors, who, he asserted, had never intended to supply his force beyond Great Island; he stated that he had resigned his command of the regiment which he had left with two months' rations and under Stephen's command. Amherst papers, fol. 275. (K)

50. After the Grant expedition destroyed fifteen middle and out towns in June 1761, the Cherokees renewed their efforts to to sue for peace. On July 1, a meeting held in the Chota townhouse was attended by headmen from all parts of the Cherokee Nation. They decided to direct their appeal for peace to Colonel Byrd and delegate Attakullakulla to deliver it. Philip M. Hamer and George C. Rogers (eds.), *The Papers of Henry Laurens*, vol. 3: *Jan. 1 1759–Aug. 31 1763* (Columbia: University of South Carolina Press, 1972), no. 49, p. 103.

Colonel Byrd, with only 684 effective soldiers, did not believe he had the strength to invade the Overhills and was forbidden by Amherst to make a treaty with them. He procrastinated in organizing and advancing his army. After prodding from Amherst, he advanced 100 miles during the first two weeks of July 1761 to Stalnakres. There he met with Attakullakulla, who brought messages of peace and conciliation. He told Byrd that he was sent by Oconostota, Ostenaco, and Standing Turkey, who had been responsible for instigating and prosecuting the war and were now cognizant of their mistakes. Byrd informed him that he must go to South Carolina and make peace with Grant. Attakullakulla left quickly for South Carolina and met with Colonel Grant. In the meantime, Grant had sent out his own emissaries imploring Oconastota to come in to talk. Oconastota, fearful of treachery, sent deputies instead. Under a military escort Attakullakulla made his way to Charles Town, where he spoke of his nation's desire for peace and the suffering brought about by the late war. His appeal for peace was strengthened by the course he chose during the war.

Less than two weeks after his meeting with Attakullakulla, Byrd resentfully resigned his command. Byrd to Amherst, August 1, 1760, Draper Mss.

4ZZ 36. From the beginning, Byrd had little stomach for a campaign against the Cherokees. Stewart to Washington, *Letters to Washington*, 111, 184. He had been appointed one of the commissioners in 1756 to solicit aid from the Cherokees for support in the war against the French. In 1756 Byrd and Attakullakulla met in treaty at the Broad River in North Carolina. Dr. Andrew Burnaby, an English clergyman who traveled through Virginia in 1760, in his *Travels through North America* related an account given to him by one of the other commissioners, indicating that Attakullakulla intervened to save Colonel Byrd's life on that occasion. The Cherokees assembled at the treaty ground became incensed upon receiving news of the murders of some of their warriors on the Virginia frontier. Burnaby reported:

> Attakullakulla, or the Little Carpenter, a steady friend of the English, hastened to the ambassadors, apprised them of their danger, and recommended to them to conceal or barricade themselves as well as they could, and not to appear abroad on any account. He then assembled his nation, over whom he possessed great influence, in the council-room; inveighed bitterly against the treachery of the English . . . 'Let us not, however, violate our faith, or the laws of hospitality, by imbruing our hands in the blood of those who are now in our power; they came to us in the confidence of friendship, with belts of wampum to cement a perpetual alliance with us." Saloue a chief from of the Valley Towns aligned with Attakullakulla for the protection of the Virginia commissioners. (Jefferson, *Notes on Virginia*, 62, 99)

James Adair, with the South Carolina forces under Grant, criticized Byrd's leadership. "The Virginia troops kept far off in flourishing parade, without coming to our assistance or making a diversion against those warlike towns which lie beyond Apalache mountains." James Adair, *The History of the American Indians* (London: Edward and Charles Dilly, 1775), 252.

51. Lieutenant Colonel Adam Stephen wrote to Amherst from the camp at Great Island on October 5, 1761, reporting his forward move fifty-eight miles west-southwest from Stalnakres to Great Island on the Holston River, his contacts with the Indians, and the lack of news from North Carolina. He enclosed copies of letters received from and sent to Cherokee leaders before their meeting on the Great Island. Amherst Papers, fols. 277–283.

Samuel Stalnakres, about 1750, with the assistance of Dr. Thomas Walker and his associates, erected a cabin home on the Holston River, about nine miles west of the cabin of Stephen Holston, for whom the river was named. Holston's cabin (1748) was on the head spring of the middle fork of the river.

On the map of 1751, this settlement is located on the middle fork of Holston River, a few miles above its junction with the south fork, which is now Washington County, formerly a part of Fincastle, and the first county in Virginia named for George Washington.

Summers' *History of Southwest Virginia*, 58, includes a register of persons killed or taken prisoner by the Indians in 1754, 1755, and 1756, on the New and Holston Rivers and Reedy Creek. The register states that Samuel Stalnakres on Holston River was taken prisoner and escaped, but that his wife, Mrs. Stalnakres, and his son, Adam, were killed. (The official report of this is found in *Dinwiddie Papers*, vol. 2, 447.) An interesting fact is that Captain

Samuel Stalnakres's house was chosen as the meeting place for treating with the Indians by His Majesty's Commissioners, at the request of the Chief of the Cherokees held at Catawba Town and Broad River in March 1756. Samuel Stalnakres was an explorer, trapper, and guide, the first white man to discover Cumberland Gap. He hunted and explored in Kentucky many years before Daniel Boone's arrival. (K)

52. Three companies under Major Andrew Lewis were sent ahead of the main body to improve the road leading to the Holston (July 6, 1761). The previous year, when a packhorseman brought news to Byrd that Fort Loudoun was about to surrender, Byrd sent Major Lewis with 300 men to their relief. They were within eighty miles of the fort when they were met by Attakullakulla and Captain John Stuart at Spring Hill on September 8, 1760, with news of the surrender and massacre. (*South Carolina Gazette*, October 11, 1760). See also note 11. (K)

53. It has also been referred to as Big Island but is best known as Long Island, at present-day Kingsport, in Sullivan County, Tennessee. Although this was the extent of the Virginia Militia's advance, it was originally intended to be the next to the last. Stewart wrote to Washington: *"Our next post is to be at Big Island and our last at Broad River, forty miles from the Imperial City of Chota. But how our small numbers are to make roads, construct posts, furnish escortes, etc., is to me quite a mystery." Letters to Washington* 111, 224. The distance from Chota to the Broad River suggests a location near the later site of White's Fort, now Knoxville, suggesting that the Virginia militia, including Timberlake (see note 67), consider the river after the confluence of the Holston and French Broad to the confluence of what later became known as the Little Tennessee to be the Broad river. Later in the 18th century and for most of the 19th century, it was officially known as the Holston. (K)

54. The fort was named in honor of John Robinson, a leading Virginia politician and a partner of Byrd in the lead mines at Fort Chiswell. It was located on the north bank of the river about 200 yards below the upper end of Long Island. It was well constructed, with walls of sufficient thickness to withstand a small cannon shot. Bastions were erected at the corners, and the gates were spiked with large nails so that the wood was completely covered. See Duane King, "Long Island of the Holston: Sacred Cherokee Ground," *Journal of Cherokee Studies* 1, no. 2 (fall 1976): 114. Williams, *Memoirs*, 38, notes that Thwaites, in his *France in America*, misidentifies it as "Fort Byrd" (196). For much of the twentieth century a historical marker between the forks of the Holston gave its location incorrectly at that place. In 1776, Fort Patrick Henry was constructed on approximately the same location as Fort Robinson. John Redd, who was there at the time, recalled:

> The place selected for the fort was where the bank of the river was very high, I suppose some 20 feet, and the water some 4 or 5 feet deep. The ground enclosed by the fort was about 100 yards square. There was only three sides enclosed, the bank of the river being almost impregnable. The fort was similar to one built by Joseph Martin in Powell's Valley, with the exception that the walls had bastions at the corners. The house for the store was in the center of the square and also the house for the commander. There were several small springs that broke out of the bank

of the river which were used, but the river was our main dependence for water.
(John Redd is quoted in "Frontier Forts," *Historical Sketches of Southwest Virginia*, Publication No. 4, ed. E. L. Henson [1968].) (K)

55. Kanagatucko is anglicized from the Cherokee /kvhna/ "turkey" /katoka/ "he is standing." He became the /ukvwiyuhi/ or "civil chief" of Chota after the death of Old Hop in December 1760. The title "Emperor of the Cherokees" was created by the British in 1721 in an attempt to force a European model on the Cherokee political system. Williams, *Memoirs*, 39, incorrectly identifies the emperor Kanagatucko as the deceased Old Hop. (K)

56. The treaty was made at Great Island Camp on November 20, 1761, by Colonel Adam Stephen of the Virginia Provincial Regiment and representatives of the Cherokee people. Two articles of this treaty were supplementary to those included in the Treaty made by Lt. Governor Bull of South Carolina. The articles related to the Tuscarora Indians and to the surrender of Cherokee Indians guilty of murder. This document was enclosed in Lt. Governor Fauquier's letter to Gen. Sir Jeffrey Amherst dated December 11, 1761. W.O. 34/37: Amherst Papers, SR 01751, Reel 300, July 1756 to November 1763, References: Lists and Indexes No. XXVIII, Supplementary vol. 1, p. 86; Andrew's List, pp. 387–392, fol. 96 (see fol. 94 for Fauquier's letter). (K)

57. This is related to the Cherokee traditional law of corporate responsibility and admission of wrongdoing. These concepts were perhaps only vaguely understood by the English and by Timberlake. Had the British broken the peace accord while Timberlake was in the company of the Cherokees, his life would indeed have been in jeopardy. See John Philip Reid, *A Law of Blood: The Primitive Law of the Cherokee Nation* (New York: New York University Press, 1970); and John Phillip Reid, *A Better Kind of Hatchet: Law, Trade and Diplomacy in the Cherokee Nation During the Early Years of European Contact* (University Park: Pennsylvania State University Press, 1976). (K)

58. A term generally used in reference to Shawnees, Iroquois, Ottawas, and other groups from the Ohio Valley and Great Lakes area. (K)

59. The sergeant was Thomas Sumter (1734–1832), from Orange County, Virginia. According to Williams, *Memoirs*, 41, his childhood friends included Joseph (later General) Martin, Benjamin (later Colonel) Cleveland, of King's Mountain fame, and John Redd, the noted frontiersman. Sumter traveled with the Cherokee delegation and Timberlake to London in 1762. Without Timberlake, he accompanied the Cherokee delegation back to their home by way of South Carolina. Back in the Overhill country in February 1763, he arrested and returned to Charleston with a French emissary, Baron des Jonnes, a French Canadian lieutenant who left the Alabama fort after killing a man in a duel. He met Oconastota in the woods and accompanied him back to Chota. *South Carolina Gazette*, March 26 and May 7, 1763.

In July 1764, Sumter requested an allowance for accompanying Ostenaco and two other Cherokees to London in 1762. He request was denied since he was not employed by South Carolina. United Kingdom, Public Record Office, C.O. 5/482, fols. 60 and 65b., cited in Anderson and Lewis, *A Guide to Cherokee Documents*, 312. After spending time in debtor's prison, Sumter married a wealthy widow in the South Carolina back country. He rose to distinction as a general in the Revolutionary War. His eagerness to engage the enemy earned him the nickname of "Gamecock." He later served as a member of Congress. Fort Sumter was named for him. He rode a horse the day he died at the age of ninety-eight in 1832. (K)

60. The interpreter was John McCormack, a fur trader married to a Cherokee woman. He served as an interpreter for at treaty negotiations at least as late 1785 when he was present at the Treaty of Hopewell. J. G. M. Ramsey, *The Annals of Tennessee to the End of the Eighteenth Century* (Philadelphia: Walker and James, 1853), 319. In 1777, he accompanied Cherokee leaders back to Long Island to serve as "linguister" for a treaty with representatives of North Carolina and Virginia. Negotiations began on June 30. Two days later, as both parties were becoming well acquainted with each other and there were good prospects for an early and amiable settlement, a Cherokee youth named Big Bullet was murdered by an unknown assailant. Big Bullet, about fifteen or sixteen years old, was the mixed-blood son of John McCormack. The Cherokees were so alarmed they immediately withdrew. The state representatives went to great lengths to demonstrate their outrage at the cowardly murder, promising to execute the slayer if he could be found. Although the state representatives offered a reward of $600, no arrest was ever made. The prime suspect was Robert Young, whose brother Charles Young had been killed several months earlier by one of Dragging Canoe's war parties. The Cherokee leaders finally agreed to return to the meeting. John McCormack, who was overcome with grief, was replaced as interpreter by Joseph Vann. Oliver Taylor, *Historic Sullivan* (Bristol, Tenn.: King Printing Company, 1909), 68. (K)

61. In the original text, Timberlake gives the following footnote: * "*What is meant here by encamping, is only making a fire and lying near it, though the Indians often prop a blanket or skins upon small poles, to preserve them from the inclemency of the weather.*" (T)

62. Williams, *Memoirs*, 47–48, noted:

> *Below Three Springs Ford, Hamblen County, Tennessee, is a cave, fifty feet above the water-level, in which stalactites are found. The cave is situated at the point of a curve in the river that is plainly observable by one going down-stream. Another cave is on the northerly bank of Holston River, in Grainger County, about fifty feet above water level. The interior contains beautiful stalagmites and stalactites; and a good-sized stream of water issues from it.*

63. December 11, 1761.

64. December 12, 1761.

65. December 13, 1761.

66. A surtout is a man's overcoat in the style of a frock coat. (K)

67. Pocket watches during this period were fairly common. Several watches and some money were found by soldiers of the Montgomery expedition in quickly abandoned Cherokee homes in the Lower Towns in June 1760. A prodigious number of watches were stolen by pickpockets from a distracted crowd viewing the Cherokee delegation at the White Conduit House in London in July 1762. (K)

68. December 14, 1761.

69. December 15, 1761.

70. The confluence of the Holston and French Broad Rivers is just above present-day Knoxville, Tennessee. Knoxville is still known in Cherokee by its pre-settlement designation of Khuwatatatlvʔi (Mulberry Grove). Below the confluence the river was called the Holston, until about 1880 when the name was changed to Tennessee (see the following notes 71, 72, and 73). (K)

71. Now called the Little Tennessee. The stream above its mouth to the mouth of the French Broad is now called the Tennessee, by force of legislative acts. This part was formerly called the Holston. The word "Tennessee," was first spelled in its current form by Timberlake at this place in his text. His spelling was not consistent; he omits one /n/ on a page further on. (K)

72. Slavecatcher was the first achievable war title. Five different individuals with this title are referenced in Corkran, *The Cherokee Frontier*. (K)

73. In this instance Timberlake spelled Tennessee with one /n/. The name Little Tennessee was first used about 1820 in recognition of the fact that the Holston River was larger than this branch of the Tennessee River at the point of their confluence. The name "Tennessee River" continued to be used for the river downstream from the point of confluence. About 1880, to take advantage of federal appropriations to improve the Tennessee River, the name was extended to the confluence of the Holston and French Broad rivers above Knoxville. Stanley J. Folmsbee, Robert E. Corlew, and Enoch Mitchell, *Tennessee: A Short History* (Knoxville: University of Tennessee Press, 1990), 12–13. (K)

74. Presently spelled Tellico. The word is possibly derived from the Cherokee words /adela/ "bead" or "money" and /e:kwa/ "big". (K)

75. The date would have been December 20, 1761.

76. After Fort Loudoun was surrendered in August 1760, Cherokee families lived in the buildings for eleven months before the fort was destroyed to prevent the approaching armies from South Carolina and Virginia from using it again.

77. Variously spelled in the records examined: Ostanaco, Ostonaco, Ustenaca, Ustenecah. Better known as Outacity (Mankiller) Ottassities, Otacie, Outassatah; or as Jud's or Judd's Friend. In one treaty all these names are written: "*Ustenah [Ustenecah], Ottassite or Jud's Friend.*" *North Carolina Colonial Records*, vol. 7, 470. He took part in the Virginia's campaign at the north in 1756, and was a chief of ability and good repute. (W) Admiralty records of his visit to London also give the following spellings: "*O Tacita (O Tasitto), Ostinaco (Ostianaco), Sky Augusta.*" Cited in Draper Mss. 2VV, 186 and 187. Sky Augusta may be an anglicized version of Skiagvsta, the highest war rank. (K)

78. Captain John McNeill, of the Byrd-Stephen regiment, was highly regarded by Colonel Washington and Governor Dinwiddie. He had been selected to command the garrison of the Virginia fort constructed (1756) on the Little Tennessee prior to the erection of Fort Loudoun. The fort was never garrisoned. See Timberlake's map. McNeill was left in command of Fort Robinson when Colonel Stephen returned to Virginia. (K)

79. The townhouse at Chota was excavated by the University of Tennessee in 1969. The archaeological record supports Timberlake's description. (K)

80. "*As in this speech several allusions are made to the customs of the Indians, it may not be impertinent to acquaint the reader, that their way of declaring war, is by smoak-*

ing a pipe as a bond among themselves, and lifting up a hatchet stained in blood, as a menace to their enemies; at declaring peace this hatchet is buried, and a pipe smoaked by both parties, in token of friendship and reconciliation." (T)

81. *"The chiefs can inflict no punishment; but, upon the signing of the peace, it was agreed by both nations, that offenders on either side should be delivered up to be punished by the offended party, and it is to this the Chief alludes."* (T) (33)

82. *"This Hot-House is a little hut joined to the house, in which a fire is continually kept, and the heat so great, that cloaths are not to be borne the coldest day in winter."* (T) (35)

83. It was called Satapo by the Spanish in the 1660s and was probably occupied by Muskogean speakers at that time. It was Cherokee-ized to Settiquo in the eighteenth century. It was Anglicized first to Settico and later to Citico, as it is spelled today. (K)

84. Captain Paul Demere (misspelled as Damere by Timberlake), commanding officer of Fort Loudoun, along with about twenty-five privates and all of the officers except Captain John Stuart, were killed by Cherokees on the morning of August 10, 1760. The survivors of the garrison were made prisoners and dispersed throughout the Nation. On August 6, Captain Demere and all the officers unanimously voted to surrender the fort. Demere reported:

    Our provisions are entirely exhausted: That we have subsisted horse-flesh, and such supply of hogs and beans as the Indian women brought us by stealth, without any kind of bread since the 7th of July; by which our men are greatly weakened and in a short time become incapable of doing any duty: That the enemy blockade us night and day: That for two nights past, considerable parties have deserted, and some even have already thrown themselves on the mercy of the enemy: That the garrison in general threaten to abandon us, and betake themselves to the woods: That we have no hope of seasonable relief, having had no intelligence from any British settlement since the 4th day of June: We are, therefore, unanimously of the opinion, that it is impracticable to maintain the fort any longer; and that such terms as can be procure from the Indians, consistent with honour, be immediately accepted of, and the fort abandoned: That capt. Stuart go to Chotee, to treat with the warriors and head-men, and procure the best terms he can. Signed by all the officers. (London Gazette, November 1760, p. 605)

    Stuart was selected for this assignment because of his rapport with the Cherokees, in contrast to Demere who was generally despised. Stuart and Lieutenant Adamson negotiated the terms of surrender with the great warrior Oconastota and other leaders, in the Chota townhouse on August 8. Upon their return to the fort, Demere wrote his last letter, attached it to the articles of capitulation, and sent it by express to Colonel Byrd. After explaining their situation, he stated:

    Tomorrow we set out, and we flatter ourselves that the Indians mean us no harm. We shall make all dispatch that our starved condition will admit of.

    The Indians expect, that immediately upon our arrival at Keowee, the prisoners confined there will all be released, all thoughts of farther hostilities laid aside, and an accommodation heartily set about; that a firm peace and well regulated trade may be established, which they say will last forever. We can discover nothing in their present behaviour that contradicts this, and hope, at least, that nothing will be undertaken which may endanger us upon the march. (*London Gazette*, November 1760, p. 605) (K)

85. Chucatah would later accompany Timberlake on his second and final trip to England in 1764–65. (K)

86. Mary Hughes was the widow of Bernard Hughes, trader at Stecoe. Timberlake's account, published in the *Gentleman's Magazine* 34 (March 1768): 142, states: "*Among these prisoners was also a woman whose husband had been murdered and who had afterward married his murderer. The Indian, though reluctant, was disposed to comply, (with prisoner release) but she absolutely refused to return with her countrymen.*" (K)

87. Thomas Boone (1730–1812) served as governor of South Carolina from 1761 to 1764. During this period the famous conflict between the governor and the assembly took place, which greatly increased the irritation of the colonies with Great Britain. As a result, Boone was recalled to England, where he spent his later life in London as commissioner of the Customs House. (K)

88. The Cherokees' sincere desire for peace is evidenced in Governor Boone's letter to Amherst on June 25, 1762, stating that the Cherokees had delivered most, if not all, remaining prisoners to the commanding officers at Fort Prince George on June 13. Public Record Office, C.O. 5/65, fol. 197, Secretary of State: Original Correspondence, Military Dispatches: 1762. (K)

89. Yachtino, also known as Youghtanno, spent four months in military service on the Virginia frontier in 1757. On February 14, 1757, he departed from the Overhills with forty warriors from Chilhowie and Tellassee. IBSC, V, 375–77; see Corkran, *The Cherokee Frontier*, 112. On the frontier, they followed Wawhatchee and Richard Pearis to Maryland and later to the forks of the Ohio to track enemy marauders. Pennsylvania Archives, Ser. 1 and III, 143–144. In mid-June 1757, he left the Virginia frontier for the Overhills with Wawhatchee and sixty other Cherokee veterans. Pennsylvania Archives, Ser. 1 and III, 175–181, 197–200. (K)

90. In spite of the substantial size of Montgomery's army traveling overland from Charleston to the Lower Towns, the Cherokees had no advance warning of the impending invasion. The army of 1,268 men reached Ninety-Six on May 28, 1760, and Twelve Mile River on June 1. Colonel Grant reported:

> *As we met no opposition at Twelve-mile river, and at the same time our scouts finding no Indian tracks near us, both Colonel Montgomery and I were convinced, that they knew nothing of our march, and we resolved to take advantage of their negligence, by a forced march that night, though the troops were a little fatigued with a march of twenty miles in the morning, from Beaver-Dams to the river: we therefore encamped in a square, upon a very advantageous ground, and leaving our tents standing, with 120 of the king's troops, a few provincials, and about 70 rangers, as a guard to our camp. Wagons, cattle, &c. we marched at eight at night thorough the woods, in order to surprise Estatoe, which by that road was about 25 miles from our camp upon the river. After we had marched about sixteen miles, a dog was heard barking at some distance in our front, and the guides informed us that there were a few houses about a quarter of a mile from the road, called Little Keowee, of which they had not informed us before: to prevent any inconvenience from these houses, the light infantry company of the Royal was*

detached to surround the houses, and put the Indians to death with bayonets. We learnt, by a scout which had been at fort Prince George that very day, they were encamped near the houses, and, upon discovering our men, they fired at them; a few of ours returned the fire, but immediately rushed in upon them, and most of those who were without the houses, and all who were in them were put to death with bayonets, except the women and children, according to the orders which had been given.

We proceeded directly on our march to Estatoe, and found a few houses on the road just deserted; the beds were warm, and every thing was left in the houses, which you may believe did not escape. We arrived early in the morning at Estatoe, which was abandoned about half an hour before: ten or a dozen, who had not time to escape, were killed: the town, consisting of about 200 houses, well provided with ammunition, corn and in short, all the necessaries of life, was plundered and laid in ashes; many of the inhabitants, who had endeavored to conceal themselves, I have reason to believe, perished in the flames, some of them I know for certain did. In order to continue the blow, and to shew those savages that it was possible to punish their insolence, we proceeded to march, took all their towns in our way, and every house and town in the Lower Nation shared the same fate with Estatoe. I could not help pitying them a little: their villages were agreeably situated, their houses were neatly built, and well provided, for they were in the greatest abundance of every thing: they must be pretty numerous. Estatoe and Sugar-Town consisted of at least 200 houses, and every other village of at least 100 houses. After killing all we could find, and burning every house in the nation, we marched to Keowee, and arrived the second of June (after a march of above sixty miles without sleeping) at four in the evening at Fort Prince George. (James Grant, *London Magazine*, August 1760, p. 425).

The siege of Fort Loudoun began on March 20, 1760. Montgomery's invasion of the Lower Towns did not bring relief to the fort, and his retreat from the Middle Towns on June 27 resulted in an intensified siege sealing the fate of Fort Loudoun. The garrison surrendered on August 9, 1760. (K)

91. James Grant, *London Magazine*, August 1760, p. 425, went on to say:

There must have been 60 to 80 Cherokees killed, with about 40 prisoners, I mean men, women, and children. Those who escape must be in a miserable condition, and can possible have no resource but flying over the mountains, in case their friends there will receive them: they can have saved nothing: some of them had just time to run out of their beds, others left their sepann warm upon the table, and in the kettles. The surprise in every town was almost equal, as the whole affair was the work of a few hours only. They had, both at Estatoe and Suger-town, plenty of ammunition, which was destroyed, and every where astonishing magazines of corn, which were all consumed in the flames: they had not even time to save their most valuable effects: the soldiers found money in many houses: three or four watches were got, their wampum, their cloathes, skins, and, in short, every thing. Many loaded guns went off when the houses were burning. I had almost forgot to tell you, that we intended to save Sugar-town, as the place nearest the fort, (where they even had a stockage fort:) centries were placed for the security of the town; but we found the body of a dead man, whom they had put to torture that very morning: it was no longer possible think of mercy.

> Our loss was inconsiderable, three or four men killed, and lieutenants Mashal
> and Hamilton, of the Royal, wounded: it is hoped that both will recover, though
> Mr. Marshal is not out of danger.

92. Ostenaco was apparently referring to Settico, Chilhowie, and Tellassee as
culpable in the late war. Oconastota had earlier informed Captain Demere
at Fort Loudoun that the towns of Chote, Tennessee, Toquo, and Timot-
ley were not guilty of the outrages. See M. De Filipis, "An Italian Account of
Cherokee Uprisings at Fort Loudoun and Fort Prince George, 1760–1761,"
North Carolina Historical Review 20, no. 3 (July 1943): 247–258. (K)

93. Governor Fauquier, *Journal of the Virginia House of Burgesses, 1761–65*, p. xvii,
noted:
> Mr. Timberlake went from our Camp down Holston's River and up the Ten-
> nessee, and he found it navigable for Batteaus which draw ten or twelve inches
> of water, all the way, by which we may find that we have a good conveyance for
> Men, Stores or Merchandise into the very heart of their Country. He has made
> a draught of the courses and bearings of the River, a fair Copy of which is by my
> order preparing for Sir Jeffery Amherst.

Timberlake's map was also reproduced in Jeffery's *Topography of North
America* (1762); in *De Brahms History of the Province of Georgia*, in Winsor's
Mississippi Basin, and in Avery's *History of the United States*, vol. 4, 346. Timberlake's map has been used by all archeologists in the nineteenth and twentieth centuries. All have relied on its accuracy for pinpointing the locations
of the eighteenth-century towns. See Cyrus Thomas, *The Cherokees in Pre-
Columbian Times*, 32; and Chapman, *Tellico Archaeology*. (K)

94. Timberlake was correct in observing that Cherokee women were farming fertile river bottoms along the Tennessee River that they had cultivated for decades, perhaps centuries, and that did not require extensive plowing. He visited in the winter, however, and did not have a chance to observe the extent of
Cherokee women's agricultural practices, creating their own varieties of corn,
beans, squash, and gourds. Bartram observed hundreds of acres of cornfields
and gardens around each Cherokee village. (K)

95. Fishing weirs in the Little Tennessee River apparently dating from at least
the eighteenth century were still clearly observable before the area was in-
undated by the Tellico Reservoir in 1980. The Cherokees also used nets for
fishing during the historic period, continuing a tradition that dates back to
the Archaic period. Timberlake may not have observed these in use because
of the time of year that he visited, from December through March. For more
information on fishing, see Adair, *History of the American Indians*, 402–404;
Harrington, *Cherokee and Early Remains on Upper Tennessee River* (New York:
Heye Foundation, 1922), 215; and Frederick W. Hodge, *Handbook of American
Indians* (Washington: U.S. Government Printing Office, 1907–10), vol. 1, 461.
(K)

96. Peaches and pears did not grow wild because they were not native to the area.
They were both introduced by Europeans very early in the historic period,
during which peaches became an important crop. According to tradition, a
peach blight occurred about 1865, after which peaches never grew as large
or plentiful again. For related material, see also Adair, *History of American*

Indians, 409ff.; William Bartram, *Travels through North and South Carolina* (Philadelphia: James & Johnson, 1791), 360; William Bartram, *Observations on the Creek and Cherokee Indians*, in *Transactions of the Ethnological Society* (New York, 1853), vol. 3, part 1, 47.

97. The Museum of the Cherokee Indian in Cherokee, N.C., and the Cherokee National Museum in Tahlequah, Okla., display Cherokee blowguns as part of their permanent exhibits. Blowgun competitions are regularly held at the Cherokee Fall Festival (N.C.) the first week in October and at the Cherokee National Holidays (Okla.) during Labor Day weekend each year. (K)

98. The Cherokee word for bison is *yv:sa*, which is very similar to the words for the animal found in most other languages in the eastern United States, suggesting a lack of antiquity for buffaloes east of the Mississippi. In the Great Plains, the introduction of the horse ca. 1680 and introduction of firearms by 1720 created greater mobility and hunting efficiency that may have contributed to the dispersal of bison outside of their normal range. The last buffalo in Tennessee was killed in 1808. (K)

99. Although traces of gold have been found in many of the streams flowing out of the Appalachian summit area, attempts to mine it commercially along Coker Creek in east Tennessee and the Oconaluftee in North Carolina were not successful. Only at Dahlonega, Georgia, where gold was discovered in 1828, was a commercial operation briefly viable within the original Cherokee Nation. (K)

100. Most notably rubies and emeralds are still periodically found in the Valley Town area near present-day Franklin, N.C. (K)

101. James Mooney collected several stories from Eastern Cherokees in 1887–88 regarding the Uktena, an anomalous creature with the body of a snake and a quartz crystal in its forehead. Anomalous creatures, in general, are afforded supernatural powers in the Cherokee oral tradition. Talismanic stones, particularly quartz crystals, were highly regarded by individuals who practiced traditional medicine. Mooney says that *"the mystic diamond crest, when in its proper place upon the snake's head, is called Ulstitlu; but when detached and in the hands of the conjurer it becomes the Ulunsuti, 'Transparent,' the great talisman of the tribe."* See James Mooney, *Myths of the Cherokees* (Washington: U.S. Government Printing Office, 1900), 459, citing Timberlake. Adair, *History of the American Indians*, 237, also gives an account of the serpent and the stone. The stones, in fact, were evidently rare specimens of rutile quartz, transparent with the exception of a single red streak running lengthways through the center of the stone. See Charles Hudson, "Uktena: A Cherokee Anomalous Monster," *Journal of Cherokee Studies* 3, no. 2 (Spring 1978): 62–75. (K)

102. Tattooing, which was widespread in the eastern woodlands during the eighteenth century, may have been used to denote military achievements and acknowledgments in addition to personal adornment. See also Bartram, *Observations*, 28. (K)

103. Piercing and stretching earlobes dates to precontact times in the Southeast, as evidenced by the popularity of ear spools and ear pins during the Mississippian period. The tradition reached new heights in the historic period with the introduction of metal tools and malleable ornaments. Louis Phillippe,

who visited the Overhill country in 1797, observed: "*The outer rim of the ear is always detached with an incision among them. They wrap it with tin and hang from it very long and heavy ear pendants. Also they often have a triangle or other dangler passed through the nasal septum. These ornaments are worn only by men.*" William Sturtevant, "Louis Phillippe on Cherokee Architecture and Clothing in 1797," *Journal of Cherokee Studies* 3, no. 4 (Fall 1978): 202. (K)

104. Long hair was considered a standard of beauty for women. Bartram, *Observations*, 30, noted: "*They preserve its perfect blackness and splendor by the use of the red covering of the berries of the common summach.*" (K)

105. Because of diet and lifestyle, obesity was virtually unknown in the eighteenth century. Bartram, *Observations*, 30, states: "*The women are tall, slim and of a graceful figure, and have captivating features and manners; and I think their complexion is rather fairer than the men's.*" (K)

106. Historically, gambling was associated with all Cherokee games of skill and chance. Serious wagers often accompanied games of skill such as stickball and chunkey. Wagering on games of chance such as the basket game was largely symbolic. Raymond Fogelson, "Cherokee in the East," *Handbook of North American Indians*, vol. 1: *The Southeast* (Washington: Smithsonian Institution, 2004), 349. (K)

107. Without being explicit, Timberlake may here again be offering contrasts between Cherokee and British societies. If so, the inference is that the British were not as deferential to or particularly careful with the elderly; and he may be calling attention to the relatively short life expectancy of Europeans during this period. When the founding fathers of the United States set the minimum age to be president at thirty-five, only half the people born would live to be that old.

108. In comparison to languages worldwide, Cherokee has a relatively small phonemic inventory, with only seventeen segmental phonemes. Eleven are consonants and six are vowels. In addition, vowel length and pitch accent are also phonemic. A distinctive feature of the inventory is the absence of bilabial stops /p/ and /b/. The Iroquoian language family is one of the few families in the world that lack this near universal tendency. The additional absence of the labio-dental spirants /f/ and /v/ leaves the bilabial nasal /m/ as the only consonant involving the lips in articulation. The phoneme /m/ has a very limited distribution. It occurs in fewer than ten aboriginal words, all of which are uninflected nouns with uncertain etymologies. This raises questions about the antiquity of the phoneme /m/ in the Cherokee language. All other phonemes constitute regularly occurring sound correspondences with sounds of other Iroquoian languages. (K)

109. In spite of the fact that Timberlake was immersed in Cherokee culture for three months and with Cherokee speakers for more than six, at no point in his *Memoirs* does he show less understanding of the richness of the culture and the language to which he was exposed than here. Structurally, the Cherokee language is much more complex than English. It is a polysynthetic language, which means that numerous units of meaning are linked together to form long words. Verbs, constituting the most important word type, must contain as a minimum a pronominal prefix, a verb root, an aspect suffix, and a modal suf-

fix. Verbs can also add a variety of prepronominal prefixes, reflexive prefixes, and derivative suffixes. Given all possible combinations of affixes, each regular verb can have more than 21,000 inflected forms. There is no shortage of ideas in Cherokee or ways to express them. Timberlake apparently did have enough exposure to understand the subtleties or the richness of the language. (K)

110. * *"As the Indians fight naked, the vanquished are constrained to endure the rigours of the weather in their flight, and live upon roots and fruit, as they throw down their arms to accelerate their flight thro' the woods."* (T)

111. * *"It is the custom of the Indians, to leave a club, something of the form of a cricket-bat, but with their warlike exploits engraved on it, in their enemy's country, and the enemy accepts the defiance, by bringing this back to their country."* (T)

112. *"The prisoners of war are generally tortured by the women, at the party's return, to revenge the death of those that have perished by the wretch's countrymen. This [57] savage custom has been so much mitigated of late, that the prisoners were only compelled to marry, and then generally allowed all the privileges of the natives. This lenity, however, has been a detriment to the nation; for many of these returning to their countrymen, have made them acquainted with the country-passes, weakness, and haunts of the Cherokees; besides that it gave the enemy greater courage to fight against them."* (T)

113. * *"Their custom is generally to engrave their victory on some neighbouring tree, or set up some token of it near the field of battle; to this their enemies are here supposed to point to, as boasting their victory over them, and the slaughter that they made."* [58] (T) On June 9, 1761, Captain Christopher French, 22nd Regiment, Grant expedition, reported seeing such a carving on a tree about ten miles from Stecou Old Town. He copied the carving of two men (one appearing to strike the other with a tomahawk) in his journal with the comment, *"This we interpreted to be either a threatening [sign], or an indication that they had a soldier of the 17th Regt. Prisoner, whom we miss'd some Days ago & had suppos'd to be drown'd."* "Journal of Christopher French," *Journal of Cherokee Studies* 2, no. 3 (Summer 1977): 283. (K)

114. At least two eighteenth-century Cherokee canoes have survived to the present. One, made from yellow poplar, was pulled from the Tennessee River in 1977 and is housed at the University of Tennessee's Frank McClung Museum. The other was made from white pine and was found in the Chattahoochee River near Helen, Georgia, in 1974. It is slightly over twenty-four feet long and two feet wide at the base. The area where it was found was most intensely occupied by Cherokees between 1700 and 1725. The canoe is preserved in the Museum of the Cherokee Indian. See Duane King, *Cherokee Heritage* (Cherokee, N.C.: Museum of the Cherokee Indian Press, 1982), 38. Both canoes match Timberlake's description for dugout canoes. (K)

115. Timberlake's observations may have been limited by his short stay among the Cherokees. Charles Hudson, on the other hand, expresses the opinion that the southeastern Indians "possessed the richest culture of any of the native people north of Mexico. It was the richest by almost any measure." Charles Hudson, *The Southeastern Indians* (Knoxville: University of Tennessee Press, 1976), vii. (K)

116. John Martin was a Presbyterian missionary. Governor Robert Dinwiddie

wrote to Governor Lyttelton on December 14, 1757, introducing John Martin and reporting that the Society for Missions and Schools wanted to establish two English schools and two missionaries among the Cherokees and other tribes. Samuel Davies, of Hanover, Virginia, wrote to Governor Lyttelton on December 16, 1757, also introducing Martin and asking the governor to give him recommendations to the Indians. Paul Kutsche, *A Guide to Cherokee Documents in the Northeastern United States* (Metuchen, N.J.: Scarecrow Press, 1986), 373. "*Mr. Martin, who comes to convoy ten Cherokees sent to our assistance by Old Hop.*" Governor Dinwiddie, June 1757, *Dinwiddie Papers*, vol. 2, 656 and 672. (K)

117. Unfortunately Timberlake's visit to the Overhill country was not at the time of year when he could have witnessed Green Corn Ceremonies. The preliminary or new Green Corn Feast was held when the young corn was first ready to eat. This feast was called *selu tsunistigistiyi* (corn, when they eat them) and was held in August. The feast was held on the night of the full moon nearest the period when the corn was ripe. There was a strong cultural prohibition against everyone eating new corn before the ceremony. The mature or ripe Green Corn Feast was held about forty to fifty days later, in mid- to late September. It was called *tu:naka?ni* and was held when the corn had become hard and perfect. The ceremonies generally lasted for four days and were preceded by fasting. Every fire in the village was extinguished; fire hearths were swept clean and rekindled from the new fire, called the sacred fire, made in the townhouse. The ceremonies promoted social unity and harmony. It was also a time of reconciliation and reaffirmation of family ties and responsibilities. See Ruth Y. Wetmore, "The Green Corn Ceremony of the Eastern Cherokees," *Journal of Cherokee Studies* 8, no. 1 (Spring 1983): 46–55. See also the Payne Manuscript, Ayers Collection, Newberry Library, Chicago. (K)

118. Timberlake's statement about the dead being thrown in the river is not corroborated by other observers of the period. Archaeological research at the townsites visited by Timberlake has revealed the dead were buried with great care. A common European perception was that Native American culture was the antithesis of European culture. Since Europeans buried their dead, Native Americans by contrast must not. It may be that Timberlake acquired his information of Cherokee culture not only by observation but from stories around campfires. (K)

119. While Timberlake and the Cherokees were in London, the *British Magazine* 3 (July 1762): 378, reported:

> *These Indians look upon the end of life to be living happily. For this purpose their whole customs are calculated to prevent avarice, which they say embitters life; and nothing is a severer reflection among them, than to say that a man loves his own. To prevent the rise and propagation of such a vice, they, upon the death of any Indian, burn all that belongs to the deceased, that there may be no temptation for the parent to hoard up a superfluity of arms and domestic conveniences, their chief treasures, for his children. They strengthen this custom by a superstition, that it is agreeable to the souls of the deceased to burn all they leave, and that afflictions follow them who use any of their goods.*

The same article is published in the *British Chronicle* for 1762 (p. 99), where the source of the information is said to be *"Lieut. Gen. Oglethorpe who often conversed with the Chiefs while he was governor of Georgia; which is the only authentic account that has ever been given of that Nation."* (K)

120. Outacity is also rendered by DeBrahm and British newspapers of the time as "Mankiller." As a military title, it has not survived to the present. The surname Mankiller is translated literally in Cherokee today as *askayadihi*. (K)

121. Because individuals were frequently referenced by military title instead of given names, the eighteenth century record is replete with location identifiers along with titles. Corkran, *The Cherokee Frontier*, distinguishes five Mankillers, five Ravens, and five Slavecatchers by town affiliation. According to *DeBrahm's Report* (DeVorsey, ed.), the first or lowest military title was "Slavecatcher," the second "Raven," the third "Mankiller," and the highest "Great Warrior." Before receiving a title, the warriors were "gunmen" or "boys." (K)

122. The most famous "War Woman" or Beloved Woman during the eighteenth century was Nane:hi or Nancy Ward. She was born at Chota in 1738 and died at her home at Woman Killer Ford on the Ocoee River in 1822. Although she was only twenty-four at the time of Timberlake's visit, she had already held the title of War Woman for seven years. At the battle of Taliwa against the Creeks in 1755, she was loading rifles for her husband, the Kingfisher, when he was mortally wounded. She immediately took his place on the firing line. Inspired by her courage, other Cherokees who had retreated returned to the battle, and the Creeks were defeated. In 1776, she used her authority as Beloved Woman to spare a war captive. In July of that year, Cherokee war parties under Dragging Canoe, Old Abram and the Raven of Chota launched a three-prong attack on white settlements in upper east Tennessee in an attempt to dislodge American patriots disloyal to the British Government. The settlers were forewarned and defeated the largest Cherokee contingent in an open battle at Island Flats (now Kingsport) on July 22, 1776. Dragging Canoe was seriously wounded and his warriors demoralized. They returned to the Overhills with only a few scalps and two prisoners from the Watauga settlements. One, a youth named Samuel Moore, was burned at the stake at Tuskeegee, home of Dragging Canoe. The other, Lydia Bean, wife of William Bean, nearly suffered the same fate atop the Toqua mound. Her life was spared by the intervention of Nancy Ward, who took Mrs. Bean back to her home at Chota. In captivity, Mrs. Bean reportedly taught Cherokee women how to make butter and cheese and weave on a frontier-style loom. Pat Alderman, *Nancy Ward, Cherokee Chieftainess* (Johnson City, Tenn.: Overmountain Press, 1978). See also John Haywood, *Natural and Aboriginal History of Tennessee* (Nashville, 1823), 278; and Mooney, *Myths of the Cherokees*, 395. (K)

123. Ostenaco is referenced by more names and titles than any other Cherokee during the eighteenth century. Only here is his given name revealed: /Woyi/ "Pigeon." (K)

124. Although Standing Turkey was the emperor at the time, he had little influence outside of the Cherokee Nation and was probably seen as a compromise between the three real power brokers: Oconastota, Attakullakulla, and Ostenaco. Oconastota gained his reputation as a warrior, and his attempts as a

diplomat were marked by a series of unmitigated failures, which greatly diminished his influence at home. Attakullakulla, much smaller in stature than Oconastota, did not intimidate anyone by his physical appearance but found favor among government and military officials for diplomatic abilities and negotiating skills. Ostenaco, by contrast, achieved prominence as both a warrior and a diplomat. Although South Carolina was the primary trading partner with the Cherokees, Ostenaco focused his attention on Virginia, making numerous trips to Williamsburg and forging an alliance with that colony during the Seven Years War. Regarding Ostenaco, Governor Fauquier noted: "*The chief is a man of great influence among the Cherokees and a man of integrity . . . He and the Little Carpenter have usually been heads of different parties, and he was for that reason one of the last who acceded to the Treaty, tho' he has been the foremost to treat our prisoners with humanity, and to release them.*" *Journal of Virginia House of Burgesses, 1761–65,* p. xvii. (K)

125. For nearly two hundred years prior to Timberlake's *Memoirs,* European writers frequently praised the freedoms perceived in Native American political systems to criticize the perceived faults in their own. Here Timberlake takes a jab at the cronyism that permeated the British government at the time by suggesting that the Cherokee system was better. On October 24, 1761, Colonel Adam Stephen wrote to General Amherst from his camp at Great Island that Connetarke had been made emperor through the influence of Great Warrior and Judd's Friend. Little Carpenter was unable to make peace until the leaders agreed with him. Stephen's letter indicates that the Cherokees were not as immune to party politics as Timberlake suggests. United Kingdom, Public Record Office, W.O. 34/38, fol. 284, Letters from the Commander in Chief to William Johnson, 1757–1763. (K)

126. Timberlake's observations may have been limited by his bias as a male and as a European observer. Cherokee women's activities occupied a different sphere from that of men, encompassing agriculture, basket making, pottery making, food preparation, house keeping, child rearing, and the obligations of the clans to maintain social order. (K)

127. Chunkey as a sport fell into disuse before the end of the eighteenth century among the Cherokees, although oral traditions about the game have continued down to the present. Timberlake's description, although meager, provides one of the few eyewitness accounts of how the game was played or scored. From the archaeological record it appears that the game had its origins in the Mississippian period, and the distribution of Chunkey discoidals is limited primarily to the Tennessee and Cumberland river valleys. Gates P. Thruston, *Antiquities of Tennessee and Adjacent States* (1897), 263. See also Bartram, *Observations,* 34; and Gene S. Stuart, *America's Ancient Cities* (Washington: National Geographic Society, 1988), 44–45. (K)

128. A chunkey stone matching this description was found in the fire hearth of the Chota townhouse when it was excavated in 1969. See Chapman, *Tellico Archaeology.* (K)

129. A gill is a liquid measure equal to one-quarter of a pint. (K)

130. The Black Drink was made from the leaves of American holly (*Ilex vomitoria*). The holly was often used in a purification ritual before council meet-

ings. Purification was obtained through sweating or vomiting. It is one of about a half dozen plants in the world that contain caffeine and is found in the coastal regions of the southeastern United States. See also Charles Hudson, *The Black Drink: A Native American Tea* (Athens: University of Georgia Press, 2004). (K)

131. See Barbara R. Duncan, "The Cherokee War Dance/Welcome Dance: From Timberlake to the Twenty-First Century," in Anne F. Rogers and Barbara R. Duncan (eds.), *Culture, Crisis and Conflict (Cherokee, N.C.: Museum of the Cherokee Indian Press, 2007).* (K)

132. Timberlake did not seem to comprehend the Cherokee Law of Corporate Responsibility at the time he departed for the Cherokee country in late November. By late January, after only a month in the Overhills, he appears fully cognizant of his vulnerability as a representative of an adversarial nation. (K)

133. On August 9, 1760 the English flag was hauled down at Fort Loudoun and a hundred men, sixty women, and a number of children, escorted by Oconostota and a large party of Indians, left the fort to travel to Prince George, 140 miles away. Exhausted by months of siege, the party traveled only fifteen miles along the Tellico River that day. During the night their escort slipped away and early the next morning guards reported Indians hiding in the bushes around the camp. John Stephen, a survivor, gave an eyewitness account of what occurred next:

> After the beating of reveille, while (the soldiers), were preparing to march, two guns were fired at Captain Demere, who was wounded by one of the shots . . .
>
> Lt. Adamson who stood beside him viewed the two Indians, returned their fire and wounded one . . . the war whoop was then setup . . . and volleys of small arms fire with showers of arrows poured in . . . from (700) Indians, who as they advanced surrounded the whole garrison and put them into the greatest confusion . . . they called to each other not to fire and surrendered. Some endeavored to escape but . . . the Indians rushed upon them with such impetuosity that it was in vain. By this time all the officers, except Stuart (who was during the assault seized by an Indian, perhaps by the Little Carpenter's arrangement and carried to the other side of the creek), with between thirty or forty privates, and three women were killed, Captain Paul Demere, whom the Indians disliked intensely suffered a cruel death. He was scalped while still alive and forced to dance while being beaten with sticks for his tormentor's amusement. When they tired of that his arms and legs were chopped off and his mouth stuffed with dirt. They taunted him as he lay dying by saying: "You English want land, we will give it to you." (John L. Nichols, "John Stuart, Beloved Father of the Cherokees," *Highlander Magazine* 31, no. 5 [September October 1993]: 37 40). (K)

134. January 28, 1762. (K)

135. The best treatment on Cherokee dance is Frank Speck and Leonard Broom, with Will West Long, *Cherokee Dance and Drama* (1983; reprint, Norman: University of Oklahoma Press, 1993). (K)

136. February 15, 1762. (K)

137. On February 24, 1762, Lt. Governor Fauquier conveyed his intent to the Board of Trade to disband the Virginia Regiment as soon as the Peace with the Cherokees was confirmed. C.o.5/1330, fol. 108, Virginia, Board of Trade: Original Correspondence, 1760–1764. On March 6, 1762, Amherst expressed

his surprise that the Virginia regiment had been disbanded. W.O. 34/48, fol. 128, Letters of the Commander in Chief to Officers serving in South Carolina and Virginia: 1760–1763. (K)

138. By mid-June 1762 most, if not all, prisoners had been delivered to Fort Prince George. The *Gentleman's Magazine* [34 (1768): 152] published an account of the prisoners that may have originated from Timberlake in London in 1765: *"Among them were above twenty boys who had become so habituated to the Indian manners that, after they were delivered up, they did nothing but cry, and would not eat."* (K)

139. A variant spelling for Timberlake's Toqua from the Cherokee (da:kwa). (K)

140. Willinawaw may have assumed that the document was a commission after having seen or heard of the one given to Oconastota less than a year earlier by the French governor of Louisiana, Louis de Kerelec. The governor appointed the great warrior as *Captaine grand chef medaille de la fond.* (K)

141. Timberlake, who had been keeping his own record of daily occurrences, believed the document to be a journal. In actuality, however, the document appears to be a hand-drawn pocket calendar designating "holy days of obligation" for a forty-week period beginning September 27, 1761, and ending July 3, 1762. After completing my analysis, I found that another researcher had come to the same conclusion several decades earlier. Harry Cantey, in 1960, realized that certain symbols on the document had religious connotations and was able to match suspected holidays with dates on the calendar. He was the first to recognize that the "curious French Journal" was actually a pocket calendar covering a period of time in 1761–62 when much of the Timberlake story took place. Harry Cantey, "An Interpretation of a Curious Secret Journal . . . ," *Tennessee Archaeologist* 16, no. 1 (Spring, 1960): 10–13.

   Timberlake was correct in identifying the longer marks as Sundays. The symbols on the lines represent religious observances. The fact that some holidays are fixed in the Christian calendar, while those associated with Easter are not, provides the best clues as to the precise time period covered. The fish symbol, located in the second week of the third column, represents fasting in the Catholic tradition, and the motif is still used on some calendars. If the fish symbol marked Ash Wednesday, it should precede Easter by forty days, excluding Sundays. Counting ahead, the date that should be Good Friday, the traditional anniversary of the crucifixion, is marked with a single cross. The date that should be Easter Sunday is shown with three *x*'s in addition to the single *x* at the beginning of the line for each Sunday. This is followed on the next day by two *x*'s and on the subsequent day by one *x*. This pattern occurs in only two other locations on the calendar, once in the third week of the second column and again at the beginning of the sixth week in the fourth column.

   From the known dates of the war party's departure and return, we can assume that the original owner of the calendar was killed in early February 1762. Assuming that the calendar was contemporary, Ash Wednesday and Easter Sunday in 1762 fell on February 24 and April 11, respectively.

   It is assumed that the x at the beginning of each line denoting Sunday indicates the regular Sunday mass, and other *x*'s indicate masses for special occasions. In the Roman Catholic Church, certain feasts, in addition to all Sundays, are designated "holy days of obligation," when all the faithful must attend Mass. In the United States, these are Christmas Day (December 25), the Octave of Christmas (New Year's Day), Ascension Day (May 20), the Assumption of the Blessed Virgin Mary (August 15), All Saints' Day (November 1), and the Immaculate Conception of the Blessed Virgin Mary (December 8). In addition to these, "days of obligation" that are celebrated elsewhere include the Annunciation (March 25), Saints Peter and Paul Apostles Day (June 29), and the Feast of Corpus Christi (June 10). Christmas, for example, has three masses: the first at midnight, the second in the morning, and the third at midday. Eight days on the calendar had three *x*'s, not counting two Sundays, which had three *x*'s in addition to the *x* at the beginning of the line.

Christmas, for example, falls on the third week in the second column, followed by three *x*'s on New Year's day (the Octave of Christmas), and the same for the Epiphany on January 6. Other dates marked by three or four *x*'s are aligned with the Annunciation on March 25, the Ascension on May 20, Pentecost on May 30, Saints Peter and Paul Apostles day on June 29, All Saints Day on November 2 (now celebrated on November 1), and the Immaculate Conception on December 8.

In addition to the *x*'s, assumed to represent masses, and the fish, symbolizing fasting at the beginning of Lent (Ash Wednesday), only three other symbols appear. First is the death's head mentioned by Timberlake, which appears at the end of the line equating to November 2, 1761, which is All Souls Day. The second is a cross that appears twice on February 7, along with the *x* for a Sunday mass. It also occurs on Good Friday, April 9, 1762, which is associated with the veneration of the cross. February 7 was the beginning of the pre-Lent season, which is peculiar to Western churches. It was developed in the sixth century as a time of special supplication for God's protection and defense in a period of great suffering in Italy from war, pestilence, and famine. It begins with the third Sunday before Lent, called Septuagesima, roughly seventy days before Easter. Although not included in the discipline of Lenten pentitence and fast, some authorities relate the season to influences from the East, especially Roman monastic customs, for a longer Lent of eight weeks.

The symbol of an anchor occurs on three dates on the calendar. The first is on Palm Sunday, April 4, 1762, when two anchors are found along with the expected *x* for a Sunday mass. The anchor is traditionally used as a symbol for hope in the Christian tradition. Palm Sunday is celebrated by the blessing of the palms and procession, with a solemn rendition of St. Matthew's Passion narrative at the Mass. Three anchors are shown on Thursday, June 10, 1762, which is the Feast of Corpus Christi. This occurs on the Thursday after Trinity Sunday, which is the first Sunday after Pentecost. The feast celebrates the real presence of Christ in the bread and wine of the Eucharist; it was instituted in 1264 by Pope Urban IV. Two anchors are shown for the date June 17, 1762. Following the anchors is a straight vertical line, suggesting the intent of the original creator or the copyist to make another anchor. If this was done by the copyist, it may have occurred after the realization that the anchors should have been placed on the following day, Thursday, June 18. The eighteenth would have been easier to explain since that date is the feast of the Sacred Heart. If the seventeenth is the correct placement, its association with a holiday is not yet discerned; however, it could be associated with a personal event such as a birthday or graduation. If so, could it be a clue to the identity of the individual killed by the Cherokees? (K)

142. The route was a well-worn path subsequently called the Great Warriors Path that connected the Overhill towns with the Great Island of the Holston and points farther north. John Stuart made his escape from the Cherokee country along this route.

143. After the surrender of Fort Loudoun, all of the arms and ammunition were moved to Chota. The second article of the Peace Treaty with Colonel Grant specified that *"Fort Loudoun and the cannon belonging thereto, now lying at Chote, shall be delivered up to any persons sent to take charge of them; and any forts shall be built hereafter in the Cherokee nation, when the same is thought necessary by the English." Annual Register . . . for Year 1761.* Property owners at Chota in the 1960s discovered two cannon barrels while plowing near the site of the town-house. It is assumed that these are the same cannons that were fired in salute of Timberlake and Ostenaco. (K)

144. Ellijay on Little River. The author's description of the locality is not over-stated. The town site was in the same valley as present-day Maryville, Tennessee. (K)

145. The part of the flesh taken from the tongue and the hump were considered choice. (K)

146. Charles McLemore was an unlicensed trader who moved freely among Cherokee and Carolina societies. He served as a messenger at various times for Demere, Oconastota, Governor Bull, and others. He helped procure food for the starving Fort Loudoun garrison during the siege in 1760 through his Cherokee family. He defended Oconastota's actions at the time of the massacre. He later showed up in the fall of 1760 in North Carolina with gold taken in raids on frontier settlements to buy supplies for the Cherokees. He was labeled by Henry Laurens as one of the "Villains of our own Country and Colour." See John Oliphant, *Peace and War on the Anglo-Cherokee Frontier* (Houndmills, UK: Palgrave Press, 2001), 184. If he was a smuggler, as Corkran, *The Cherokee Frontier*, 295, suggests, he seems to have applied his trade for the assistance of the beleaguered people on both sides. See also John P. Brown, "Eastern Cherokee Chiefs," *Chronicles of Oklahoma* 16, no. 1 (March 1938): 1–33.

147. It was located at Stalnakres, and was constructed by the Virginia regiment on their way to the Great Island. It was named by Colonel Byrd as a tribute to Attakullakulla and his efforts to bring about peace between the warring Nations. The tribute to Attakullakulla by Byrd was obvious. He was credited with saving Byrd's life in 1756 and had come to visit with Byrd at Stalnakres upon Byrd's arrival in July 1761. (K)

148. Israel Christian had been a captain in the Virginia regiment since at least 1756. He was a member of the House of Burgesses in 1759–61. He was the father-in-law of Colonel William Fleming and Colonel Stephen Trigg and the Father of Colonel William Christian, who led an invasion of the Overhill

country in October 1776; he served as commissioner at the Treaty of Long Island in 1777 and a subsequent treaty with the Cherokees in 1781. Israel Christian was born on the Isle of Man and came to Virginia by way of Dublin. He was the founder of Christiansburg, Virginia. He died in 1784. (K)

149. Named for Major Andrew Lewis, near Salem, Virginia, it was built in 1755 and was one of several supply stations on the road from Williamsburg to the Overhill country. Troops under Major Lewis cleared much of this road in advance of the Byrd-Stephen Expedition to the Great Island in 1761. Lewis also supervised the construction of the Virginia fort near Chota in 1756. See Corkran, *The Cherokee Frontier*, 124ff. (K)

150. William Shorey was an interpreter at Fort Loudon (1756–1760). He married Ghigooie about 1740. They had three children: Annie (ca. 1746–May 28, 1825); William Shorey, Jr. (ca. 1750–1809) and Elizabeth Shorey (ca. 1762–ca. 1842). Annie married John McDonald (ca. 1747–August 29, 1824). Their daughter, Mary Molly McDonald Ross (November 1, 1770–October 5, 1808) was the mother of Principal Chief John Ross (October 3, 1790–August 1, 1866). (K)

151. Cherokee visits to Williamsburg during this period were not out of the ordinary. The Cherokees sent fourteen delegations to Williamsburg between 1746 and 1777. (K)

152. Another traveler to this part of the world found Virginia, the land of Timberlake's nativity, strange and curious. In April 1759, as Reverend Andrew Burnaby was preparing to leave London for a trip to the colonies, he later recalled:

> A few days before I embarked for America, being in a coffee-house with some friends, and discoursing of things relative to that country, an elderly gentleman advancing towards the box where we were sitting, addressed himself to me in the following manner: "Sir," said he, "you are young, and just entering into the world; I am old, and upon the point of leaving it: allow me therefore to give you one piece of advice, which is the result of experience; and which may possibly, some time or other, be of use to you. You are going to a country where every thing will appear new and wonderful to you; but it will appear so only for a while; for the novelty of it will daily wear off; and in time it will grow quite familiar to you. Let me, therefore, recommend to you to note in your pocket-book every circumstance, that may make an impression upon you; for be assured, sir, though it may afterward appear familiar and uninteresting to yourself, that it will not appear so to your friends who have never visited that country, and that they will be entertained by it.

The young minister took the old man's advice and kept a journal of his travels. His recollections of Williamsburg give us a good description of the environment and the people the Cherokee delegation may have encountered in 1762. Andrew Burnaby, *Travels through the Middle Settlements in North America in the Years 1759 and 1760* (Ithaca, N.Y.: Cornell University Press, 1960). (K)

153. Andrew Burnaby concluded:

> The public or political character of the Virginians, corresponds with their private one: they are haughty and jealous of their liberties, impatient of restraint, and can scarcely bear the thought of being controuled by any superior power. Many of them consider the colonies as independent states, not connected with Great

Britain, otherwise than by having the same common king, and being bound to her with natural affection. There are but few of them that have a turn for business, and even those are by no means adroit at it. I have known them, upon a very urgent occasion, vote the relief of a garrison, without once considering whether the thing was practicable, when it was most evidently and demonstrably otherwise.*

The garrison here alluded to, was that of Fort Loudoun, in the Cherokee country, consisting of a lieutenant, and about fifty men. This unfortunate party being besieged by the Cherokee Indians, and reduced to the last extremity, sent off runners to the governors of Virginia and Carolina, imploring immediate succour; adding that it was impossible for them to hold out above twenty days longer. The assembly of Virginia, commiserating their unhappy situation, very readily voted a considerable sum for their relief. With this, troops were to be levied; were to rendezvous upon the frontiers 200 miles distant from Williamsburg; were afterward to proceed to the fort 200 miles farther through a wilderness, where there was no road, no magazines, no posts, either to shelter the sick, or cover a retreat in case of any disaster; so that the unfortunate garrison might as effectually have been succoured from the moon. The author taking notice of these difficulties to one of the members, he frankly replied, "Faith, it is true: but we have had an opportunity at least of showing our loyalty." In a few days after arrived the melancholy news, that this unfortunate party was intirely cut off. (Ibid., 25)

154. Andrew Burnaby, recording his first impressions of Williamsburg on July 5, 1759, wrote:

The next morning, having hired a chaise at York, I went to Williamsburg, about twelve miles distant. The road is exceedingly pleasant, through some of the finest tobacco plantations in North-America, with a beautiful view of the river and woods of great extent. . . . Williamsburg is the capital of Virginia: it is situated between two creeks; one falling into James, the other into York river; and is built nearly due east and west. The distance of each landing-place is something more than a mile from the town; which, with the disadvantage of not being able to bring up large vessels, is the reason of its not having increased so fast as might have been expected. It consists of about two hundred houses, does not contain more than one thousand souls, whites and negroes; and is far from being a place of any consequence. It is regularly laid out in parallel streets, intersected by others at right angles; has a handsome square in the center, through which runs the principal street, one of the most spacious in North-America, three quarters of a mile in length, and above a hundred feet wide. At the ends of this street are two public buildings, the college and the capitol: and although the houses are of wood, covered with shingles, and but indifferently built, the whole makes a handsome appearance. There are few public edifices that deserve to be taken notice of; those, which have mentioned, are the principal; and they are far from being magnificent. The governor's palace, indeed, is tolerably good, one of the best upon the continent; but the church, the prison, and the other buildings, an all of them extremely indifferent. The streets are not paved, and are consequently very dusty, the soil here about consisting chiefly of sand: however, the situation of Williamsburg has one advantage, which few or no places in these lower parts have; that of being free from mosquitoes. Upon the whole, it is an agreeable residence; there are ten or twelve gentlemen's families constantly residing in it, besides merchants and tradesmen: and at the times of the assemblies, and general courts; it is crowded with the gentry of the country: on those occasions there are balls and other amusements; but as soon as the business is finished, they return to their plantations; and the town is in a manner deserted. (Ibid., 4–5)

155. Andrew Burnaby concluded in his observations of Virginians:

From what has been said of this colony, it will not be difficult to form an idea of the character of its inhabitants. The climate and external appearance of the country conspire to make them indolent, easy, and good-natured; extremely fond of society, and much given to convivial pleasures. In consequence of this, they seldom show any spirit of enterprize, or expose themselves willingly to fatigue. Their authority over their slaves renders them vain and imperious, and intire strangers to that elegance of sentiment, which is so peculiarly characteristic of refined and polished nations. Their ignorance of mankind and of learning, exposes them to many errors and prejudices, especially in regard to Indians and Negroes, whom they scarcely consider as of the human species; so that it is almost impossible, in cases of violence, or even murder, committed upon those unhappy people by any of the planters, to have the delinquents brought to justice: for either the grand jury refuse to find the bill, or the petit jury bring in their verdict, not guilty.*

* There are two laws in this colony, which make it almost impossible to convict a planter, or white man, of the death of a Negroe or Indian. By the first it is enacted, that "if any slave shall die by reason of any stroke or blow, given in correction by his or her owner, or by reason of any accidental blow whatsoever, given by such owner; no person concerned in such correction, or accidental homicide, shall undergo any prosecution or punishment for the same; unless, upon examination before the county court, it shall be proved by the oath of one lawful and credible witness, at least, that such slave was killed wilfully, maliciously, and designedly; nor shall any person indicted for the murder of a slave, and upon trial found guilty only of manslaughter, incur any forfeiture or punishment for such offence or misfortune." (See John Mercer, Abridgment, 345.)

By the second, *"No Negroe, Mulatto, or Indian, can be admitted into any court, or before any magistrate, to be sworn as a witness, or give evidence in any cause whatsoever, except upon the trial of a slave for a capital offence."* (Mercer, *Abridgment*, 419; Burnaby, *Travels*, 22–23)

EDITOR'S NOTE: Mercer's *Abridgment*, referenced by Burnaby, is the *Abridgment of the Laws of Virginia*, published in 1737. The author, John Mercer (1704–1768) of Marlborough, Stafford County, was also the publisher of the First Code of Virginia, in *Laws* (1759). (K)

156. Rev. James Horrocks was a professor in William and Mary College at the time of Ostenaco's visit. He later served as president of the college between 1764 and 1771. Andrew Burnaby, who visited the institution in 1759, recalled:

The progress of arts and sciences in this colony has been very inconsiderable: the college of William and Mary is the only public place of education, and this has by no means answered the design of its institution. It has a foundation for a president and six professors. The business of the president is to superintend the whole, and to read four theological lectures annually. He has a handsome house to live in, and 200£ sterling per annum. The professor of the Indian school has 60£ sterling, and a house also; his business is to instruct the Indians in reading, writ-

ing, and the principles of the Christian religion: this pious institution was set on foot and promoted by the excellent Mr. Boyle. The professor of humanity has the care of instructing the students in classical learning: he has an usher or assistant under him. The four other professors teach moral philosophy, metaphysics, mathematics, and divinity. Each of the professors has apartments in the college, and a salary of about 80£ per annum*. The present chancellor of the college is the bishop of London. (Burnaby, *Travels*, 21–22) (K)

157. It is believed that this was a copy of the official coronation portrait of King George III by Allan Ramsay. Numerous copies of this portrait were painted by Ramsay's students in his studio in London and sent to various parts of the empire. The copy from William and Mary is now in the National Portrait Gallery in Washington, DC. (K)

158. Francis Fauquier, the new governor of Virginia, was well aware of the factionalism within the Cherokee Nation at this time. One advantage that Ostenaco's rival, Attakullakulla, had was the prestige of a trip to England thirty years earlier and the distinction of being the only living Cherokee to have had an audience with a British monarch. By sending Ostenaco to London, Fauquier was calculating a stronger tie between the Cherokee Nation and Virginia with the ascendancy of Ostenaco. Fauquier justified his decision by pointing out:

> *As the Little Carpenter had formerly been in England, he [Ostenaco] most earnestly solicited me and the Council that he might have permission to go to England to see the great King, his Father, and judge whether the Little Carpenter had not told them lies . . . I have accordingly put him, two of his followers and a faithful Interpreter on board Captain Blake's Sloop* [L'Epreuve] *to be transported to England . . . The Indians will be accompanied by Mr. Timberlake, an ensign in our Regiment, who has been in the Cherokee Over Hill Towns and is much respected by the Indians, etc. (Journal of the House of Burgesses, May 1, 1762).* (K)

159. On May 1, 1762, Gov. Fauquier wrote a letter of introduction for Ensign Timberlake to Lord Egremont. He credited Timberlake with opening a new route to the Cherokee country and noted that he was accompanying the Cherokees at his own expense. C.O. 5/1345, fol. 1, Virginia, Secretary of State: Original Correspondence, 1762–1767, 3 pages. (K)

160. Thomas Jefferson was a sixteen-year-old student at William and Mary at the time of Ostenaco's visit. Many years later he wrote:

> *I knew much of the great Outasseti, the warrior and orator of the Cherokees. He was always the guest of my father on his journeys to and from Williamsburg. I was in his camp when he made his great farewell oration to his people the evening before he departed for England. The moon was in full splendour, and to her he seemed to address himself in his prayers for his own safety on the voyage and that of his people during his absence. His sounding voice, distinct articulation, animated action, and the solemn silence of his people at their several fires, filled me with awe and veneration, although I did not understand a word he uttered.* (Francis W. Hirst, *The Life and Letters of Thomas Jefferson* [New York: Macmillan, 1926], 16) (K)

161. Williams, *Memoirs*, 132 fn75, states: "*One of the two Indians who accompanied*

Ostenaco was mentioned in the St. James Chronicle *(London, July 22–24, 1762) as 'Tohanohawighton.' No mention of the name of the other has been found."* Captain Peter Blake, who commanded the ship that took them to England and brought them back, recorded their names more than once. In the muster books on the return trip, he listed the Cherokees on August 22 at Portsmouth as (1) Otacita Ostinaco Sky Augusta, (2) Wooe Pidgeon, and (3) Conney Shota. When they were discharged at Charleston on November 3, he recorded their names as (1) Otassitto Ostianaco Sky Augusta, (2) Woee Pidgeon, and (3) Conney Shoatt. On the return trip they were accompanied by Thomas Sumter and Charles Bullin. Copy of Admiralty Records in Draper Mss. 2VV, 186–187. Cunne Shote or Stalking Turkey was the subject of a much published portrait by Thomas Parson. The original is in the Gilcrease Museum, Tulsa, Oklahoma. Woyi or Pidgeon died at Williamsburg in 1777, after having been recruited to serve in Washington's army by Nathanial Gist. (K)

162. *Lloyd's Evening Post and British Chronicle,* June 16–18, 1762, p. 582, reported:
    The Epreuve *frigate, Peter Blake, Esq. Commander, is arrived at Plymouth from Virginia. She sailed thence on the 17th of May with fifteen sail merchant-men under convoy, which were parted on the 30th of May in a gale wind, 400 leagues to the westward of the Lizard. In the fleet were the Theodorick, Hall; Leeds Merchant, Clarkstone; Bettesworth, Catren; Grand Duke, Morris; and Randolph, Walker.—There is come over in this frigate three Cherokee Indians, with whom a peace is concluded, and they set out directly for London.* (K)

163. The *HMS Revenge* was a relatively new warship. It was launched in May 1760 and sailed until 1789. (K)

164. Wilton House is at Salisbury in Wiltshire. Wilton Abbey was founded in 773. The current Tudor-style house was started in 1543 by Henry Herbert (b. 1506), who was the 1st Earl of Pembroke (1551–1570). William Herbert (b. 1978) is the 18th Earl of Pembroke (2003–present). (K)

165. The classical marble statue of Hercules was collected by Thomas Herbert, the 8th Earl of Pembroke, between 1683 and 1733. In 1692, he became the First Lord of the Admiralty and in that capacity was able to collect many of the paintings and sculptures that are displayed in the house today. At the time of the Cherokee visit, Henry Herbert (b. 1734), the 10th Earl of Pembroke (1750–1794), was the master of the house. He was Lord of the Bedchamber to King George III. In 1778, King George III visited the house to inspect troops preparing to depart for service in the War of American Independence. The house was also used as the Allied command center to plan the D-Day invasion of World War II. The slightly larger-than-life statue of Hercules described by Timberlake is still on view in the entry foyer of the Wilton House. (K)

166. They did stay in Salisbury long enough to do a newspaper interview.
    On Thursday last [June 17, 1762] arrived in this city [Salisbury] on his way to London, the King of the Cherokee Indians in North America, attended by two of his chiefs. They landed in Portsmouth from Virginia, and came over in the Epreuve frigate, Capt. Peter Blake. They are tall well made men, near six feet high, dressed with only a shirt, trowsers, and mantle about them; their faces are painted a copper colour, and their heads are adorned with shells, feathers, ear-rings, and other trifling ornaments. They neither can speak to be understood,

and very unfortunately their interpreter died in the passage, which obliges them to make their wishes know by dumb signs. They are shy of company, especially in a crowd, by whom they avoid being seen as much as possible. Their only business over, as far as we can learn is to pay their respects to the King of Great Britain, for whom they express the greatest veneration. (*Lloyd's Evening Post and British Chronicle* 10, no. 771 [June 21–23, 1762] and *St. James Chronicle*, June 19, 1762) (K)

167. June 18, 1762. (K)

168. Timberlake seems to imply they hired two chaises, one for the Cherokees and one for Blake, Sumter, and himself. (K)

169. On the morning of June 19, Blake went to Lord Egremont's house. Lord Egremont was Charles Wyndham (1710–August 21, 1763), who succeeded his uncle, Algernon Seymour, 7th Duke of Somerset, as the 2nd Earl of Egremont in 1750. Wyndham was a member of Parliament from 1734–1750, and in October 1761 he was appointed Secretary of State for the Southern Department in succession to William Pitt. He worked closely with his brother-in-law, George Grenville, during his time in office, which was mainly focused on the declaration of war with Spain and the negotiations for with peace with France and Spain. He was also involved in the proceedings against John Wilkes. Horace Walpole was among his detractors. (K)

170. Although Fauquier's letters of introduction (except for Timberlake's letter of introduction), which were written on May 1, were undoubtedly delivered by Blake during their first meeting on June 18, Egremont did not acknowledge receipt of them until July 10, 1762. On that date, he wrote to Fauquier from Whitehall that Captain Blake had delivered Fauquier's letters and the three Cherokees, but their visit was causing problems because their interpreter had died and a replacement had not been found. C.O. 5/1345, fol. 9, Virginia, Secretary of State: Original Correspondence, 1762–1767, 4 pages. (K)

171. The Cherokees must have been impressed with the Egremont house at No. 94 Piccadilly. It was designed by Matthew Bettingham, and Lord Egremont was its first resident in 1760. Egremont set a new fashion for living in the western section of Piccadilly. Egremont lived there until his death in 1763. A later resident was Lord Palmerston. Until recently it was occupied as the Naval and Military Club and popularly known as the In and Out Club from the signs on the gate posts. Today, it is one of the last surviving mansions on Piccadilly. (K)

172. Here Timberlake gives a subtle clue as to the identity of Caccanthropos, in the first letter of his first name, N. Caccanthropos was Nathan Carrington, a Royal Messenger in Ordinary. (K)

173. "*A House is taken for them in Suffolk Street, and cloaths given them in the English fashion.*" *Gentleman's Magazine*, Monday, June 21, 1762. A similar report was published by the *London Chronicle*, June 24, 1762, p. 597, but adding: "*They are to be clothed in Scarlet.*" The Quin House on Great Suffolk Street was a short carriage ride from the Egremont house in Piccadilly. (K)

174. "*On Monday, June 21st, About 7 o'clock in the evening, the King of the Cherokees, his son-in-law, & one of his chiefs waited upon Lord Egremont.*" *Lloyd's London Evening Post*, June 21–23, 1762. *Editorial note*: This is the only reference to any member

of the delegation being Ostenaco's son-in-law. Was this a reference to one of the other Cherokees or an admission by Ostenaco or Timberlake that the latter had made a commitment to Ostenaco's daughter Sekinny?

Egremont was among the first to use the visiting delegation for show. After dinner at Egremont House on Monday, June 21, he invited his sister, her husband George Grenville, and Lord and Lady Aylesford to visit the Cherokees in their house at Suffolk Street. John Oliphant, "Lord Egremont and the Indians: Official, Educated and Popular Reactions to the Cherokees in London," in Anne F. Rogers and Barbara R. Duncan (eds.), *Culture, Crisis and Conflict* (Cherokee, N.C.: Museum of the Cherokee Indian Press, 2007); see also John Oliphant, "The Cherokee Embassy to London, 1762," *Journal of Imperial and Commonwealth History* 27, no. 1 (January 1999): 1–26. (K)

175. This is the letter written by Lt. Governor Fauquier on May 1, in which Timberlake is credited with opening a new route to the Cherokee country. C.O. 5/1345, fol. 1, Virginia, Secretary of State: Original Correspondence, 1762–1767, 3 pages. (K)

176. Although the first "cloaths" that were ordered were in the English fashion, Timberlake may have soon realized that dressing like Indians made them more conspicuous and more of a curiosity. By the end of June they were sitting for two of the leading portrait painters in the country. Sir Joshua Reynolds, in his small pocket diary, recorded the names of his sitters for the month of June. He listed "The King of the Cherokees" with eight prominent Englishman as sitters. Algernon Graves and William Vine Cronin, *A History of the Works of Sir Joshua Reynolds*, P.R.A., vol. 4, 1533.

The British Chronicle (June 30–July 2, 1762) reported on June 29:

One of the Cherokee Chiefs sat for his picture to Mr. [Francis] Parsons in Queens Square. He expressed much pleasure to the interpreter on the occasion, saying, "His friends would now have something to remember when he is gone to fight the French." . . . a throng of ladies coming out of Mr. Parsons' room from seeing the pictures of the Cherokee Chief, one of them had the misfortune to fall down the Stairs and dislocate her knee; two surgeons were sent for, and she was carried home in a [sedan] Chair.

See also Carolyn Foreman, *Indians Abroad 1493–1938* (Norman: University of Oklahoma Press, 1943), 70.

Reynolds's appointment book indicates a single appointment with the King of the Cherokees on July 1, 1762 (at 9:00 A.M.) and one with *"Miss Cherocke on 5 July (at two)."* Grieg, *The Diaries of a Duchess* (London: Hodder and Stoughton, 1926), 47. In 1758, Reynolds raised his prices to twenty, forty, and eighty guineas for head, half length, and full length portraits. In 1762, he was making six thousand pounds a year, perhaps the highest-paid artist in England. The portrait of Ostenaco should have cost forty guineas. The government only gave the Cherokees a guinea a day to cover their expenses. Who had the money to commission it? Probably not the king, who purchased Buckingham House (later Palace) for £28,000 in 1762. Perhaps Lord Ergemont, perhaps Lord Eglinton, or perhaps the artists painted the portraits without commissions for the publicity which the London papers readily provided.

Two newspapers reported that *"the Cherokee Chiefs are sitting for their pic-*

tures to Mr. [afterward Sir Joshua] Reynolds." St. James Chronicle, July 3, 1762, and *Lloyd's Evening Post* (no. 777), 17: July 5–7, 1762. A separate portrait was made of Ostenaco from which was made an illustration for the *Royal Magazine* (London) of July 1762. (K)

The portrait of Ostenaco by Reynolds and the portrait of Cunne Shote (Stalking Turkey) by Francis Parsons are now at the Gilgrease Museum in Tulsa, Oklahoma. The portrait of Stalking Turkey shows what appears to be a slit in a stretched left earlobe and tattooing on the neck. He is also shown wearing a GR III military gorget and strands of black trade beads. He is wearing a white lace shirt and a scarlet mantle with black and gold trim draped over his left shoulder. He is also wearing silver arm and wrist bands and holds a knife is ready position in his right hand. Two medallions are suspended just below the shirt collar.

The detail of the painting is sufficient to identify the medallions. The first is a wedding medallion by J. Kirk. The obverse shows the conjoined busts of George III and Queen Charlotte facing right. He, laureate, hair long tied behind, in armor with lion's head on breast, mantle fastened on shoulder with brooch; she, hair in diadem and drapery fastened in front with brooch; GEORGE III & CHARLOTTE KING & QUEEN. On the reverse is Eros, Roman god of love, who stands fanning the flames of two hearts burning on an altar. THE FELICITY OF BRITAIN. In exergue: MARRIED SEPT. THE / VIII MDCCLXI. See Laurence Brown, *Catalogue of British Historical Medals, 1760–1960*, vol. 1 (Ringwood, Hampshire, UK: Seaby Publications Ltd., 1980), 5.

The second medal worn by Cunne Shote is the proclamation medal of King George III. It is also by the royal engraver J. Kirk. The obverse is the draped bust of George III with long hair tied in queue. GEORGIVS.III.REX. The reverse has a heart in the center of a wreath of laurel and oak on a plinth inscribed BORN MAY 24 / 1738 / PROCLAIMED / OCT^r 26. 1760. The patriotic legend around the medallion reads: ENTIRELY BRITISH. See Brown, *Catalogue*, 4.

The painting of Ostenaco by Reynolds may show the same medal, only with obverse side out. (K)

177. Although Timberlake was not aware of it, the king was actually sick. On June 9, George III had developed an early but disabling attack of porphyria and did not resume normal duties until the end of June. Oliphant, "Lord Egremont and the Indians." (K)

178. To divert them while waiting for an audience with the king, Timberlake took them out on the town. Their first public appearance was June 23 in Kensington Gardens. At that time they were *"all dressed in English Fashion and seemed highly delighted with the Place."* Two days later they visited Westminster Abbey. Two English officers who had seen service in America and learned something of their language accompanied them to aid as interpreters. Sir Alexander Cuming, who accompanied the Cherokee delegation in 1730 and was imprisoned upon his arrival for his participation in a stock fraud scam in Charleston, was reported to have begun *"reviewing his manuscripts of the Cherokee Language in order to enable him to converse with the Indian Chief."* St. James Chronicle, June 26 and July 1, 1762.

The *South Carolina Gazette*, October 2, 1762, reported that after walking for some time in Kensington Gardens on June 26, they dined with Governor Ellis. (K)

179. Their audience with King George III was held in the Drawing Room of St. James's Palace on July 8, 1762, and was widely covered in the press. In the *Annual Register . . . for the Year 1762*, vol. 5, 92–93, is the account:

> *Three Cherokee Chiefs, lately arrived from South Carolina in order to settle a lasting peace with the English, had their first audience with his majesty. The head chief is called Outacite or Mankiller, on account of his many gallant actions, was introduced by Ld. Eglinton, and conducted by Sir Clement Cotterell, master of ceremonies. They were upwards of an hour and a half with majesty, who received them with great goodness, and they behaved in his presence with remarkable decency and mildness. The man who assisted as interpreter on this occasion, instead of the one who set out with them, but died in passage, was so confused that the king could ask but few questions.*

Monthly Chronicle, July 8, 1762, reported:

> *Ostenaco dressed for the occasion in a mantle of rich blue covered with lace. On his breast he wore a silver gorget-engraved with His Majesty's arms. The other two Cherokees wore scarlet richly adorned with gold lace, and gorgets of plate on their breasts . . .*

Gazetteer or London Daily Advertiser, July 9, 1762:

> *The Cherokees came from their Audience of the King highly pleased with His Majesty's gracious Manner of treating them, and talked earnest to each when they came out of the Presence Chamber; and the King seems very proud of his Gorget or Breast Plate, which is very handsome.*
>
> *They spent more than an hour and a half with his Majesty. . . . They were received by his Majesty and their Behavior was remarkably humble and meek. . . . There seemed to be a Mixture of Majesty and Moroseness in their Countenances. . . . The man who assisted as Interpreter was so much confused that he [the King] could ask but few Questions.*

Public Advertiser, July 10, 1762:

> *The Cherokees came from their audience of the King highly pleased with His Majesty's gracious manner of treating them, and talked earnest to each when they came out of the Presence Chamber; and the King seems proud of his Gorget or Breast Plate, which is very handsome.* (K)

180. It is apparent from the newspaper reports that the reason Timberlake was asked few questions during the hour and a half meeting was that "*the man who assisted as Interpreter was so much confused that he [the King] could ask but few Questions.*" *Public Advertiser*, July 10, 1762. (K)

181. The Duchess of Northumberland in her diary wrote on August 8, 1762:

> *The Chief (Ostenaco) had the Tail of a Comet revers'd painted in blue on his forehead, his Left Cheek black & His Left Eyelid Scarlet his Rt Eyelid Black and his Right Cheek Scarlet, all of his teeth were cut through like Rings, He had a Blue Cloth Mantle laced with Gold & a silver Gorget. The second had nothing particular except his Eyelids were painted Scarlet, the 3d had painted in Blue*

on his cheeks a large pair of wings which had an odd Effect as he look'd directly
as if his Nose & Eyes were flying away. The last two were in Scarlet with Silver
Gorgets. (Grieg, *The Diaries of a Duchess*, 47; also see Oliphant, "Lord
Egremont and the Indians") (K)

182. Oliver Goldsmith, the noted writer and poet, was among those who called
on the Cherokees at their Suffolk Street Residence. Goldsmith waited in the
crowd for three hours while Ostenaco prepared himself to receive guests.
When the poet was admitted he gave Ostenaco a present, which was acknowledged by an embrace from the chief, leaving Goldsmith's face well bedaubed
with vermillion. Goldsmith emerged on the street, his face smeared with vermillion, much to the amusement of the awaiting crowd. Goldsmith concluded
from this encounter that vanity of dress was a fundamental weakness of mankind, not a folly of modern civilization. Oliver Goldsmith, *An History of the
World and Animated Nature*, vol. 2 (London: J. Nourse, 1774), 97–98; Foreman, *Indians Abroad*, 71, 76–77. (K)

183. On Wednesday, June 30, the Cherokee chiefs went to the Tower of London
to see the curiosities there (including the zoo and the royal jewels). *London
Chronicle*, Saturday, July 3, 1762. On July 1, 1762, they went to St. Paul's and
were impressed with the magnificence of the structure and greatly admired
the "golden gallery." From there they went on to both houses of Parliament
and from there to Westminster Abbey. *Gazette of London Daily Advertiser*,
July 8, 1762, and the *St James Chronicle*, July 3–6, 1762. (K)

184. "*This evening the King of the Cherokees, with the two chiefs, will be at Sadler's
Wells.*" "*This evening at Sadler's Wells (musical entertainment: musical glasses by
Miss Wilkinson), the whole to be concluded with a new entertainment of music and
dancing called the Harlequin Quack or the Modes of the Moderns, starting at 6:00
p.m. doors open at 5:00 p.m.*" *Public Advertiser,* July 2, 1762.

On Saturday, July 24, "*The Cherokees will return to Sadler's Wells at 5:00 p.m.
for a variety programme of music, song dance, and gymnastics.*" *Public Advertiser,*
July 24, 1762. On Friday, July 30, the *Public Advertiser* announced: "*This Evening, the king of the Cherokees and the two Chiefs will be at Sadler's Wells.*" It was
later reported that on August 11, Wednesday evening: "*The Cherokee King and
one of his chiefs, accompanied by Capt. Timberlake, were again at Sadler's Wells, the
diversion of the place they seemed always highly delighted with, particularly with the
agility of Mr. Matthews, the wire dancer, whom they are so very fond of, that they
expressed a great liking to have him accompany them home.*" *Lloyd's Evening Post*,
August 11–13, 1762. (K)

185. "*On Saturday night, [July 3] The Cherokees were at Sadler's Wells and expressed
great satisfaction with the entertainment of that place.*" *Lloyd's London Evening
Post*, July 2–5, 1762. "*The gentleman who accompanied them [obviously Timberlake]
said that they would frequently come there.*" *London Evening Post*, July 3–6, 1762.
The Cherokees were at Sadler's Wells on July 2, 3, 24, and 30, and August 11.
(K)

186. On Monday, July 5, with no fewer than three officers (including Timberlake
and Sumter), they went to Ranelagh gardens, where the Cherokees compared
the rotunda to the Townhouse at Chota. *Gazette or London Daily Advertiser*,
8 July 1762. (K)

187. The Ranelagh rotunda was larger, almost 150 feet in diameter. The Chota townhouse was about half that size. This is the only recorded architectural comparison the Cherokees made while in London. (K)

188. The *London Chronicle*, July 6, 1762, p. 22, reported: "*When the Cherokees were at Vauxhall last week they had very sumptuous entertainment.*" "*The Wines first set before them were Burgundy and Claret, which however, they did not seem greatly to relish. Others were then placed on the Table, when they fixed upon Frontiniac, the sweetness of which highly hit their Palates, and they drank of it very freely.*" (K)

189. In spite of Timberlake's protests, he apparently accompanied the Cherokees to Vauxhall on at least six occasions. In addition to their visit the week before July 6, they returned to Vauxhall on July 9, 16, 21, 23, and 29. (K)

   In early July, the press endorsed the entertainment schedule of the Cherokees: "*To tie the knot of amity still further the Cherokee Chief now in London was brought over. We approve of his being carried to places of diversion such as Vauxhall, Sadlers-Wells, etc. and to Westminster-Abby, St. Paul's and the Tower of London.*" *British Chronicle*, July 7–9, 1762.

   Jackson's Oxford Journal, July 10, 1762, approved of the diversions offered the Cherokees but questioned the priorities in hosting the Cherokee guests, stating that to show "*a proper idea of the King's Grandeur, the Gentlemen Pensioners, the yeomen of the Guard and the Life Guards*" should "*at one time be drawn up in View . . . Should not their Chief be carefully instructed in the Principals of the Christian religion? Should not he and his attendants have been taken frequently to our Cathedrals, to hear the grand Service there?*" By late July the novelty of their visit had worn off and instead of endorsements, there were calls for their safe passage home. (K)

190. On July 9, they were back "*at Vauxhall Gardens—greatly pleased with the entertainment and beauty of the place. They shook hands with hundreds of gentlemen who crowded to see them.*" *South Carolina Gazette*, October 2, 1762. (K)

   On Friday, July 16, 1762, and Wednesday, July 21, the *Public Advertiser* (no. 8642) announced: "*The Cherokees will be at Vauxhall this evening.*" The *Daily Advertiser* alerted the public on Friday, July 23, 1762: "*The King of the Cherokees, and his two chiefs, will be this Evening at Vauxhall Gardens.*" (K)

191. In particular, the most embarrassing incident occurred on July 29, 1762, which appears to have been their farewell party at Vauxhall. The day of the event, it was announced that "*the King of the Cherokees with the two chiefs will be at Vauxhall Gardens this Evening for the last Time, they will be leaving England in a Day or two.*" *Public Advertiser*, July 29, 1762.

   At Vauxhall, on Thursday last [July 29, 1762] it is supposed that not less than ten thousand persons crowded thither to obtain a sight of these Indians. At the same time a songstress of the Grove attempted the honor of traversing the walks with the swarthy monarch dangling on her arm; but the press was so much as to oblige him to retire, with his chief (and many ladies of the town) into the orchestra, where they entertained themselves and the gaping multitude, by sounding the keys of the organ, scraping upon the strings of the violin, clapping their hands in return for the claps of applause bestowed upon them, and swallowing by wholesale, bumpers of frontiniac.

   Between two and three in the morning their Cherokeeships began to think of departing and being duly supported, made shift to reach their coach for that purpose. The chief, who was in the best plight stepped in first, with his friend; but the garment of his Majesty unluckily falling foul of a gentleman's sword hilt, in the crowd, a sort of scuffle mistakenly ensued, the sword by some accident was drawn and broke, and the Indian's hands in pretty bloody condition, were exposed to the spectators with much seeming remonstrance and complaint. He then threw himself into a fit of sullenness or intoxication, or both, on the ground, and obstinately remained there for a considerable time. Force, however, effected what persuasion could not, for he was, neck and heels lifted in, and laid a long the bottom of the coach. Soon after his legs, which had obstructed the shutting of the door, being carefully packed up with the rest, the coachman, by driving away put an end to this wretched scene of British curiosity and savage debauchery. Lloyd's Evening Post, July 30–August 2, 1762. (K)

192. Although Timberlake says that the irregularities were committed by one of the younger Cherokees, at the time of the event, he admitted that two of the Indians were involved. The allegations seemed so scandalous that Timberlake felt compelled to write to the *Public Advertiser* to refute the charges that Ostenaco was seen cavorting with a songstress of the Grove or was even at Vauxhall the night in question. He reported: *"It is true that two of the chiefs were [there], and intoxicated; the Reason of which was, the ungovernable curiosity of the People, who would force upon them, and oblige them to drink; and for the future, I shall take particular Care to confute as unjust Paragraphs I may hereafter meet with in any of the Papers."* Timberlake to the Printer, Suffolk Street, *Public Advertiser,* Wednesday, August 4–Saturday, August 7, 1762. (K)

193. Although not mentioned in the memoirs, another favorite of the Cherokees in London was the Star and Garter in Chelsea. The *Public Advertiser* recorded five visits by the Cherokees to this establishment during the month of July: July 8, 10, 12, 14, and 17. The *Public Advertiser* announced (no. 8632) on Monday, July 5, that *"Mr. Johnson will perform feats of horsemanship for the Cherokees at the Star and Garter in Chelsea on July 8."* The paper also provided a note on the status of the Cherokee chief among his people. Again on Saturday, July 10, the *Public Advertiser* (no. 8638) announced: *"Mr. Johnson will perform his horsemanship for the Cherokee King and his two Chiefs at the Star and Garter to-night. Admission price was one shilling."* For Monday, July 12 (no. 8639), *"Mr. Johnson thanks the nobility and gentry for approbation in presence of Cherokee Chiefs on Saturday, will perform for a few days more at the Star and Garter."* The paper (no. 8641) advertised on Wednesday, July 1, *"Mr. Johnson's Performance on Saturday last proved so entertaining to the King and Chiefs of the Cherokees, that they have signified their Intention to see him perform again This Evening at Nine o'Clock, at the Star and Garter at Chelsea; and it is humbly hoped by Mr. Johnson that the Company will suffer no dogs to follow them upon the Ground."* Finally, on July 17 (no. 8643), *"the Star and Garter, the End of the Five-Fields Row, Chelsea, This Day, the 17th of July Instant, Mr. Carlo Genovini, the Italian artificier, from Rome, in Honour of the last Victory gained by the Forces of His Majesty over the French Army in Germany, will exhibit A Decorated Grand Fire Work with several large new pieces, not yet exhibited there. By Desire of the Cherokee King and his Chiefs. (Description of fireworks follows). To begin at 9 and lasts til 10."* (K)

194. Mr. Henry Baldwin wrote a letter to the printer of the *St. James Chronicle*:

> *I hope it will not be thought crimen laesae majestates, or High Treason in me to censure the behaviour of his Cherokee Majesty, and to say that such Practices as he was guilty of in this Nation would have been subjected him to be deposed in his own country. . . . Could are newspapers be translated . . . and could the Cherokee read, what must they think of their great Warrior, when they are told, that he spent Time in England getting Drunk at one Place, picking up common Squaws at another, and making himself Ridiculous and Contemptible wherever he went?*
>
> *And they must look upon the English People as a Pack of Idiots, Beats and Barbarians, when the King shall relate . . . he was exposed to publick View as a Monster? The Indian was brought over to give him an idea of Great Britain, but what could he gather from Sadler's Wells . . . or . . . Vauxhall, but that Squaws were tempting . . . May it not . . . conjectured, that this strange Sight was exhibited . . . to divert our Attention from the present political Squabble?*

The writer commented that puppeteers had made Punch over into a Cherokee. The letter was signed *"I am your humble Servant, You Know who."* See Foreman, *Indians Abroad*, 80–81. (K)

195. Other advertised visits by the Cherokees that seemed to have the sole purpose of attracting customers include the following:

Sunday, July 11, 1762

> The *Daily Advertiser*, July 12, 1762, says: *"on Friday last the Cherokee king and his two chiefs were so greatly pleased with the curiosities of the Dwarf's Tavern, in Chelsea Fields, that they were again there on Sunday, (7/11/62) at seven in the evening, to drink tea, and will be there again in a few days."* The Dwarf's Tavern was kept by John Coan, a diminutive person from Norfolk. The reputation of the tavern was brief, as the "unparalleled Coan," as he was styled, died in early 1764.

Saturday, July 17, 1762

> The concourse of people at the White Conduit House to see the Cherokee king and one of his chiefs, (the other one being indisposed) on Saturday afternoon last (7/17/62) was inconceivable; and during the time they were there a prodigious number of watches, etc. were stolen. See Draper Mss., 2VV, 140; *Lloyd's Evening Post*, Friday, July 16, and Monday July 19, 1762.

Saturday July 17, 1762

> The *Public Advertiser* (no. 8643) noted: *On Tuesday next by Desire of the Cherokee King and Chiefs the 31st performance of Mr. Foote's Oratorical Course preceded by the Minor. Doors open at Six to begin at Seven.*

Other advertisements in the *Public Advertiser* include:

Friday, July 16, 1762

> *On Tuesday next (July 20) by Desire of the Cherokee King and Chiefs the 31st performance of Mr. Foote's Oratorical Course preceded by the Minor. Doors open at Six to begin at Seven.* The Indians will parade *"upon the Green for a sufficient Time to satisfy the Curiosity of the Public, in hopes that they may receive the like Politeness from the Populace, in their Retirement to the Apartment appointed for Them."*

No. 8645 Tuesday, July 20, 1762

At the Haymarket Theatre, This Day by Desire of the Cherokee King and Chiefs the 31st performance of Mr. Foote's Oratorical-Course preceded by the Minor. Doors open at Six to begin at Seven.

No. 8649 Friday, July 23, 1762

This Day, the King of the Cherokees, and his two chiefs, will go to see the Curiosities at the Dwarf's Tavern, Chelsea Fields, where they will likewise dine and drink Tea. Tickets at 1 S. each, will be taken in the Reckoning, either for Wine, Punch, Tea, &c. The Tea this Day will be 1S. a Head, which will be an excellent Sort on purpose. Dinner will be upon the Table at Three o'Clock.

No. 8651 Monday, July 26, 1762

NEWS: *The Cherokee King and the two chiefs will dine and drink Tea at Marybone Gardens on Thursday next. A Grand Box is intended to be fitted up for their Reception.*

We hear the Cherokee King and the Chiefs are advised to drink the Waters at Bagnigge, and To-morrow they go to taste them, and breakfast there.

Bagnigge Wells was in Clerkenwell straddling the Fleet, a tributary of the Thames. As a spa, the Bagnigge Wells were opened to the public about 1760. There were two wells, each twenty feet in depth; the water was brought from them to one point and then drawn from two pumps. These were enclosed in a small architectural feature called the "Temple," which was a circular colonnade covered by a roof. One well was chalybeate, located at the back of the house, and was about two yards in diameter. The water was said to be especially clear. The second well was located forty yards north of the first, and was reported to contain cathartic properties. At the time of the Cherokee visit, Bagnigge Wells was a fashionable meeting place with a bowling green and skittle alley. Tea and ale was served to patrons. It was the subject of much satire, including a humorous song, "Bagnigge Wells," by W. Woty (1760), which begins with the lines,

Wells and the place I sing, at early dawn
Frequented oft, where male and female meet
and strive to drink a long adieu to pain . . .

Bagnigge's popularity declined in the early nineteenth century and was almost in ruin by 1842.

No. 8653 Wednesday, July 28, 1762

AD: *By Authority for the entertainment of the Cherokee King and Chiefs at the New Threatre in the Haymarket this day July 28 will be performed a Scots Musical Pastoral call THE GENTLE SHEPHERD Doors open at Six and begin at Seven. Care will be taken to keep the house cool.*

The play was followed by dancing as will be express'd om the Day's Bill,' would be performed that evening For the Entertainment of THE CHEROKEE KINGS AND CHIEFS' the price was five shillings for a box, the pit was three and the gallery was two shillings.

No. 8654 Thursday, July 29, 1762

AD: *Marybone Gardens. The Cherokee King and the two Chiefs will dine in public This day, at Three O'Clock, where a grand open Box is prepared for their reception. To prevent improper Company, each Person to Pay 6d. Admittance. Tea, Coffee, Cakes, Wine, &c. at the usual Price.*

No. 8655 Friday, July 30, 1762
AD: *Armonica, To-morrow at Twelve o'Clock in the Forenoon, the Cherokee King and the two chiefs will be at the Great Room in Spring Gardens, to hear Miss Davies perform on the Armonica, and sing several favourite songs, particularly some out of the Opera of Artaxerxes. She is likewise to play on the German Flute and Harpsciord. This is the last public entertainment in London, at which the Cherokee King and Chiefs will be present.*

No. 8656 Saturday, July 31, 1762
AD: *Armonica, This day at Twelve o'Clock in the Forenoon, the Cherokee King and the two chiefs will be at the Great Room in Spring Gardens, to hear Miss Davies perform on the Armonica, and sing several favourite songs, particularly some out of the Opera of Artaxerxes. She is likewise to play on the Gernman Flute and Harpsichord, accompanied occasionally by Mr. Davies. This is the last public entertainment in London, at which the Cherokee King and Chiefs will be present. (K)*

196. The Cherokees did dine with nobility on occasion. In addition to dinner at Egremont on June 21, and dinner with Governor Ellis on June 23, the Cherokees also dined at the Mansion on June 15. "*The Cherokee Chiefs have been invited by the Lord Mayor to the Mansion House and are soon to go there.*" London Chronicle, Thursday, July 15, 1762, p. 49.

Friday, July 16, 1762
Yesterday at 1 o'clock the Cherokee chief and one of his Chiefs with the interpreter went to the Mansion House where they spent three quarters of a hour viewing the several apartments in one of which was a table set with wines, sweet meats and fruits; and after refreshing themselves, they departed highly pleased with the building and their entertainment. The other chief was indisposed that he could not be there. The Lord Mayor it being sessions time, was at the Old Bailey. London Chronicle, Friday, July 16, 1762, p. 61. "*They seem greatly pleased with the number of ladies and gentlemen who crowded the Windows to see them pass.*" London Evening Post, July 15–17, 1762.

Tuesday, July 27, 1762
This day the Cherokee Chief and his two chiefs were to dine with the Earl of Macclesfield at Twickenham. South Carolina Gazette, October 2, 1762. (K)

197. Timberlake's reference to the disparity in age provides another subtle clue to the man he calls Caccanthropos. Nathan Carrington, the prime suspect, had been in the king's service as a Messenger in Ordinary since at least 1729. He would have been at least in his fifties at the time of this confrontation. Timberlake, on other hand, was about twenty-six years old. (K)

198. This was probably one of two women named Lady Letitia Trelawney living in London at the time. The first Letitia was recently widowed. Her husband was Sir Harry Trelawny (February 15, 1687–April 7, 1762), the 5th Baronet.

She died on May 28, 1775, and was buried June 6, in Egg Buckland, Devon, England. The second Letitia Trelawny was christened June 16, 1728, in St. Burdeaux, Cornwall. She was married to Sir William Trelawny, the 6th Baronet and son of Captain William Trelawny, R.A. Letitia Trelawny died on August 24, 1772, and her husband died December 11, 1772, in Jamaica, where he served as governor. (K)

199. A portrait of Ostenaco that appeared in the *British Magazine* in July 1762 was reported to be drawn from life at the Cherokee King's palace on Suffolk Street. Although it was not a palace, it was the Quin home rented for the Cherokees. Suffolk Street is only about two blocks in length. The building facades have much the same appearance today that they did in the eighteenth century. The Quins may have been related to James Quin, the Irish-born actor who claimed credit, as the elocution instructor for the young prince, for teaching King George III to speak. James Quin retired from acting in 1757. (K)

200. Mr. Edward Montague, the agent from Virginia, took the Cherokees on a tour of the lower Thames about July 22, 1762, to impress the Cherokees with the military might of Great Britain. "*In their passage to Woolwich, in the admiralty-barge, they were much surprised at the number of ships in the river, as well as at the vast quantity of cannon, bombs, and bullets, &c. in Woolwich-warren.*" *British Magazine*, vol. 3 (July 1762), p. 378.

201. Robert Wood served as an assistant to Lord Egremont, with the title of Under Secretary of State. (K)

202. Almost a decade and a half after Sir Joshua Reynolds painted a portrait of a Cherokee, he made the following observation in his *Maxims of Art: Seventh Discourse* in 1776:

> I have mentioned taste in dress, which is certainly one of the lowest subjects to which this word is applied; yet, as I have before observed, there is a right even here, however narrow its foundation, respecting the fashion of any particular nation. But we have still more slender means of determining, to which of the different customs of different ages or countries we ought to give the preference, since they seem to be all equally removed from nature. In an European, when he has cut off his beard, and put false hair on his head, or bound his own natural hair in regular hard knots, as unlike nature as he can possibly make it; and after having rendered them immovable by the fat of hogs, has covered the whole with flour, laid on by a machine with the utmost regularity; if when thus attired, he issues forth, and meets a Cherokee Indian, who has bestowed as much time at his toilet, and laid on with equal care and attention his yellow and red oker on particular parts of his forehead and cheeks, as he judges most becoming; whoever of these two despises the other for this attention to the fashion of his country, whichever first feels himself provoked to laugh, is the barbarian. (K)

203. Londoners could not get enough of the Cherokees even after they left. In November 1762, a new pantomime play called *The Witches, or Harlequin Cherokee* was performed at the Theatre Royal in Drury Lane. The opening review was over two quarto columns, and concludes with the statement:

> To attempt an enumeration of every scene and action would be unnecessary as it would be only recounting the particular escapes and surprises, which Harlequin and Columbine are, as usual in pantomines, exposed to. After a variety of them,

in the course of which a great deal of machinery is exhibited, it concluded with a view of the sea at a distance. A great number of Cherokees, both male and female now enter, dressed in the habit of that country, preparing with great joy to receive the three chiefs who had been in England, and who land from a large vessel, attended by several English sailors, and decorated with gorgets, bracelets, etc. wherewith those chiefs were presented while in this country, and the piece ends with a complicated dance of the English sailors and the Cherokees. Evening Post, November 26–29, 1762. (See also note 231) (K)

204. Wax figures of the Cherokees for a life-size diorama were also created. In a traveler's guide entitled *A Companion to Every Place of Curiosity and Entertainment in and about London and Westminster* is a description of "Salmon's Royal Wax Works, near Temple Bar." An exhibit, "The Cherokee king, with his two chiefs," is listed in the first edition of this text, which was printed in 1767 and is still listed in the 8th edition published in 1797. (This source was called to my attention by Ian Chambers, Department of History, University of California, Riverside, and Barbara Duncan, Museum of the Cherokee Indian, Cherokee, N.C.) (K)

205. Lord C-t-f-d was undoubtedly Lord Chesterfield—Philip Stanhope, 4th Earl of Chesterfield (September 22, 1694–24 March 24, 1773). He was a British statesman and man of letters. In 1762, he lived at the Ranger's House, Chesterfield Walk, Greenwich, London. A Whig, Lord Stanhope, as he was known until 1726, was born in London and educated at Cambridge. In 1715 he entered the House of Commons as Lord Stanhope of Shelford and member for St. Germans.

In 1726 his father died, and Lord Stanhope became Earl of Chesterfield. He took his seat in the House of Lords, and his oratory, which had been ineffective in the Commons, was suddenly appreciated. In 1728 Chesterfield was sent to The Hague as ambassador. In 1732 a liaison with a certain Mlle. du Bouchet of Flanders resulted in the birth of an illegitmate son, Philip Stanhope, for whom he provided advice and instruction at Westminster School in the famous *Letters*. He negotiated the second Treaty of Vienna in 1731, and in the next year, his health and fortune damaged, he resigned as ambassador and returned to Britain. A few months' rest enabled him to resume his seat in the House of Lords, of which he was one of the acknowledged leaders.

In 1768 Philip Stanhope, his son, died. The constant care bestowed by his father on his education resulted in an honorable but not particularly distinguished career for young Stanhope. His death was an overwhelming grief to Chesterfield, and the discovery that he had long been married to a lady of humble origin must have been galling in the extreme to his father after his careful instruction in worldly wisdom. Chesterfield, who had no children by his wife, Melusina von der Schulenburg, Countess of Walsingham (an illegitimate daughter of George I by Ehrengard Melusina von der Schulenburg, Duchess of Kendal and Munster), whom he married in 1733, adopted his godson, a distant cousin, also named Philip Stanhope (1755–1815), as heir to the title and estates.

As a politician and statesman, Chesterfield's fame rests on his short but brilliant administration of Ireland. As an author he was a clever essayist and epigrammatist. But he stands or falls by the *Letters to His Son*, first published by Stanhope's widow in 1774, and the *Letters to His Godson* (1890). The *Letters* are brilliantly written, full of elegant wisdom, keen wit, admirable portrait painting, and exquisite observation and deduction.

Although the collection of 395 letters was private and not intended for publication, the work attained immediate popularity, and it remains an essential literary and historical document of the eighteenth century. See *Letters written by the late Right Honourable Philip Dormer Stanhope, Earl of Chesterfield, to his son, Philip Stanhope . . . together with other several pieces on various subjects. Published by Mrs. Eugenia Stanhope, from the originals in her possession* (London: J. Dodsley, 1774). The first edition includes the engraved bookplates of Richard Hammond. Chesterfield County, Virginia, and Chesterfield County, South Carolina, in the United States were named in his honor. (K)

206. The editor of the *London Chronicle*, July 24–27, 1762, criticizing the spectacle made of the Cherokees, states:

> *These poor creatures make no more than theatrical figures, and can be seen with no satisfaction by a throng: why then are people mad in their avidity to behold them?. . . I doubt nor but they [the Cherokees] think them [the British] stupid and unnatural. The Cherokees in contrast never "throwing down a pipe to run and gaze at any of us."*
>
> Monday, August 2: *The intemperence of his Cherokee Majesty and his chiefs and the selfish views of the proprietors of our public gardens, in the plentifully treating them with strong liquors give occasion to the considerate, sincerely to wish them safely shipped off for their own country.* (K)

207. *"It is said that as order has been seen to prevent the Cherokee King and his chiefs from being taken to any more places of public entertainment, as it has been productive of much rioting and mischief."* London Chronicle, August 6, 1762, p. 130.

"It is said that three men personating the Cherokee kings and having their faces painted like them have been shewn at many of the public places for the real Indians." Evening Post, August 4–6, 1762.

The Advertiser published a mock appeal from an innkeeper driven by his overbearing wife to exploit the Cherokees against his will. *"For this reason he exhibited the Indians in a railed of corner of the bar . . . To have a man outside with a constable staff, who is to cry, "Walk in Gentlemen, see'em alive!" To advertise a special beer for the occasion worse than normal and twice the price. He begged the paper to announce to the world it was his wife's fault."* London Daily Advertiser, August 5, 1762.

The *Gazette* even more mockingly printed: *"It is said that the Cherokees King and the chiefs will be present at the next pillory exhibition, as also near Newgate at the very next execution, then see the mob throw dogs and cats at each other, till the criminals make their appearance, and then attend them to Tyburn to see whether they die game, and afterwards the battle of the mob [to determine] who shall have the body, in order to form an idea of European savages as well as his own."* Gazette, 5 August 5, 1762.

"On Friday (August 6) their baggage was sent away for Portsmouth, and they will set out on their return home." Lloyd Evening Post, Friday, August 6–Monday, August 9, 1762.

"Blake will be ordered to return the Cherokee chiefs to Virginia." C.O. 1/47, ADM 2/721, fol. 215, Secretary of the Admiralty's Common Letters 1762, August 6, 1762, Lords of the Admiralty to Capt Blake, 1 page. (K)

208. "Introduced by Lord Eglinton, and conducted by Sir Clement Cottrell, master of ceremonies, they were upward of an hour and a half with his Majesty. The dress of Ostenaco was a very rich blue mantle covered with lace; on his breast a silver gorget with his Majesty's arms engraved. The other two Indians were in scarlet richly adorned with gold lace, and gorgets of plate on their breasts. 'They were received by his Majesty and their Behavior was remarkably humble and meek . . . There seemed to be a Mixture of Majesty and Moroseness in their Countenances . . . The man who assisted as Interpreter was so much confused that he [King George III] could ask but few Questions.'" Gazetteer and London Daily Advertiser, July 9; Annual Register . . . for the Year 1762, vol. 5, 92.

Williams mistakenly identifies Lord Eglinton as Colonel Montgomery, who led six hundred Highlanders and six hundred Royal Americans against the Cherokees in 1760. Williams, Memoirs, 143. Lord Eglinton was Alexander Montgomerie (February 10, 1723–October 25, 1769), the 10th Earl of Eglinton and older brother of Colonel Archibald Montgomerie (May 18, 1726–October 30, 1796), who became the 11th Earl after the 10th Earl was murdered in 1769. The earl was shot on his own estate near Androssan by the excise officer Mungo Campbel on October 24, 1769, following a dispute about the latter's right to bear arms on the earl's estate. He died from his wounds the following day.

Archibald Montgomery joined the army in 1743 and was a colonel of the 77th Highlanders when he invaded the Cherokee Nation in 1760. He was promoted to major general in 1772, lieutenant general in 1777, and general in 1793. He was elected for two seats in parliament in the 1761 general election. He chose to give up Wigtown Burghs, to sit for Ayrshire. He served in the House of Commons from 1761 to 1768. He died in 1796, and was succeeded by his cousin Hugh, age fifty-seven, as the 12th Earl of Eglinton. At that time Hugh Montgomery moved from the House of Commons to the House of Lords. Hugh Montgomery was a lieutenant in the 77th Highlanders, commanded by his cousin Colonel Archibald Montgomery, during the invasion of the Cherokee Nation in 1760. Twenty years later, he commissioned a portrait of himself by John Singleton Copley. The 1780 portrait shows Montgomery in the uniform of the Argyll Fencibles, the unit in which he served during the American Revolution. The background scene showing British forces overpowering Cherokees perhaps relates to the surprise attack at Little Keowee, in which Cherokee noncombatants were bayoneted to death to prevent disclosure of the army's position before the attempted surprise attack on Estatoe. On June 27, 1760, Montgomery's army suffered heavy losses at the Battle of Cowee Pass, south of present-day Franklin, N.C. Reaching the town of Cowhee that evening, Montgomery suddenly declared his mission complete. He ordered that campfires be left burning at each of the houses while his troops under the cover of darkness retreated toward Charleston. His regiment, the 77th Highlanders, was disbanded in 1763, and officers such as Hugh Montgomery were reduced to half pay. Hugh Montgomery was elected to Parliament from Ayrshire in 1784–89 and again in 1795. He died in 1819. (K)

209. On this occasion Ostenaco wore a silver gorget. The other two wore gorgets of plate. *Gazetteer* and *London Daily Advertiser*, July 9; *Annual Register . . . for the Year 1762*, vol. 5, 92. (K)

210. Ostenaco's speech to King George III that was translated and sent back from Charleston was as follows:

> *Some time ago my nation was in darkness, but that darkness is now cleared up. My people were in great distress, but that is ended. There will be no more bad talks in my nation, but all will be good talks. If any Cherokee shall kill an Englishman, that Cherokee shall be put to death.*
>
> *Our women are bearing children to increase our Nation, and I will order those who are growing up to avoid making war with the English. If any of our head men retain resentment against the English for their relations who have been killed, and if any of them speak a bad word concerning it, I shall deal with them as I see cause. No more disturbance will be heard in my Nation. I speak not with two tongues, and I am ashamed of those who do. I shall tell my people all that I have seen in England.* (K)

211. Timberlake here seems to refer to the first meeting with King George III which took place on July 8. There was a second meeting in which the Cherokees said their farewells to the king. This meeting took place on Friday, August 6. *"Yesterday. The Cherokees were at St. James to take their leave of His Majesty."* London Chronicle, August 7, 1762, and *Lloyd's Evening Post*, August 6–9, 1762.

The queen at the time was only a few days from the delivery of the first child, so she viewed the proceedings from a distance.

> *The Chiefs took leave of the King; the Queen, Princess Augusta* [the King's eldest sister] *and the Prince of Mechlenburg stood at one of the windows fronting the courtyard to see them. The name of the head chief is Outacite, one of the Greatest warriors in the Cherokee Nation. His name signifies 'Mankiller.'* London Magazine August 8, 1762.
>
> [They] *stood in one of the windows, with Sashes up, above Half an Hour, to take a View of them. St. James Chronicle,* August 5–7, 1762.

A week later the Cherokees joined in the public celebration of the royal birth of the prince, who, fifty-eight years later in 1820, would become King George IV.

> *St. James, August 12. The morning at half an hour past 7, the Queen was happily delivered of a Prince. His Royal Highness, the Princess Dowager of Wales, several Lords of his Majesty's Most Honorable Privy Council, and the Ladies of her Majesty's Bed Chamber, being present. London Gazette Extraordinary,* August 12, 1762.
>
> *This great and important news was immediately made known to the town, by the firing of the tower guns; and by the Privy Council, being assembled as soon as possible Thereupon; it was ordered that a form of Thanksgiving for the queen's safe delivery, etc. be prepared etc. Lloyd's Evening Post,* August 11–13, 1762.

> On Thursday Night, [August 12, 1862] The Chief of the Cherokees visited
> the most public streets on this metropolis. He was no stranger to the cause of
> illuminations, bonfires, etc. and testified a great approbation at their appearance,
> and heartily joined with those that cheerfully huzza'd for King George, Queen
> Charlotte, and the new born Prince. Lloyd's Evening Post, August 13–16, 1762.

212. "This Day the Cherokees will go in the Admiralty Barge to Deptford, Greenwich,
and Woolwich, to see the Military Stores, &c. And as there are now six Capital ships
on the Stocks, it must give them a high opinion of our Strength and Grandeur, which
is the rather to be wish'd, as the French and Spaniards had always intimated to them
that we were an inconsiderable People. and unable to protect them in case of War."
Public Advertiser, July 23, 1762.

The tour was sponsored by Edward Montague; the Virginia agent took the
Cherokees on a tour of the lower Thames on an admiralty barge provided by
Lord Halifax. They were entertained at breakfast in the King's Bench Walk
in the Temple by Mr. Montague; they were shown Templar's Church, and
the halls and curiosities of the societies. They inspected the law school at the
Temple, but did not understand the need for lawyers. They went down the
Tower stairs to the river and an admiralty barge, *"to attend and convey them
down the Water: the shipping was an object greatly exceeding their Expectation. First,
they went to Woolwrich and saw many experiments, and were in the utmost astonishment at the vast preparations for War which that Magazine is always furnished
with."* Six capital ships on the stocks impressed the Indians with the strength
of the British navy, *"which is rather to be wish'd, as the French and Spanish had
always intimated to them that we are an inconsiderable People, and unable to protect
them in case of War."* They inspected the ships of the line building at Woolwich, before returning to Greenwich with its grand seventh-century palace,
naval hospital, observatory, and park. After lunch at the Greyhound Inn and a
tour of the grounds of the 174-acre Greenwich Park and the famous observatory, they returned to London by coach. Ostenaco talked into the night about
the wonders he had seen. Oliphant, "Lord Egremont and the Indians."

> When Mr. Montague, conducted the Indians to a parade of the grenadiers,
> they entered the guard room just as the grenadiers in drill were fixing their
> bayonets; the Indians were much agitated, having a suspicion of treachery; and
> were impatient to leave desiring "to see no more of those warriors with capes."
> St. James Chronicle, July 22, 1762.

They also visited the Honourable Artillery Company, dined in the Armory
Room, and saw gunners exercise in Hyde Park. Public Advertiser, August 4,
1762; London Evening Post, July 22–24, 1762. (K)

Edward Montague was one of two agents representing Virginia at the time
Montague represented the House of Burgesses from 1759 to 1770. The other,
Charles Abercrombie, served as agent for the council during the same period.
(K)

213. The decision to return the Cherokees to Charleston instead of Virginia was
made shortly before their departure. On August 9, 1762, Captain Blake was
ordered to return the three chiefs to Virginia. United Kingdom, Public Record Office, ADM. 2/88, fol. 492, Secretary of the Admiralty, Secretary's De-

partment, Out Letters, Orders and Instructions: 1762, 2 pages. On August 20, Captain Blake was ordered by the Lords of the Admiralty to proceed to Charleston, not Virginia. Ibid., fol. 535, 1 page. (K)

214. The *Epreuve* was actually stationed in Savannah, Georgia. (K)

215. In the North Papers in the Oxford Library is an undated (probably August 1762) two-page petition from Henry Timberlake to Earl of Bute, asking for reimbursement for expenses in accompanying three Cherokees to London. See Anderson and Lewis, *A Guide to Cherokee Documents*, 510. (K)

216. Egremont viewed Timberlake's requests for additional funds as unreasonable and bordering on extortion. Charles Bullin replaced Timberlake as an escort for the Cherokee delegation, along with Sumpter. (K)

217. *"On Friday [August 20] The King of the Cherokees and his two chiefs, attended by their interpreter, set out for Portsmouth in a coach and six; as their train were two other officers, who are to proceed with them to America."* (*Evening Post*, August 20–23, 1762)

"The Cherokee chiefs set out for Portsmouth on their return for America. In their way thither they visited Winchester camp, and dined with Lord Bruce at the Wilshire Suttling Booth before attending a play. The next day they were conducted to the French prison, which they viewed with uncommon curiosity, expressing in the strongest terms their detestation of a people, from whom they had received so many instances of the most perfidious and cruel usage. In the afternoon they watched six regiments parade, were shewn the college, and were entertained with fruit and wine by the Warden. The pupils at Winchester college were drawn up in two lines, through which the Indians passed." (*Public Advertiser*, August 20, 1762)

(In the same issue of the *Evening Post*, August 20–23, 1762, was a report: *"Last week Benjamin Franklin, Esq. Postmaster General of North America, set out from his house in Craven Street for Portsmouth, in order to embark for Philadelphia."* History does not record whether Franklin and the Cherokee delegation crossed paths while they were in England.)

"The next morning the Wiltshire Militia diverted them with an infinite variety of firings and evolutions for near two hours, which they beheld with remarkable attention and satisfaction. They then proceeded with Mr. Montagu and their interpreter to Portsmouth, and saw the fortifications, ships, and dockyards there, which struck them with such astonishment as they could not find words to express. Their general observation on being shewn these great objects is: That their English brethren can do everything." (*Gentleman's Magazine*, Friday, August 20, 1762, and *Scots Magazine*, August 1762, p. 44)

"At Portsmouth they were taken to the theater to see the comedy Amphitryon or the Two Sofias, which was attended by a splendid and crowded audience. The next morning they were politely entertained by Mrs. Brett at the Dock-Yard, with a variety of fruits and wines. They boarded the L'Epreuve at 10:00 a.m. in the morning on the 24th. The winds being fair, they sailed immediately." (See Foreman, *Indians Abroad*, 78) (K)

218. At sea on October 14, the *Epreuve* *"Gave Chase and took in Latitude 31 N the schooner Runner belonging to Isaac and Nepthali Hart of Rhode Island with 42 casks and 114 bags of coffee all French Property." South Carolina Gazette*, October 30,

1762. The Cherokees were issued muskets and cartridge pouches and turned out on deck prepared for action. The schooner quietly surrendered. Blake wrote Egremont: "*I suffered the Indians to think she was a Frenchman, & gave them some Tobacco, Cocoa nutts,& other little things as their share.*" C.O. 5/390, fols. 6–7, Blake to Egremont, Charleston, 27 November 1762. (K)

219. Sumter (misspelled as Sumpter by Timberlake) was charged with carrying a letter from Lord Egremont to the governor of South Carolina, in which was expressed concern that the Indians might not have been pleased by the reception accorded them in England: "In case you shall perceive they have been offended or disgusted with anything that may have happened, you will endeavour to remove any ill impression, etc." United Kingdom, Public Record Office, American and West Indies, vol. 77, Colonial Transactions: 236. (K)

220. Although Timberlake may not have gained from the trip to England, Ostenaco did. His standing with colonial officials and within the Cherokee Nation was substantially enhanced.

A Talk between His Excellency, Thomas Boone Esquire, Captain General,
Governor & Commander in Chief of His Majesty's Province of South Carolina
And Judd's Friend, the Headman of the Cherokee Nation
Delivered in the Council Chamber, at Charles Town
Wednesday the 3rd day of November 1762

Governor: *I am extremely glad to see you, Judd's Friend, and your two Warriors who accompanied you to London, safely arrived here. I have been made acquainted with all the notice that has been taken of you in England, and am persuaded you are well satisfied, as indeed you ought to be, with the attention that has been paid to you.*

I am ordered to mention to you that the King was sorry that your Interpreter died on the Passage to England; whereby your words, and your Intention by going thither, could not be so well understood, as if the Interpreter had lived, tho' you have not suffered materially on that account, for upon a supposition that your going to England was in person to confirm the declarations, and promises, which the Nation has made of being hereafter in peace and friendship with the King and his Subjects, it was his Majesty's pleasure that you should be so universally well received, and kindly treated, and upon his suggestion also, he ordered you the valuable and distinguished presents, which I am informed he had given you; But if however, you had anything more particular to say, I am commanded by His Majesty to hear and to faithfully report it: Speak out therefore, freely open your mind, that it may be known what by the death of your Interpreter you were not enabled to communicate.

Judd's Friend: *This day your Excellency and I are met in the Council Chamber, and the Great Being above will hear and bear witness to what I shall say.*

I went from my own Nation to Virginia, but it was not my Intention to stay there; I was desirous of going over the wide water to see the Great King George, and if I was refused a passage from thence, I was resolved to go to New-York and get a passage from thence to England in order to see the great King George.

The Governor of Virginia told me there were many French on the Sea; therefore it was dangerous least I should be taken; but I told him I was not afraid of the

French, and I was determined to go, because I had a strong desire to see the Great King, that I might Talk with him upon what was good for his people and mine, and to prevent any harm happening to either of them for the future. Altho' I met with a good deal of trouble in going over the wide water, yet, that is more than recompensed by the satisfaction I have had in seeing the King, and the kind reception I met with from him, being treated as one of his own Children, and finding the treatment of everyone there good towards me.

And now I am arrived in Charles Town, his Excellency might take it amiss, if I did not make a Talk to you on my return from England, before I leave this place, especially as you desire to hear from my own mouth how I liked England, and what I intended to have said to the Great King, had the Interpreter lived.

The Governor of Virginia procured a place for me in one of the Great King's canoes, in which I crossed [?] the wide water to the Country where my father lives. When I was admitted into his Presence he was glad to see me, and he would not see [say?] what had been amiss [unclear] now relieved between his people and mine; as the Interpreter who went with me died on the Passage, and the person who attended me understood very little of my language, I could not say what I intended, but I had a paper from the Governor of Virginia, which I showed to the Great King, and told him that I was desirous there should be a firm peace and [unclear] between his people and mine for the future. But there being no Interpreter he heard or could understand but a few words of what I said, or had to say. I therefore desire Your Excellency will write to the Great King and tell him this, and when he hears what I intended to have said to him, I hope he will write an Answer, and that your Excellency will send it to me.

Some time ago my Nation was in darkness, but that darkness is now cleared up. And my people were in great Distress, but that is now at an End; and I desire Your Excellency will acquaint the Great King that there will be no more bad Talks in my Nation, but all will be good; and that there will be no more war between the English and my people, and that if any Cherokee shall kill an Englishman, the Cherokee shall be immediately put to Death. Our women are breeding Children Night and Day to increase our People, and I will order those who are growing up to avoid making War with the English. When I return unto my Nation I will inquire if any of the headmen retain a Resentment against the English on account of their Relations which have been killed, and if any of them are found to Speak a bad word concerning it, I will deal with them as I shall see Cause.

I speak not with two Tongues & am ashamed of those who do.

My heart is now set upon going home, and no more disturbances will be heard of in my nation; this is what I intended to have declared to the Great King.

The Head Warrior of the Canoe that brought us over used us exceeding well; he desired us not to be afraid of the French, for he and his Warriors would fight like men and die rather than be taken.

The Number of Warriors and people being all of one Colour which we saw in England, far exceeded what we thought possible could be; and that we might see everything that was strange to use or what we desired to see, the Great King was pleased to order a coach to carry us, and a Gentleman to attend us all Day, and at Night till bedtime and I shall relate to my People, all that I have seen in England.

When I went away from my Nation in order to go to England, I told my people that they should remain in peace, and if any of them have done mischief, I will call them to account. I have now finished what I had to say to Your Excellency.

GOVERNOR: *There has been no disturbance in your Nation since you left it, except in this Instance (Viz) When the persons, employed to collect the white prisoners in May last, came to Old High [unclear: Hiwassee?] Town, Kinneta of Old Tellico took a man and a woman who were prisoners to him aside, and shot them both Dead; I now mention this Circumstance to You that you may upon your return to your Nation make a proper Inquiry into this matter.*

JUDD'S FRIEND: *On my way home I will make a full Inquiry into that matter, and if Kennteta is guilty, I shall give orders for his being put to death.*

GOVERNOR: *Your so doing will prove as you have declared, that you have only one Tongue.*

I am now to acquaint you that I have received the King's orders for furnishing you with the proper means for conveying yourselves and the presents you have received into your Nation, and you shall likewise have an order from me for your being supplied with plenty of Provisions.

JUDD'S FRIEND: *I beg Your Excellency will write a Letter to the Headmen of the Nation and acquaint them that I am safely arrived here and that you will also be pleased to deliver me a Copy of the Talk that has now passed; that I may carry it with me into the Nation.*

GOVERNOR: *I will send a letter by a White man tomorrow, to the headmen of your nation, acquainting them of Your safe arrival here, and shall likewise order a Copy of the Talk that has now passed to be delivered to You; and I am to acquaint you, that I am ordered by the King to ask You, whether the Gentleman who was employed to attend you from England hither has taken proper care of You & behaved well toward You, for he will be taken notice of & rewarded accordingly; and at the same time I must observe to You that by this you perceived that His Majesty's Care and Concern for You, was not confined to your Stay in England only; but that his Goodness and Friendship is apparent, also, by his ordering, that you should be agreeably and safely conveyed back again.*

JUDD'S FRIEND: *That Gentleman has treated me exceeding well, and has been very good to us, and I desire the King may be likewise acquainted that we have been well received and kindly treated by everybody here.*

The Indians thereupon shook hands and withdrew. (K)

221. Amherst wrote to Fauquier on October 18, 1762, acknowledging receipt of orders to reward Timberlake. Timberlake is appointed lieutenant in the Royal Highland Regiment. W.O. 34/37, fol. 269, Letters of the Governor of Virginia and the Commander in Chief: 1758–1763, 1 page. (K)

222. They sailed from Portsmouth on August 24 and arrived in Charleston on October 28, 1762. Captain Blake in his muster books gives the dates that the Cherokees were taken in and discharged as August 22 and November 3, 1762. Draper Mss., 2VV, 186–187. (K)

223. The departure of the Cherokee did not end the embarrassment. Less than three weeks after the Cherokees sailed, William Hogarth, who made a living

ridiculing contemporary British society, referenced the Cherokee visit in one of his prints. On September 7, 1762, he published *The Times* Plate 1. It satirizes the carnival-like atmosphere surrounding the Cherokee visit to London with a billboard of a scantily clad native captioned "Live from America."

Also embarrassing to the government was the publication of a humorous song by Henry Howard. The song alludes to the reception of the three Cherokees and is inscribed to the Ladies of Great Britain. It was sung to the tune of "Caesar and Pompey were both of them Horned?" The masthead shows line drawings of the three Cherokee chiefs adapted from the Joshua Reynolds engravings; they are identified as the Stalking Turkey, the Pouting Pidgeon, and the Mankiller. Printed copies were sold for six pence by the author opposite the Union Coffee-House, in the Strand, near Temple-Bar, as well as by other print and pamphlet sellers. (K)

224. Martin. (W) Probably Samuel Martin with the Lords of the Treasury. (K)

225. Possibly Gabriel Wright, an employee and salesman for the noted optician Benjamin Martin, the maker of the only pair of eyeglasses found in the archaeological investigations at Chota. (K)

226. In a grave believed to be that of Oconastota, a pair of mid-eighteenth-century eyeglasses were found. They were made by an optician named Benjamin Martin. The glasses were known as Martin's Margins. They probably date to the early 1760s, although Oconastota died in the spring of 1783. (K)

227. A reference to Ostenaco. (K)

228. This is the same Samuel Martin of the Treasury Office that Timberlake earlier references as Mr. M-t-n. (K)

229. This is an obvious reference to the Dunk Warrant scandal. See note 27. (K)

230. The *St. James Chronicle*, which previously published the erroneous story about Shorey's poisoning, used the Cherokee visit for one last jab at the British monarchy and the selection of John Stuart of Scotland, Earl of Bute, as prime minister. On August 21, the newspaper reported: "*Everyone knows that the reason why the Cherokee King came over hither was on Account of the Antipathy, which that sensible Nations bears to the two Chiefs that accompany him, one of whom is Creek and the other is Catawba. When Kings choose foreigners as their Favourites, the Nation is sure to be undone.*" (K)

231. While Timberlake was trying to escape London, the visit of the Cherokees was still to be relived. A playbill for His Majesty's Company at the Theatre Royal in Drury Lane read:

> *This present Tuesday, being the 21st of December (1762)*, Rule a Wife and have a Wife. *Leon by Mr. Garrick . . . To which will be added (Being the 22nd Day) a New Pantomine, call'd* The Witches: Or, Harlequin Cherokee. "*Principal Witches by Mr. Vernon, Mr. Lowe, Mr. Champnes, Mr. Johnston, Signor Grimaldi, Mrs. Vincent, Mrs. Dorman, &c. Harlequin by Mr. Rooker, Misers, Mr. Blakes and Mr. Castle, Misers servants, Mr. Clough and Mr. Ackman, Columbine by Miss Baker, Lilliputian Harlequin Miss Rogers, Columbine Miss Ford, The Whole to conclude with The Landing of the CHEROKEES in America. Cherokees by Sig. Grimaldi, Mr. Vincent, Sig Lochery. Siga. Fiorentini, Siga. Giorgi, Miss Baker, &c. &c. With new habits, Scenes, Decorations and*

Music. +Nothing under full price will be taken. ("Guide to the Playbills in the Folger Shakespeare Library Relating to the Theatrical Career of David Garrick, 1741–1776," Folger Shakespeare Library [2002])

Based on the playbill and the newspaper account, it would seem that the pantomime was a typical harlequinade, a kind of theatrical performance developed in England during the mid–eighteenth century. Harlequinades usually involved four main characters: Harlequin, the comic; Columbine, the innocent beauty and Harlequin's love interest; Clown, the foil of Harlequin's tricks; and Pantaloon, the greedy patron of Columbine. In this version, the witches probably filled the role of the Clown, and the misers filled the role of Pantaloon. See also note 203. (K)

232. Timberlake's pay as a lieutenant would have started on October 18, 1762. W.O. 34/37, fol. 269, Letters of the Governor of Virginia and the Commander in Chief: 1758–1763, Amherst to Fauquier, October 18, 1762, 1 page.

233. On January 27, 1762, Henry Timberlake married Eleanor Binel. According to the marriage allegation signed by her father, Peter Binel, and Timberlake, Mr. Binel gave his permission for the marriage. (K)

234. Wood Street Compter was a notorious debtor's prison that operated throughout the eighteenth century. It was located in Mitre Court on Wood Street near Cheapside in the heart of London. The prison was demolished in 1816. Only a stairwell and cellar that was the common section for debtors survive today. (K)

235. The committee was comprised of Richard Henry Lee, Benjamin Harrison, and Edmund Pendleton. *Journal of the Virginia House of Burgesses, 1764*, p. 208.

236. Nathanial Walthoe, Clerk of the Council, the Upper House of the Virginia Legislature. He was a resident of Williamsburg. (K)

237. Here Timberlake allows the reader to fill in the most appropriate descriptive term.

238. John Stuart (September 25, 1718–March 21, 1779) was born in Inverness, Scotland, and made his way to America in the spring of 1748. He was commissioned a captain in the South Carolina Provincial Militia in 1755. He was stationed at Fort Loudoun and was the only officer to escape the massacre on August 10, 1760. He made his way to Virginia with the help of Attakullakulla and others. He was appointed Royal Superintendent of Indian Affairs for the Southern Districts on January 5, 1762. He held the position for eighteen years. He died of consumption in Pensacola in 1779. (K)

239. Lord Halifax. (W) Lord Halifax, was George Montague-Dunk Halifax (October 6, 1716–June 8, 1771).

He was the son of the 1st Earl of Halifax, and was known as Viscount Sunbury until succeeding his father as 2nd Earl of Halifax in 1739. He was educated at Eton College and at Trinity College, Cambridge. In 1742 he married Anne Richards, who died in 1753. She had inherited a great fortune from Sir Thomas Dunk, whose name Halifax took. In 1748, Lord Halifax became president of the Board of Trade. While in this position he helped found Halifax, the capital of Nova Scotia, which was named after him, as are counties in North Carolina and Virginia.

In March 1761 Halifax was appointed Lord Lieutenant of Ireland, and for a while was also First Lord of the Admiralty. He became Secretary of State for the Northern Department under Lord Bute in October 1762, switching to the Southern Department in 1763. He was one of the three ministers to whom King George III entrusted the direction of affairs during the premiership of George Grenville. In 1762, in search of evidence of sedition, he authorized a raid on the home of John Entick, which was declared unlawful in the case of *Entick v. Carrington*. He signed the general warrant under which John Wilkes was arrested in 1763, for which action he was made to pay damages by the courts of law in 1769. Together with his colleagues, Lord Halifax left office in July 1765, returning to the cabinet as Lord Privy Seal under his nephew, Lord North, in January 1770. He had just been restored to his former position of Secretary of State when he died. Halifax, who was Lord-Lieutenant of Northamptonshire and a lieutenant general in the army, was very extravagant. He left no children, and his titles became extinct on his death. Lord Orford wrote disparagingly of Halifax, saying that he and his mistress, Mary Anne Faulkner, had sold every employment in his gift. (K)

240. Actually Lang's Court, just off St. Martin's Street, one block south of Leicester Fields. (K)

241. Stanhope. (W) This was probably Lovel Stanhope, the law clerk for the office of Secretary of State Dunk Halifax. His name also surfaces in the intrigue of the Dunk Warrant and the trial of Nathan Carrington and the other Royal Messengers, in *Entick v. Carrington* (1765). The papers confiscated at Entick's house were taken to Lovel Stanhope instead of Halifax, which the prosecution argued was an unlawful delegation of authority. Stanhope, a bachelor, died October 31, 1783, at sixty-two. He was buried in the Shelford Church in Nottinghamshire. (K)

242. Mohawk from New York. (K)

243. The petition from Timberlake to the Board of Trade was received in January 1765. Timberlake requested that the crown pay expenses for the three Cherokees brought over by Aaron Trueheart. They wanted to return home since they could not obtain an audience with the king. C.O. 323/18, fol. 79, Board of Trade: Original Correspondence, 1764–1766, 2 pages.

244. The Earl of Halifax wrote to the Board of Trade on February 1, 1765, stating that Timberlake would not be reimbursed since he brought the Cherokees without permission and against the will of the lieuenant governor of Virginia. The Indians would be sent back safely and speedily. C.O. 323/18, fol. 80, Board of Trade: Original Correspondence, 1764–1766, 3 pages.

245. Lord Hillsborough. Lord H-h was Wills Hill, 1st Marquess of Downshire (May 30, 1718–October 7, 1793). He was usually called the Earl of Hillsborough in America when he served as Secretary of State for the Colonies in 1768–1772. He was the son of Trevor Hill, 1st Viscount Hillsborough, born at Fairford in Gloucestershire. He became an English member of Parliament in 1741 and an Irish viscount on his father's death in the following year, thus sitting in both the English and Irish parliaments. In 1751 he was created Earl of Hillsborough in the Irish peerage; in 1754 he was made Comptroller of the Royal Household and an English privy counsellor; and in 1756 he became a peer of Great Britain as Baron Harwich.

For nearly two years he was president of the Board of Trade and Plantations under George Grenville, and after a brief period of retirement he filled the same position, and then that of joint Postmaster-General, under the Earl of Chatham. From 1768 to 1772 Hillsborough was both Secretary of State for the Colonies and president of the Board of Trade, becoming an English earl on his retirement; in 1779 he was made Secretary of State for the Southern Department, and he was created Marquess of Downshire seven years after his final retirement in 1782. Both in and out of office he opposed all concessions to the American colonists, but he favored the project for a union between England and Ireland. Reversing an earlier opinion, Horace Walpole says Downshire was a pompous composition of ignorance and want of judgment. Hillsborough County, New Hampshire, and Hillsborough County, Florida, are named in his honor. Upon his death in 1793, his titles were passed to his son Arthur (1753–1801). (K)

246. The Earl of Hillsborough, learning that the destitute Cherokees were wandering the streets of London, ordered them removed from the care of *"a tavern-keeper and a Jew who had advertised them to be seen for money at the tavern-keeper's house"*; he sent tradesmen to fit them out genteelly at his own expense. On February 14, 1765, they were taken before the House of Lords, to whom they made complaint of encroachments by the whites on their hunting grounds, and *"expressed surprise that, having often heard of learned persons being sent to instruct them in the knowledge of things, none had ever appeared, and entreated that some such men might soon be sent among them to teach them writing, reading and other things."* King George III ordered presents to be distributed to them, and the tavern keeper and the Jew were severely reprimanded. *Annual Register . . . for the Year 1765*, vol. 7, 65. (K)

247. Edward Montague. On March 4, 1765, Montague provides an account of the expenses attending the passage of three Indians from England to Virginia and of providing them with a few presents. C.O. 323/18, fol. 95, Board of Trade: Original Correspondence, 1764–1766. See also fols. 79, 80, 82, and 84 (Anderson and Lewis, *A Guide to Cherokee Documents*, 416). (K)

248. Williams, *Memoirs*, 173, wrote:

> Two missionaries, John Daniel Hammerer and companion, both Germans, accompanied the Indians to Virginia. The party arrived there June 24th and went to Williamsburg, where the missionaries were informed that the "Indians, one of whom had passed in England for a Chief and Man of Authority in his Nation, were people of little Account; and, at the same time, that the Little Carpenter, a man well affected to the English and of known influence among his People, was coming to Williamsburg on Account of what lately happened in Augusta County." The missionaries awaited the coming of the great chief to see whether he would approve their plan. The Little Carpenter on arriving at the capital promised to take them under his protection; and he conducted them to his home, starting July 18th and journeying by way of Fort Chiswell. From that place Hammerer wrote to the Moravians in Salem, North Carolina, offering co-operation, and sending his plan "to civilize and humanize" the Cherokees. September 27th news reached the Moravian town that the missionaries had been well received by the Indians, "but that the entire Nation had been called out for war against the Shawanoes, Little Carpenter among them." Support had

been promised the missionaries by a group of Englishmen, in London; and the governor and council of Virginia bestowed a bounty of forty pounds. The Earl of Hillsborough had given approval of their efforts. Hammerer wrote to the Moravians (Sept. 26, 1765) that he had "made but a small beginning in learning the language and in teaching the Indians."

He estimated the total Cherokee population to be 16,000 souls. Fries, *Record of the Moravians in North Carolina* (Raleigh, N.C., 1922), vol. 1, 304, 311, 337. Hammerer, born in Straussburg, Alsace, was a Lutheran who had been forced by religious oppression to leave his native land for England.

249. At the time Timberlake completed his *Memoirs*, he still had some hope of recovering from his decline in circumstances. About the time his memoirs came off the press, the *Gentleman's Magazine*, vol. 34 (1765), p. 491, reported: "*Died, September 30, 1765, Lieut. Henry Timberlake of the 42d Regiment. He came in with the Cherokee Indians, and attended them.*" He was about twenty-nine years old. (K)

250. This was Timberlake's final reference to his wife, whom he never identifies. The marriage records in the Guildhall Library indicate that a marriage took place: "*on January 27, 1763, Henry Timberlake of St. Martin's in the Fields, Esq, B(achelor) and Eleanor Binel of this parish*" [(St. Georges Hanover), S(pinster), L.A.C. (license from the Archbishop of Canterbury)].

Two decades after his death, Mrs. Timberlake was using the name Helena Theresa Timberlake Ostenaco. In 1786–87, she petitioned the British government, citing her late husband's service to the crown, for assistance in securing passage to North America for reasons clarified in supporting documents. Her petition was supported by Lord Amherst and others. (See note 26.) The supporting documents have not survived in the public record. We can only guess why Lord Jeffrey Amherst would have supported her petition to have the British government pay for her travel to North America and whether her use of Ostenaco as a surname indicates a justification for her appeal. (K)

Bibliography

MANUSCRIPT SOURCES

Bodleian Library
  North Papers 1702–1778
  Petition of Henry Timberlake to the Earl of Bute

Gilcrease Museum, Tulsa, Oklahoma
  Alexander Monypenny, Order Book and Journal 1761

Henry E. Huntington Library, San Marino, California
  Abercromby Papers
  Draper Manuscripts (on microfilm)
  Loudoun Papers

Lambeth Palace Archives, London
  The Marriage Allegation of Henry Timberlake

Library of Congress, Washington, D.C.
  The Journal of Christopher French

Newberry Library, Chicago
  John Howard Payne, Payne Manuscript, Ayers Collection

North Carolina State Archives, Raleigh
  North Carolina Colonial Records, Vols. 1–9 (compiled 1886–1890)

Pennsylvania Archives, Harrisburg
  French and Indian War Records, Ser. 1 and III, 143–144, 175–181, 197–200

United Kingdom, Public Records Office, National Archives, Kew
  Board of Trade: Original Correspondence, 1760–1764 and 1764–1766
  Colonial Office (C.O.): America and West Indies, for Virginia, South Carolina,
    North Carolina, and Georgia
  Entry Book of Commissions, Warrants, and Instructions, 1760–1764
  Secretary of Admiralty: Common letters, 1762
  Secretary of State: Original Correspondence
    Military Dispatches: 1760, 1761, 1762, 1763
    Indian Affairs: 1760–1763 and 1766–1767
    Entry Book of Letters and Dispatches, 1759–1763
  Sessional Papers
  Treasury Board Papers: in Letters 1787
  War Office (W.O.): Amherst Papers

U.S. National Archives, Washington
  Lost Cherokee Archives, Papers of Oconastota

William L. Clements Library, University of Michigan
  Sir Jeffrey Amherst Papers
  William Henry Lyttelton Papers

Wisconsin State Historical Society
  Draper Manuscripts: Series VV (Sumter Papers)
  and Series ZZ (Virginia Papers)

NEWSPAPERS AND JOURNALS

Annual Reviews

The Annual Register or a View of the History, Politics and Literature for the Year 1761
The Annual Register or a View of the History, Politics and Literature for the Year 1762
The Annual Register or a View of the History, Politics and Literature for the Year 1765

Colonies

The Maryland Gazette
The Pennsylvania Gazette
The South Carolina Gazette
The Virginia Gazette

England

The British Chronicle
The British Magazine
The Daily Advertiser
The Gazette and London Daily Advertiser
The Gentleman's Magazine
Jackson's Oxford Journal
Lloyd's Evening Post
The London Chronicle
The London Evening-Post
The London Gazette
London Gazette Extraordinary
The London Magazine
The Monthly Chronicle
The Public Advertiser
The Royal Magazine, or Gentleman's Monthly Companion
The Scots Magazine
The St. James's Chronicle

Travel Guide

*A Companion to Every Place of Curiosity and Entertainment in and about London and
  Westminster* [a description of Salmon's Royal Wax Works, near Temple Bar. An
  exhibit, "The Cherokee king, with his two chiefs," is listed in the first edition of
  this text, which was printed in 1767 and is still listed in the 8th edition published
  in 1797]

Adair, James. *The History of the American Indians, Particularly Those Nations adjoining to the Mississippi, East and West Florida, Georgia, South and North Carolina and Virginia.* London: Edward and Charles Dilly, 1775.

Alden, John R. *John Stuart and the Southern Colonial Frontier.* Ann Arbor: University of Michigan Press, 1944.

Anderson, William L., and James A. Lewis. *A Guide to Cherokee Documents in Foreign Archives.* Native American Bibliographical Series, no. 4. Methuen, N.J.: Scarecrow Press, 1983.

Axtell, James. *The European and the Indian: Essays in the Ethnohistory of Colonial North America.* New York: Oxford University Press, 1981.

Bartram, William. *Travels through North & South Carolina, Georgia, East & West Florida, the Cherokee country, etc.* Philadelphia: James & Johnson, 1791. Reprint, London, 1792.

———. *Observations on the Creek and Cherokee Indians.* In *Transactions of the American Ethnological Society,* vol. 3, pt. 1. New York, 1853.

Brock, R. A. *The Official Records of Robert Dinwiddie [Dinwiddie Papers].* 2 vols. 1883. Reprint, New York: AMS Press, 1971.

Brown, John P. *Old Frontiers: The Story of the Cherokee Indians from Earliest Times to the Date of their Removal to the West.* Kingsport, Tenn.: Southern Publishers, 1938.

———. "Eastern Cherokee Chiefs" *Chronicles of Oklahoma* 16, no. 1 (March 1938): 1–33.

Brown, Laurence. *A Catalogue of British Historical Medals, 1760–1960.* Vol. 1. Ringwood, Hampshire: Seaby Publications, 1980.

Bull, J. Kinloch. *The Oligarchs in Colonial and Revolutionary Charleston: Lieutenant Governor William Bull and his Family.* Columbia: University of South Carolina Press, 1991.

Burnaby, Andrew. *Travels through the Middle Settlements in North America in the Years 1759 and 1760 with Observations upon the State of the Colonies.* Ithaca, N.Y.: Cornell University Press, 1960.

Calmes, Alan. "The Lyttelton Expedition of 1759: Military Failures and Financial Successes." *South Carolina Historical Magazine* 77 (1976): 10–33.

Cantey, Harry. "An Interpretation of a Curious Secret Journal . . ." *Tennessee Archaeologist* 16, no. 1 (Spring 1960): 10–13.

Carroll, B. R. *Historical Collections of South Carolina.* 2 vols. New York: Harper & Bros., 1836.

Cashin, Edward J. *Governor Henry Ellis and the Transformation of British North America.* Athens: University of Georgia Press, 1994.

Chapman, Jefferson. *Tellico Archaeology: 12,000 Years of Native American History.* Knoxville: Tennessee Valley Authority, 1985.

Cook, Thomas H. "Old Fort Loudoun: The First English Settlement in What Is Now the State of Tennessee." *Tennessee Historical Magazine* 7 (1921): 111–33.

Corkran, David H. "The Unpleasantness at Stecoe." *North Carolina Historical Review* 32 (1955).

———. *The Cherokee Frontier: Conflict and Survival 1740–1762.* Norman: University of Oklahoma Press, 1962.

Crane, Verner W. *The Southern Frontier 1670–1732.* Durham, N.C.: Duke University Press, 1929.

De Filipis, M. "An Italian Account of Cherokee Uprisings at Fort Loudoun and Fort Prince George, 1760–1761." *North Carolina Historical Review* 20, no. 3 (July 1943): 247–58.

De Vorsey, Louis Jr. *The Indian Boundary of the Southern Colonies 1763–1775.* Chapel Hill: University of North Carolina Press, 1966.

——— (ed.). *DeBrahm's Report of the General Survey in the Southern District of North America.* Introduction by Louis DeVorsey Jr. South Carolina Tricentennial Commission, Tricentennial Edition 3. Columbia: University of South Carolina Press, 1971. [Transcribed from Kings Mss. 210 and 211 in the British Museum, London]

Duncan, Barbara R. "The Cherokee War Dance/Welcome Dance: From Timberlake to the Twenty-First Century." In Anne F. Rogers and Barbara R. Duncan (eds.), *Culture, Crisis and Conflict: Cherokee-British Relations 1756–1765.* Cherokee, N.C.: Museum of the Cherokee Indian Press, 2007.

Fogelson, Raymond. "Cherokee in the East." *Handbook of North American Indians.* Vol. 1: *The Southeast.* Washington, D.C.: Smithsonian Institution, 2004.

Folmsbee, Stanley J., Robert Ewing Corlew, and Enoch Mitchell. *Tennessee: A Short History.* Knoxville: University of Tennessee Press, 1990.

Foreman, Carolyn Thomas. *Indians Abroad 1493–1938.* Norman: University of Oklahoma Press, 1943.

Franklin, W. Neill. "Virginia and the Cherokee Indian Trade 1753–1778." *East Tennessee Historical Society Publications* 5 (1933): 22–38.

Fries, Adelaide L. *Records of the Moravians of North Carolina.* Vols. 1 and 2. Raleigh: Edwards & Broughton Printing Company, 1922.

Gearing, Fred. *Priests and Warriors: Social Structures for Cherokee Politics in the Eighteenth Century.* Memoir 93. Menasha, Wisc.: American Anthropological Association, 1962.

Goldsmith, Oliver. *An History of the World and Animated Nature.* Vol. 2. London: J. Nourse, 1774.

Goodwin, Gary C. *Cherokees in Transition: A Study of Changing Culture and Environment Prior to 1775.* Research Paper No. 181. Chicago: University of Chicago, Department of Geography, 1977.

Graves, Algernon, and William V. Cronin. Introduction. *A History of the Works of Sir Joshua Reynolds.* 4 vols. London: Henry Graves and Co., 1899–1901.

Grieg, James (ed.). *The Diaries of a Duchess: Extracts from the Diaries of the First Duchess of Northumberland.* London: Hodder and Stoughton, 1926.

Hamer, Philip M. "Anglo-French Rivalry in the Cherokee Country 1754–1757." *North Carolina Historical Review* 2 (1925): 303–22.

Hamer, Philip M., and George C. Rogers (eds.). *The Papers of Henry Laurens.* Vol. 3: *Jan. 1, 1759–Aug. 31, 1763.* Columbia: University of South Carolina Press, 1972.

Hamilton, S. M. (ed.). *Letters to Washington and Accompanying Papers,* 5 vols. Boston: 1898–1902.

Harrington, M. R. *Cherokee and Early Remains on Upper Tennessee River.* New York: Heye Foundation, 1922.

Hatley, Tom. *The Dividing Paths: The Cherokees and South Carolina Through the Era of Revolution.* New York: Oxford University Press, 1993.

Haywood, John. *The Natural and Aboriginal History of Tennessee, etc.* Nashville, Tenn., 1823.

Hening, W. W. *Statutes of Virginia*. Vols. 1–13. Richmond, 1818–1823.

Henson, E. L. "Frontier Forts." *Historical Sketches of Southwest Virginia*. Publication No. 4. 1968.

Hewatt, Alexander. *An Historical Account of the Rise and Progress of the Colonies of South Carolina and Georgia*, 2 vols. London: Printed for Alexander Donaldson, 1779. Reprint, Spartanburg, S.C.: The Reprint Co., 1971.

Hirst, Francis W. *The Life and Letters of Thomas Jefferson*. New York: Macmillan, 1926.

Hodge, Frederick W. *Handbook of the American Indians*. Washington, D.C.: U.S. Government Printing Office, 1907–1910.

Hudson, Charles. *The Southeastern Indians*. Knoxville: University of Tennessee Press, 1976.

———. "Uktena: A Cherokee Anomalous Monster." *Journal of Cherokee Studies* 3, no. 2 (Spring 1978): 62–75.

———. *The Black Drink: A Native American Tea*. Athens: University of Georgia Press, 2004.

Hudson, Charles, and Paul E. Hoffman. *The Juan Pardo Expeditions: Explorations of the Carolinas and Tennessee, 1566–1568*. Scranton, Pa.: Smithsonian Institution Press, 1990.

Jacobs, Wilbur R. *Dispossessing the American Indian: Indians and Whites on the Colonial Frontier*. Norman: University of Oklahoma Press, 1985.

——— (ed.). *The Appalachian Indian Frontier: The Edmond Atkin Report and Plan*. Lincoln: University of Nebraska Press, 1967.

Jefferys, Thomas. 1772 *Collection of the dresses of different nations, antient and modern. Particularly old English dresses: after the designs of Holbein, Vandyke, Hollar and others. With an account of the authorities from which the figures are taken; and some short historical remarks on the subject; to which are added the habits of the principal characters on the English stage*, Vol. 4. London: Published by Thomas Jefferys, geographer to His Royal Highness the Prince of Wales, in the Strand., MDCCLVII–MDCCLXXII, 1772.

King, Duane H. "Long Island of the Holston: Sacred Cherokee Ground." *Journal of Cherokee Studies* 1, no. 2 (Fall 1976): 114.

———. *Cherokee Heritage*. Cherokee, N.C.: Museum of the Cherokee Indian Press, 1982.

——— (ed.). *The Cherokee Indian Nation: A Troubled History*. Knoxville: University of Tennessee Press, 1979.

King, Duane, with Ken Blankenship and Barbara R. Duncan. *Emissaries of Peace: The 1762 Cherokee and British Delegations*. Cherokee, N.C.: Museum of the Cherokee Indian Press, 2006.

Kutsche, Paul. *A Guide to Cherokee Documents in the Northeastern United States*. Methuen, N.J.: Scarecrow Press, 1986.

Malone, Dumas (ed.). *Dictionary of American Biography*, Vol. 9. New York: Charles Scribner's Sons, 1936.

McCrady, Edward. *History of South Carolina under the Royal Government, 1719–1776*. New York: Macmillan Company, 1899.

McDowell, William L. (ed.). *Colonial Records of South Carolina*. Series 2: *Documents Relating to Indian Affairs 1754–1765*. Columbia: University of South Carolina Press for the South Carolina Department of Archives and History, 1970.

McIlwaine, H. R., and John Pendleton Kennedy (eds.). *Journals of the House of Burgesses, 1761–1765.* Richmond, Va., 1905–1913.

Mercer, John. *The Abridgment of the Laws of Virginia.* Williamsburg, Va.: Private Printing, 1737.

Mooney, James. *Myths of the Cherokee.* 19th Annual Report of the Bureau of American Ethnology, Part 1. Washington: U.S. Government Printing Office, 1900.

Nichols, John L. "John Stuart, Beloved Father of the Cherokees." *Highlander Magazine* 31, no. 5 (Sept.–Oct. 1993): 37–40.

O'Donnell, James Howlett. *Southeastern Frontiers: Europeans, Africans, and American Indians, 1513–1840. A Critical Bibliography.* Bloomington: Indiana University Press for the Newberry Library, 1982.

Oliphant, John. "The Cherokee Embassy to London, 1762." *Journal of Imperial and Commonwealth History* 27, no. 1 (January 1999): 1–26.

———. *Peace and War on the Anglo-Cherokee Frontier.* Houndsmills, UK: Palgrave Press, 2001.

———. "Lord Egremont and the Indians: Official, Educated and Popular reactions to the Cherokees in London." In Anne F. Rogers and Barbara R. Duncan (eds.), *Culture, Crisis and Conflict: Cherokee-British Relations 1756–1765.* Cherokee, N.C.: Museum of the Cherokee Indian Press, 2007.

Philopatrios [pseud. of Henry Laurens]. *Some Observations of the Two Campaigns against the Cherokee Indians.* Charleston, S.C.: Printed by Peter Timothy, 1762. [Microprint copy, Huntington Library]

Ramsey, J. G. M. *The Annals of Tennessee to the End of the Eighteenth Century.* Philadelphia: Walker and James, 1853.

Randolph, J. Ralph. *British Travelers Among the Southern Indians, 1660–1763.* Norman: University of Oklahoma Press, 1973.

Reid, John Phillip. *A Law of Blood: The Primitive Law of the Cherokee Nation.* New York: New York University Press, 1970.

———. *A Better Kind of Hatchet: Law, Trade and Diplomacy in the Cherokee Nation During the Early Years of European Contact.* University Park: Pennsylvania State University Press, 1976.

———. "A Perilous Rule: The Law of International Homicide." In Duane H. King (ed.), *The Cherokee Indian Nation: A Troubled History,* 33–45. Knoxville: University of Tennessee Press, 1979.

Rogers, Anne F., and Barbara R. Duncan (eds.). *Culture, Crisis and Conflict: Cherokee-British Relations 1756–1765.* Cherokee, N.C.: Museum of the Cherokee Indian Press, 2007.

Speck, Frank, and Leonard Broom, with Will West Long. *Cherokee Dance and Drama.* Berkeley: University of California Press, 1983. Reprint, Norman: University of Oklahoma Press, 1993.

Stanhope, Eugenia (ed.). *Letters written by the late Right Honourable Philip Dormer Stanhope, Earl of Chesterfield, to his son, Philip Stanhope . . . together with other several pieces on various subjects.* (Published by Mrs. Eugenia Stanhope, from the originals in her possession.) London: J. Dodsley, 1774.

Stuart, Gene S. *America's Ancient Cities.* Washington: National Geographical Society, 1988.

Sturtevant, William. "Louis Phillippe on Cherokee Architecture and Clothing in 1797." *Journal of Cherokee Studies* 3, no. 4 (Fall 1978): 202.

———. "The Cherokee Frontiers, the French Revolution, and William Augustus Bowles." In Duane H. King (ed.), *The Cherokee Indian Nation: A Troubled History*, 61–91. Knoxville: University of Tennessee Press, 1979.

Summers, Lewis Preston. *History of Southwest Virginia 1746–1786.* Richmond, Va.: J. L. Print Co., 1903.

Taylor, Oliver. *Historic Sullivan.* Bristol, Tenn.: King Printing Company, 1909.

Thruston, Gates P. *The Antiquities of Tennessee and the adjacent states . . .* 1897. Reprint, New York: AMS Press for Peabody Museum of Archaeology and Ethnology, Harvard University, 1973.

Thwaites, Reuben G. *France in America, 1497–1763.* 1905. Reprint, Haskell House Publishing Company, 1969.

Thwaites, Reuben G., and Louise Phelps Kellogg. *Documentary History of Dunmore's War.* Madison: Historical Society of Wisconsin, 1905. Reprint, Bowie, Md.: Heritage Books, 1989.

Timberlake, Henry. *Memoirs of Lieut. Henry Timberlake.* London: Printed for the author, 1765. [See also Samuel Cole Williams (ed.), *The Memoirs of Lieut. Henry Timberlake*]

Tinling, Marion (ed.). *The Correspondence of the Three William Byrds of Westover, Virginia 1684–1776.* Vol. 2. Charlottesville: University Press of Virginia for the Virginia Historical Society, 1977.

Wetmore, Ruth Y. "The Green Corn Ceremony of the Eastern Cherokees." *Journal of Cherokee Studies* 8, no. 1 (Spring 1983): 46–55.

Williams, Samuel Cole. "An Account of the Presbyterian Mission to the Cherokees 1757–1759." *Tennessee Historical Magazine*, 2nd ser., 1 (1931): 125–38.

———. *Early Travels in the Tennessee Country 1540–1800.* Johnson City, Tenn.: Watauga Press, 1938.

——— (ed.). *The Memoirs of Lieut. Henry Timberlake.* Johnson City, Tenn.: Watauga Press, 1927. Reprint, Marietta, Ga.: Continental Press, 1948.

Index

Viscount Sunbury. *See* Lord Halifax
von der Sculenburg, Melusina, 144n

Wade, S., Cunne Shote, the Indian
   Chief (drawing), 90
Walker, Dr. Thomas, 109n
Walpole, Horace, 133n, 156n
Walthoe, Nathanial, 79, 80–81, 154n
Wampum, collar of, 25
War. *See under* Cherokees.
War, Lord Dunnore's (1774), 106n
Ward, Nancy, 122n
Warriors, 36, *Plate 8*
   titles of, 122n
Warriors, by Robert Griffing, *Plate 14*
Washington, Colonel George, xxiii–
   xxiv, *xxiv*, 5, 6, 103n, 104n, 105n,
   106n, 109n, 113n
Wax figures of Cherokees, for diorama,
   144n
Westminster Abbey, *60–61*, 135n, 137n
White Conduit House, *61*, 140n
White's Fort, 110n
Wilkes, John, 102n, 133n
William and Mary, College of, Rev.
   Andrew Burnaby's impressions of,
   130–131n

Williams, Samuel Cole, xxiii, xxx
Williamsburg, 81, 156n
   arrival in 1761, 55
   Rev. Andrew Burnaby's impressions
     of, 129–130n
   in 1759, 129–130n
   visit(s) to, 55, 128n
Willinawaw, 35, 45–47, 125n
Wilshire Suttling Booth, 149n
Wilton House, Salisbury in Wiltshire,
   58–59, *59*, 132n
Wiltshire Militia, 149n
Winchester College, 149n
Wine glass, circa 1760, *69*
Woey. *See* Ostenaco
Wood, Robert, 67, 73, 143n
Wood Street Compter, 77, 154n
Wooe Pidgeon, 132n
Wright, Gabriel, 73, 153n
Wyndham, Charles. *See* Egremont,
   Lord

Yachtino, 21, 115n
Yawyawgany River, 7–8
Youghtanno, 21, 115n
Young, Robert, 112n

Acknowledgments

MANY YEARS AGO, as an undergraduate at the University of Tennessee, I was fortunate to have the opportunity to work at several Cherokee town sites that were visited by Henry Timberlake more than two centuries earlier. Long silenced by the ravages of time, the remains of the material culture recovered from the refuse pits and post molds of architectural features bore silent testimony to the people Timberlake met and the communities they built. His *Memoirs* became the travel guide for archaeological field crews attempting to save for future generations some record of the once bustling Cherokee settlements—sites destined for inundation by the nearly completed Tellico Dam and its reservoir. I recall contemplating the importance of Timberlake's *Memoirs* on many evenings in the field camp. In particular, I remember the deference given to Timberlake's eye-witness account by my colleagues, some of whom began their distinguished careers working on sites identified in the *Memoirs*. In this group were Jeff Chapman, Gerald Schroedl, George Nick Fielder, Danny Olinger, Carey Oakley, Richard Polhemus, Howard Earnest, and Robert Newman. The field crew I supervised at Chota, including Lloyd Wolfe, Moses Walkingstick, Robert Crowe, Owen Walkingstick, Jim West, Alan Sequoyah, and Larry Miller, offered many insights into Cherokee culture and language.

Over the years, the experiences of four field seasons have helped shape my view of combining data from various disciplines to create a more complete understanding of any subject studied. I have been able to apply these lessons in the classroom at the University of Tennessee, Western Carolina University, and Northeastern State University in Tahlequah as well as in exhibits and programs at museums where I have had the privilege of working—including the Museum of the Cherokee Indian, the Cherokee National Museum, the National Museum of the American Indian, and the Autry National Center's Southwest Museum of the American Indian.

I am especially grateful to Ken Blankenship, director of the Museum of the Cherokee Indian, who was willing to undertake a major exhibit on this subject. Funding for the exhibit and publication was provided by the National Endowment for the Humanities as a "We the People" project. Additional funding for the "Emissaries of Peace" exhibit was provided by The Cherokee Preservation Foundation, Harrah's Foundation, First Citizens Bank, and the Cannon Foundation. Support for the exhibit was also contributed by the Frank McClung Museum and the National Museum of Natural History. Roseanna Belt, Walker Calhoun, Marie Junaluska, Garfield

Long, Jr., Carmelita Montieth, John "Bullet" Standingdeer, and James "Bo" Taylor served on the community review panel and provided wise counsel. The scholarly review panel, William Anderson, Jeff Chapman, Barbara R. Duncan, Tom Hatley, Cecile Ganteaume, Jonathan C. King, Anne Rogers, Gerald Schroedl, Robert Scott Stephenson, and William C. Sturtevant offered sage advice. The story was brought to life by those involved in the content development, design, and fabrication of the exhibit, including Nancy Seruto, John Low, Ben Hurst, Pat Allee, Anna Schlobohm de Cruder, and Ralph Nielson. Those objects and images assembled by the Museum of the Cherokee Indian for the exhibit serve as the basis for the illustrations of this book.

Barbara R. Duncan, Director of Education, Museum of the Cherokee Indian, selected images and provided editorial oversight. Anne Rogers, Department of Anthropology, Western Carolina University, served as general editor. Lee Callander, Kianga Lucas, and Pam Hannah helped with proof-reading. William C. Sturtevant did the research and writing for Appendix A and his wife, Sally McClendon, edited his work. John Low created the placements for the London map of Appendix B. Jonathan King and Sheila O'Connell of the British Museum; Jerry Clark, U.S. National Archives; and Victoria Steele, Department of Special Collections, Charles E. Young Research Library, University of California at Los Angeles; all helped with images for this publication. Robert Griffing and Paramount Press, and H. Tom Hall and the National Geographic Society generously allowed their art to be reproduced in this book. The staff of BW&A Books Inc., especially Barbara Williams, Julie Allred, Virginia Daniel, and Darwin Campa, did outstanding work in typesetting, designing, and coordinating the publication. Mark Simpson-Vos, of the University of North Carolina Press, offered wise counsel throughout the process. To each of these individuals and institutions, I express my most sincere gratitude.

Most importantly, I am indebted to Angela, Travis, and Lee for allowing me the time to do the research and writing for this book and for making sure that my work is always balanced by family life.

Duane King
Executive Director
Southwest Museum of the American Indian
Autry National Center, Los Angeles, California